cial
Accounting

. . . .

ook is to be returned on or before
stamped below.   3016

Longman modular texts in business and economics

· ·

Series Editors Geoff Black and Stuart Wall

Financial
Accounting

....

*Christopher Waterston
& Anne Britton*

London and New York

Addison Wesley Longman Limited,
Edinburgh Gate,
Harlow, Essex CM20 2JE, England
and Associated Companies throughout the world.

*Published in the United States of America
by Addison Wesley Longman, New York*

First published 1996

ISBN 0 582 262577 PPR

British Library Cataloguing-in-Publication Data

A catalogue record for this book is
available from the British Library

Library of Congress Cataloguing-in-Publication Data
Waterston, Christopher, 1955–
    Introduction to financial accounting/Christopher Waterston and
Anne Britton.
        p. cm. – (Longman modular texts in business and economics)
    Includes bibliographical references and index.
    ISBN 0–582–26257–7
    1. Accounting. I. Britton, Anne. II. Title. III. Series.
HF5635.W335 1996
    657 – dc20   95–50115
                                                              CIP

set by 30 in Stone serif 9/12 pt

Printed in Great Britain by Henry Ling Ltd, Dorset Press,
Dorchester, Dorset.

Contents

Preface

Welcome to your studies of financial accounting. Here we suggest how to use this book to gain the maximum benefit from your studies.

The book is divided into 15 chapters, each dealing with a separate area of financial accounting. The sequence of chapters is important, and you should normally work through the book following the chapter order. If you try to jump ahead, you may find that the material doesn't make much sense because you haven't yet picked up the necessary underpinning knowledge and skills.

Each chapter starts with a brief list of its objectives. This is a check-list of the things you should be able to do by the time you have worked through that chapter. Check back to this list when you finish each chapter to ensure that you have understood it all. If you are unsure about one or more aspects, don't leave the chapter, but have another look at the relevant part. If you are still no more confident in your abilities, you will find suggestions for alternative approaches to the topic at the end of each chapter.

It is very tempting to forget this advice and to move on. However, we also know that the next topic will be much easier if you have thoroughly covered the previous one.

At a number of points in the book we suggest that you jot down your own ideas about a question raised, or that you calculate a figure, prepare an account, etc. You should therefore have at your side when you read this book,

▶ a pad of paper
▶ a pen
▶ a calculator.

Where an activity is designed to help you to learn the material, an answer is given in the text immediately following. It can be difficult to discipline yourself to make the effort to do the suggested activity instead of just reading ahead to the answer, but it is well worth the effort. Where an activity is designed to assess whether you have understood the topic, and can apply the required skill, a question and an answer is provided at the end of the chapter.

Notice that in each case we have provided *an* answer, not necessarily *the* answer. As you will see as you explore accountancy, it is not the exact science that many people suppose it to be. Almost all the answers in accountancy, at least in the UK, are contingent and dependent on ideas of what is to be achieved – which is why Chapter 1 is concerned with such fundamental issues. We must be clear about what we are trying to achieve before we start on the mechanics of doing it.

Review questions can be found in a separate resource pack which accompanies this book and is available to lecturers. These are a selection of questions providing additional practice in the topics covered in the following chapters.

Remember, if you *work through* the issues for yourself you will learn and retain them much more effectively than if you just read about them. Ultimately, it is your choice how much benefit you derive from this book.

Acknowledgements

We are grateful to the Accounting Standards Board for permission to reproduce extracts from 'Statement of Principles', Chapter 1, 'Statement of Principles', Chapter 3, 'Foreword to Standards', 'SSAP 2', 'SSAP 9' and 'FRS 5'.

What is accounting?

Objectives:

By the end of this chapter you should be able to:-

▶ Discuss the need for, and purposes of, accounting.
▶ Outline the nature and types of accounting.
▶ Describe the major formats in which accounting information is presented.
▶ List the users of accounting, and describe their particular informational needs.

Introduction

This chapter aims to introduce the purposes and the types of accounting, and to consider who might be interested. Since you are reading this book, you presumably have some interest in accounting, or at least a need to study it. Nevertheless, you may not be aware of the range of activities that make up accounting, nor be quite sure about what, and who, accounting is for. In this chapter we look at these issues under three headings – the purposes, the types, and the users.

If you have done some accounting before you may be tempted to skip over this chapter. Don't. The last few years have seen a strong trend towards accounting for the spirit of transactions, rather than the letter. If you are to understand what the spirit of a transaction is, then you must be clear about the fundamental issues dealt with in this chapter.

Purposes of accounting

Before we look at the purposes of accounting, it is helpful to review briefly the contexts in which accounting occurs. In other words, we examine the different types of organisation which need accounting.

ACTIVITY **1.1**

What types of organisation can you think of? Jot them down and then put a cross against any that have no need of accounting.

Answer

The following list of organisations covers the main types. You may have included others, or have expressed the same ones in different words.

▶ Sole trader. This means one person who runs a business on their own, or perhaps with a few employees. The main aim is to make a profit.

▶ Partnership. This is two or more people who carry on a business in common, intending to make a profit.

▶ Limited company. A limited company is a legal organisation set up under the Companies Acts of 1985 and 1989. The owners are called the shareholders, and it is run by directors, who are appointed by the shareholders. In small companies it is common for the shareholders to appoint themselves as directors. Larger companies are often public limited companies, or PLCs. You will find out more about limited companies in Chapter 8.

▶ Public sector bodies, such as local councils or the National Health Service. Traditionally, these bodies have not existed to make a profit, but to provide a service.

▶ Clubs and societies, such as a local cricket club. Again the intention is not to make a profit.

All of these organisations require some form of accounting, however simple. Our next task is to explore why this should be so.

ACTIVITY **1.2**
· · · · · · · · · · · · · ·

Accounting is undertaken by organisations for a variety of reasons. What do you think they are? Jot down at least three reasons before you read on.

Answer

This is probably the most fundamental question in accountancy. Nevertheless, there are no agreed, clear answers to it. In principle, therefore, your answers are as valid as any others, but we would expect you to include some or all of the following.

1 To record what money has come into the organisation and what has gone out.
2 To help managers make decisions about how to run the organisation.
3 To tell other people about the activities and consequent profit or loss of the organisation during the past year, or other period.
4 To tell other people about the present financial state of the organisation.
5 To provide a basis for taxation.
6 To help assess whether the organisation is beneficial to society as a whole.
7 To control the organisation, by controlling the finances.
8 To provide a basis for planning future activities.
9 To support legal relationships, for example how much one business owes another.

The above is not a comprehensive list, and you may have listed other items, or have expressed similar points in different ways. Points 2 and 8 in the list arguably overlap. However, if you look at our list and your own, you should see that the purposes are broadly of two types.

First, there are purposes that relate to the running of the business, that is those that form a basis for decision making. In Chapter 9 you will see that part of the regulatory framework of financial accounting in the UK is a document called the 'Statement of Principles'. This is a publication by the Accounting Standards Board

(ASB), which is itself an authoritative group of accountants. Chapter 1 of the 'Statement of Principles' states that the prime objective of financial statements is to aid decision making.

Second, there is a group of purposes that can be classified as 'stewardship'. This term means that accounting is used to keep track of what has been done with the financial resources entrusted to its managers. Historically, this was the original purpose of financial accounting, whereby managers ('stewards') had to account to the owners for their stewardship of the owners' money. Chapter 1 of the 'Statement of Principles' is clear that stewardship is now secondary to decision making as a general aim of financial accounting. This means that accounting is now less a matter of keeping track of the money, and more a matter of using the resulting information to actively manage the organisation, and for outsiders to make decisions about the organisation.

DID YOU KNOW ...?
The UK has more qualified accountants per head of population than any other European country.

If this is what accounting is for, what does that imply for the nature of accounting? Well, for one thing, it means that accounting is not just a matter of recording data, or even of processing it in an organised way. It is both these things, but an increasingly large part of accounting is concerned with subsequently presenting the resultant information to those who are interested in the welfare of the organisation. The next section looks in more detail at the consequent nature of today's accounting.

Types of accounting

Accounting can be divided very roughly into two areas, financial accounting and management accounting. Bear in mind that the division is a rather arbitrary one, and many functions in the accountancy world spread across both areas. Nevertheless, it is a distinction that is often made, and which can help to make accountancy as a whole more manageable.

Financial accounting is concerned with the recording, processing and presentation of economic information after the event to those people outside the organisation who are interested in it. By contrast, management accounting deals with similar activities, but geared to providing information about the organisation to its managers to help them run it. In other words, the heart of the distinction is the *purpose* of the accounting, rather than what is done. This may become clearer if we look at each of the three functions of recording, processing and presentation.

Recording

All accounting requires the prior collection of raw data and its organisation into some form of structured record. In principle, this could be as crude as writing down each transaction in a single book, as it occurs. It should be obvious, however, that it would not be easy to get information out of this book. You may be aware that, in fact, almost all accounting systems across the world rely on 'double entry' recording in some form. This method has been so successful over the past 500 years since it was codified precisely because it is relatively easy to get information out of it. In Chapter 5 you will start to learn about this system.

Before we can start on the practicalities of recording data, however, there remains one major question to be answered.

ACTIVITY **1.3**

What sorts of transaction does an accountant record? Note down at least four.

Answer

There are many kinds of transactions, and you may have noted others than those listed below, or expressed similar items in different ways.

1 Sales made.
2 Money received for the sales – remember that you don't always get paid as soon as you sell something.
3 Production materials bought.
4 Expenses incurred, for example electricity used.
5 Production materials and expenses paid for – again we don't always pay for something as soon as we buy it.
6 Borrowing money from the bank.
7 Persuading other people to put money into our organisation.
8 Buying big items that we intend to keep, such as buildings or machinery.

Note that what accountants therefore record is almost always restricted to what can be valued reasonably objectively in money terms. In other words, if you can't attach a £ sign to it, accountants ignore it. Furthermore, accountants tend to focus on the organisation, rather than taking a broader societal view.

ACTIVITY **1.4**

List three things about an organisation that accountants might not record, but which you would regard as useful things to be told about.

Answer

As with most of the questions raised in this chapter, there is no single, correct answer. Some of the things we consider to be currently important are:

1 The value added to the economy by the activities of the organisation.
2 The measurement and inclusion of human resources. Some football clubs, for example, include a valuation of their players in their balance sheet, that is the summary of what the organisation owns and owes. Others claim that it is impossible to say objectively what a player is worth, and so omit them from the balance sheet. Which approach do you think gives the best picture of what the organisation owns? We think this area of accounting is one of the more interesting ones, and it is dealt with more fully in the next chapter and in Chapter 12.
3 Environmental accounting, which tries to report the impact of the organisation on the environment, perhaps in terms of tonnes of pollutants emitted, compared with previous years, other similar organisations, or standards of some sort.

4 Social accounting, which provides information about the social impact of the organisation. This could include looking at, say, the employment of minority groups, or the effect of purchasing policies, especially where supplies come from the Third World. In the UK, Body Shop plc is one of the more notable companies already moving down this road.

The above possibilities are not part of generally accepted accounting practice at the moment. However, there are signs that this is changing. Ethical investment is a growing force in the UK, with about £800 million invested by investment funds which claim some ethical basis. An organisation trying to attract such investment could find that providing some of the information suggested above could help. Against this, there is a view that organisations in the UK, especially limited companies, already have to provide so much information that the costs of doing so prevent them from concentrating on their core business. All we can do here is note that accounting is constantly changing, and that there are signs that it is moving towards some of the issues indicated above.

In Chapter 5 we will start to explore exactly how organisations record data and turn it into useful financial statements of various sorts. For the moment all we need to consider is what data should be recorded and why. To consolidate your knowledge so far, try putting a tick in the correct box in the table shown in Activity 1.5.

ACTIVITY **1.5**
·············

In conventional accounting, which of the events listed in the table would usually be recorded and which would be ignored?

	Recorded	Ignored
1 Selling one of the organisation's cars		
2 Paying the wages		
3 Making the tea		
4 Moving staff between jobs in the office		
5 Incurring a fine for polluting a local river		
6 Paying the fine		

Answer

You should have ticked the 'recorded' column for items 1, 2, 5 and 6, since all these result in objectively measurable resources coming into or leaving the organisation. On the other hand, items 3 and 4 do not change the economic relationship with the outside world, and would therefore not be recorded in a financial accounting system. You should therefore have ticked the 'ignored' column for these two.

You might expect the law to specify what records are required. In fact, the Companies Acts are quite vague about exactly what records need be kept, and say only that they should be 'sufficient to show and explain' the transactions and consequent position of the company. This means that the records differ between companies, each organising the recording as it thinks best. It need not be like this. In France, for example, the 'Plan Comptable', that is the government's accounting plan, specifies exactly which ledger accounts must be kept, and exactly what can and can't be recorded in each. Ledger accounts are explained in Chapter 5.

ACTIVITY **1.6**
. . . .

Which approach, the UK or the French, do you think is best? Why?

Answer

As usual, the answer depends on what you think accounting is for. The UK system has the benefit of flexibility, in that it allows each organisation to set up an accounting system that best suits its own circumstances and needs. If we are aiming to present information for users to make decisions about that organisation, then gearing the system to the peculiarities of the organisation is most likely to result in relevant information.

On the other hand, allowing each organisation to design a different system is unlikely to result in information that is comparably prepared and presented between organisations. Despite rules set down by the Companies Acts and by the ASB in accounting standards, lack of comparability is a major problem in the UK. We leave it to you to judge whether state control of accounting would be politically and culturally acceptable in the UK. Ultimately, we get the accounting that reflects our society.

Processing

By 'processing' is meant turning the raw data that we have recorded into useful information that can be presented to those interested in knowing about the organisation. As we have already seen, the processing will be determined by what information we want from our accounting system, and by the underlying method of recording that we have adopted. Given these two, the processing is simply the way we turn the recorded data into the required financial information.

Beginning in Chapter 5, you will see how we not only record data but then process it so that we can produce the financial statements that most users of the information require. Having looked at the essential features of recording, it may help to appreciate what is involved in processing if we now turn our attention to the end product. In other words, it is time to look at the forms in which financial information is most usually presented.

Presenting

We saw above that there are very lax rules in the UK about what records need be kept and how the data in them is then presented. However, as you will see as we progress through this book, limited companies in the UK are closely governed with respect to the presentation of information to the users of the accounts. The Companies Acts require a profit and loss account and a balance sheet. Furthermore, accountants' own rules, the accounting *standards*, also require a cash flow statement. We will examine all three financial statements later in the book – indeed you will learn to prepare them yourself – but they are so fundamental to accounting that it is worth taking a brief look at them now.

The profit and loss account

This is a list of the expenses incurred by the organisation, set against its revenues, the net results being a profit, if revenues are more than expenses, and a loss if the reverse is true. It covers a specific period, usually one year.

The balance sheet

This is a summary of the assets and liabilities of the organisation at a specific time. In simple terms, assets are what the organisation owns and liabilities are what it owes. As you will see in the next chapter, these definitions are not strictly true, but they are good enough for a basic understanding.

DID YOU KNOW ...?
The main reason for business failure is not a lack of profitability. It is because they have insufficient cash to pay their debts.

The cash flow statement

This is the last of the major financial statements. Like the profit and loss account, it covers a specific period, but it differs by listing the actual cash received and paid out. The profit and loss account, by contrast, lists the amounts incurred. The difference will become clearer when you look at the profit and loss account adjustments in Chapters 6 and 7.

It may have occurred to you that all three of these statements are summaries of different aspects of the organisation, prepared for those outside the business. They therefore fall within the area of *financial* accounting. The presentation of *management* accounting information is not governed by the Companies Acts or the accounting standards. This means that management accounting statements vary between organisations. Nevertheless, most organisations of any size will produce some or all of the following, and these would normally be regarded as management accounting statements.

▶ A structured guess about what revenues and expenses will be in the future. This is usually called a budget.
▶ A comparison of the previously estimated revenues and costs with the actual revenues and costs. Such a statement allows managers to see where things have not gone according to plan, by highlighting the variances between estimated and actual figures. It is therefore sometimes known as a variance report, or variance analysis report.
▶ An analysis of the cost of a particular product or service provided by the organisation, showing the cost of each item that has gone into that product or service.
▶ An estimate of what money will come into and flow out of the organisation over the coming months. This is usually known as a cash flow forecast.

ACTIVITY **1.7**
• • • • • • • • • • • • •

Earlier in this chapter we referred to the cash flow statement. This is not the same thing as a cash flow forecast. To ensure that you appreciate the difference, and hence something of the difference between financial and management accounting, state the difference in your own words.

Answers

A cash flow statement is a summary of what cash flow actually occurred during the past accounting period. It is a record of what happened, prepared primarily for those outside the business, It would therefore normally be regarded as part of financial accounting. The cash flow forecast is an educated, structured guess about what we think the cash flows will be in the next accounting period(s). It is mainly prepared for managers, to help them plan the activities of the organisation in the future. It is thus probably best classified as management accounting.

As you may have guessed from its title, this book is only about financial accounting. We will therefore not be dealing with management accounting topics any further. If you want to know more, refer to the Management Accounting text in the same series as this book, and consult the suggestions for further study at the end of this chapter.

Who cares anyway? – the users
• •

You should have noticed in our discussion above that what accounting is ultimately depends largely on who we think the end users will be. If, for example, you think that the information produced by the accounting process is primarily for the managers of the organisation, you would probably want to focus on recording and processing data about, say, the estimated and actual costs of products, and estimates of future revenues and costs. You could then present the resulting information to managers in the form of comparisons of estimated and actual costs for making each product.

DID YOU KNOW ...?
A typical annual report of a large plc may consist of 60 pages of detailed financial information.

Alternatively, if you think those with the greatest need of information about the organisation are those who work there, you might be more concerned to record and process information about changes in rates of pay, health and safety records, emission levels of toxic products, or employment of minority groups. Think for a moment about how such a perspective would change the nature of accounting.

ACTIVITY **1.8**
• • • • • • • • • • • • •

As a way of getting to grips with the various groups who are usually held to need financial information, and why they need it, try completing the following table. To get you started, we have already filled in some of the table.

	User group	User needs
1	Investors	Return on money invested. Growth in the total value of the organisation.
2		Security of employment. Wage rates, and the share of generated wealth going to the employees, compared with owners and the Inland Revenue.
3	Lenders	
4	Suppliers and other trade creditors	
5	Customers	
6		Tax assessments and trade statistics
7	Public	

Answer

At this point, we should admit that we have cheated a little here, and taken the list of users from Chapter 1 of the ASB's 'Statement of Principles'. You may recall that we came across Chapter 1 earlier, where it gave us an authoritative statement about the purposes of financial accounting. The list above is very similar to previous lists, notably that provided by the 'Corporate Report' in 1975. The Corporate Report was published by the forerunner of the ASB, the Accounting Standards Committee. The importance of this list is its up-to-date authority. The suggested user needs are our own. The completed table is as follows.

	User group	User needs
1	Investors	Return on capital. Growth in the total value of the organisation.
2	Employees	Security of employment. Wage rates, and the share of generated wealth going to the employees, compared with owners and the Inland Revenue.
3	Lenders	Ability to make repayments of capital and interest. Security, in the event of non-repayment.
4	Suppliers and other trade creditors	Credit worthiness of the organisation. Time typically taken to pay suppliers.
5	Customers	Security of supply, ie will the organisation still be in business next year?
6	Government and their agencies	Tax assessments and trade statistics.
7	Public	A 'catch-all' category, covering local communities, pressure groups and industry watchers.

As a final point on users, note that they will not only be interested in commercial businesses. You saw at the start of this chapter that accounting is required by all organisations, not just commercial ones. We have therefore used the term 'organisations' in this chapter to cover not only businesses, but also charities, public sector organisations such as the NHS, voluntary bodies and social clubs. Each will have a different weighting of users, and different information needs.

The future of financial accounting

If nothing else, you should be finishing this chapter with the idea that accounting is a dynamic subject. This means that it is constantly changing to reflect changing practices and the requirements of competing user groups. It may be helpful to conclude this first chapter with a brief exploration of where financial accounting may be going over the next few years.

Notice what the table of users above is suggesting. A single set of financial statements has to meet all the user needs in the list above. This is an ambitious aim. Is it likely that it is achievable? If not, are we to try to satisfy all users partially, or to put the needs of some users above the needs of others? Who decides? Would it be acceptable to produce a number of financial statements, each geared to the needs of a different user? If we did, what would happen to comparability, and who would pay for all the extra reports? You should be getting used to the idea that there are few definite answers to many of the questions in accounting, and the questions we have raised here are simply more examples of such questions. All we can suggest is that you think about them in the light of what you have learned in this chapter, and bear them in mind for later chapters.

For a specific example of how accounting is currently changing, we could take the growing area of social and environmental accounting. We touched on what is involved in this form of accounting earlier in the chapter. All we want to emphasise here is that it constitutes an extension – some would say an alternative – to existing generally accepted accounting practice. It has arisen because of changing societal concerns over the environment and over the impact of business on social issues. In turn, the more responsible and responsive businesses have reacted to the changed context by changes in their commercial practices. This is resulting in some, so far limited, changes in accounting.

Summary

This first chapter asked what accounting is all about. We saw that it is concerned with the recording, processing and presentation of economically measurable information. The precise form this takes is defined by the law and by standards set by the ASB, but these are themselves a reflection of what users want to know about the organisation. Where the users are primarily concerned about information for the internal running of the organisation, the resultant accounting systems and reporting would usually be classified as management accounting. Otherwise, it will be the subject of this book, financial accounting.

Many text books simply describe accounting as it is, while this chapter has tried also to suggest how accounting might be. After all, if you continue with your studies of accountancy, you will one day be one of those who will determine the nature and purposes of accountancy.

Before you can tackle such issues seriously, however, you should be competent in the existing practice of financial accounting. The rest of this book will help you achieve that competence, but always remember that all accounting is ultimately determined by the issues we have covered in this chapter.

Further study

All introductory texts on accounting will include the above material to some extent. You may find it helpful to browse through one or two in a library to get an alternative viewpoint. If you have access to the Chartered Association of Certified Accountants open learning pack for 'The Accounting Framework', then there is a useful discussion of some of these issues on the audiotape that comes with that pack. As far as we are aware, there is no computer-based learning material which covers the topics in this chapter to any useful degree.

Rather more formally, Chapters 1 and 2 of the ASB's 'Statement of Principles' deal authoritatively with many of the issues we have explored in this chapter.

If you want to know more about the management accounting that was touched on in this chapter, there is a companion book in this series called *Management Accounting*.

SELF-
CHECK
QUESTION

Chapter 1 of the 'Statement of Principles' outlines two rationales for financial accounting, namely decision making and stewardship. It suggests that accounting is done to help users make decisions (decision making) and to confirm what has happened (stewardship). Which of these two purposes do you consider to be the more important? Give reasons for your answer.

Your answer should be in the form of a short essay, of about 300 to 500 words, or at least in the form of comprehensive notes for such an essay. There is no single right answer, nor will you find the answer by looking it up in this chapter. You will have to apply the ideas and facts introduced in this chapter to formulate your own answer – indeed, requiring you to work through the issues like this is the point of this self-assessment question. Our answer below is based on Chapter 1 of the 'Statement of Principles', and lists the main points that you should have covered.

Answer

1   List and consider the users, and their needs. In particular, financial statements in the UK are mostly used by existing and potential investors and lenders.

2   Such users are concerned with whether the entity is now, and/or is likely to be in future, a good source of financial return and security. This means that they are looking to the statements for, in the words of Chapter 1 of the 'Statement of Principles', 'information about the financial position, performance and financial adaptability of an enterprise that is useful . . . in making economic decisions'.

3   Other users' needs should also be considered, in terms of the decisions they need to make about the entity. For example, employees' use of the financial statements could be considered in relation to decisions about whether to join or leave the entity, or pay rises.

4   Note the shortcomings of UK financial statements in that they only provide historical information, while decision making is inherently forward looking.

5   Nevertheless, the usefulness of historical information for confirmatory purposes should be considered in relation to specific users. With regard to investors and lenders, for example, Chapter 1 of the 'Statement of Principles' says that 'financial statements also show the results of the stewardship of management, that is the accountability of management for the resources entrusted to it'.

6   The generally accepted conclusion, then, is that the main rationale for financial accounting and reporting in the UK is to aid users in decision making, but that the confirmatory stewardship role, while secondary, is also valid.

Further review questions are available in a separate resource pack which is available to lecturers.

CHAPTER 2

The balance sheet

Objectives:
....

By the end of this chapter you should be able to:

▶ List and explain the major sources and applications of funds for a commercial entity.
▶ Construct a simple balance sheet.
▶ Outline the alternative methods of valuing assets and liabilities.

Introduction
....

In Chapter 1 we looked at the purposes of accounting, and saw how accounting information is conventionally presented. One of the main methods of presentation was the balance sheet. This is a statement of the financial position of the undertaking at a specific point in time. In this chapter we look at the balance sheet in more detail, and you will learn how to prepare one.

Before we tackle the construction of a balance sheet, however, we need to turn our attention to where the money typically comes from and where it is spent. You discovered in the last chapter that a balance sheet is simply a list of the assets and liabilities of an entity. The entity must have got the assets by spending money on them, and must have got that money in the first place by incurring a liability to third parties. This should become clearer if we now examine what are more formally known as the sources and applications of funds.

The sources and applications of funds
....

The starting point is to consider where an entity gets its money from. Some entities will have unusual sources. Charities, for example, receive donations, whereas most other entities don't. Nevertheless, we can identify some sources of funds which will be widely applicable.

ACTIVITY **2.1**
....

List three sources of funds for a typical business. You may find it helpful to think about your present or past employer, or another business you know of.

Answer

Our list would include the following:

1 Money borrowed from an outsider, often a bank. Money borrowed is known as 'debt finance'.

2   Money invested by the owners. For a sole trader or a partnership this is known simply as 'capital'. For a limited company, such money is called 'share capital'.

3   Once a business is up and running it will hopefully make profits. Profit is then another source of funds, and can be used in the business as soon as it is received. The total of capital or share capital, together with such profit, is then called 'equity finance'.

4   More subtly, the credit allowed to an entity by a supplier is also a source of funds. If I agree to supply you with goods and accept payment next month, what I am effectively doing is lending you the goods for a month. Such a loan in kind is analogous to the loan in money that we listed as point 1 above.

There are thus two broad classifications of funding sources: equity and debt. These are both liabilities of the business because the business has an obligation to repay them eventually. Loans will have to be repaid and even the capital invested by the owners of the business will have to be repaid to them if and when the business comes to an end. Similarly, the profits ultimately belong not to the business, but to the owners, since the whole business belongs to them. The profits will therefore have to be paid by the business to the owners. In other words, the profits made in the past and retained by the business are a liability of the business.

In the meantime, the business can spend the equity and debt funds on buying a range of goods and services. Some of the things it buys will have a transitory existence, such as the labour of the workforce. The immediate benefit that comes from buying one hour of an employee's time ends at the end of that hour. Similarly, there will be nothing to show for money applied to paying the electricity bill. Note that the labour and the electricity may well have been used to produce the business' product, and any stock of that product will have a continuing existence. The distinction we are aiming for, however, is that the labour and the electricity no longer exist as labour and electricity, but as part of the stock value.

For comparison, some of the things the business applies its funds to will have a continuing existence. We have already seen that one such example could be stock. Others could be, for example, buildings, vehicles or machinery. Items like this which have a continuing existence in themselves, and are of future benefit to the business, are called assets.

In Chapter 1 we defined assets as things we own and liabilities as things we owe. We can now adopt more accurate definitions, namely:

▶   'The essence of an asset is the right to receive future economic benefit.'
▶   'A liability is the obligation to transfer economic benefit.'

Both of these definitions come from Financial Reporting Standard 5 'Reporting the Substance of Transactions'. In Chapter 9 we will look at the significance of Financial Reporting Standards, but for the moment you only need to be aware that they are very authoritative in the world of financial accounting.

The situation we have arrived at may become clearer if we look at an activity.

ACTIVITY **2.2**

A new business starts up as a limited company called Sunrise Ltd by raising £10,000 from its owners, ie its shareholders. It puts this money into a new bank account. What would be the asset(s) and liability(ies)?

Answer

The asset would be a bank account with £10,000 in it, and the liability would be share capital of £10,000. Remember that the share capital is a liability because it represents money that has been contributed to the company by the shareholders.

ACTIVITY **2.3**

Sunrise Ltd then uses £6,000 of its bank account to buy a delivery van. List the asset(s) and liability(ies) after this transaction.

Answer

The list should have been fairly easy to construct, ie:

Assets:	Delivery van	£6,000
	Bank account	£4,000
Liability:	Share capital	£10,000

What you may not have noticed is that you have just constructed your first balance sheet. In other words, a balance sheet is simply a listing of all assets and liabilities. As we saw in Chapter 1, the actual layout of the balance sheet is presented in a specific, detailed format, especially for limited companies, but its basic nature is no more than you have just done.

ACTIVITY **2.4**

Finally, Sunrise Ltd buys some stock for £3,000 but does not yet pay for it. That is, it buys on credit from Daytime Suppliers, agreeing to pay them the £3,000 next month. List the asset(s) and liability(ies) after this transaction.

Answer

Our suggestion is shown below.

Assets:	Delivery van	£6,000
	Stock	£3,000
	Bank account	£4,000
Liabilities:	Share capital	£10,000
	Creditor	£3,000

Note one very important matter – the total assets equal the total liabilities. This is not a coincidence, or just a feature of this example. It is inevitable because the liabilities are providing the funds that we are then spending on these assets. This equality is fundamental to all financial accounting, and is often expressed as the 'balance sheet equation'. This equation is usually set out so as to make a distinction between the capital liability and all other liabilities. This is done in order to maintain the distinction we saw earlier between equity and debt. In the case of Sunrise Ltd, for example, the equity is the share capital, while the debt is the creditor, After all, giving us goods with only a promise to pay in return could be thought of as a loan in kind.

The balance sheet equation thus becomes:

ASSETS = CAPITAL + LIABILITIES

Note that the equation can be re-expressed in a number of different ways, including:

CAPITAL = ASSETS – LIABILITIES

It is also worth noting here that this equality forms the basis of the double entry book-keeping which we will deal with in Chapter 5.

The format of the balance sheet

We have seen that a balance sheet is no more than a list of assets and liabilities (including capital) at a particular point in time. However, we have also noted that there is a specific format for the balance sheet. In the case of limited companies, this format is specified by law, in Schedule 4 to the Companies Act 1985. The next step in learning to construct a balance sheet is therefore to apply the standard format to a list of assets and liabilities.

A few days later, on 30 June 1996, Sunrise Ltd has the following assets and liabilities:

Assets: Delivery van £6,000; Stock £3,000; Bank £500; Machinery £2,200;
    Debtors £700.
Liabilities: Share capital £10,000; Creditors £400; Loan repayable in five years
    £2,000.

The first step is to divide the assets into 'fixed assets' and 'current assets'. Fixed assets are those where the expected life, ie how long we think the asset will last in our business, is more than one year. Current assets are then those that we do not expect to still have one year from now. This is a rather crude pair of definitions, and we will see in Chapter 8 that it will not always be valid, but is nevertheless acceptable for our present purposes.

ACTIVITY **2.5**

List the fixed assets and total them. Then list the current assets beneath the fixed assets, and total them separately.

Answer

Your answer should look like the one below. There are a number of specific points relating to our layout, which are explained below.

Fixed assets		£
Machinery		2,200
Delivery van		6,000
		8,200

Current assets		
Stock	3,000	
Debtors	700	
Bank	500	
	4,200	

Note the following points about the layout above. These are not optional issues, but matters you must normally comply with.

▶ There are two columns of figures, with the current assets being inset. The reason for this will become clear soon.

▶ Both the fixed and current assets are listed in reverse order of liquidity. This means that both lists start with the asset which is likely to be hardest to turn into cash. We have assumed, for example, that a van is easier and quicker to sell than machinery, and that debtors are more liquid than stock. The bank account is obviously the most liquid asset and therefore comes last in the list of current assets.

▶ There is a subtotal for each group of assets.

You might expect that the next step is to list and add up all the liabilities. However, this is not the case. The standard format actually now proceeds by deducting the current liabilities from the current assets. The net amount is called 'net current assets' or, more commonly, 'working capital'. This amount is then carried out into the right-hand column and added to the fixed assets subtotal. The long-term liabilities are then deducted from the total of fixed assets and working capital.

ACTIVITY **2.6**

Extend your balance sheet to include the liabilities. Total your figures, and double underline the total. Now list the share capital below the rest of the balance sheet.

Answer

Your completed balance sheet should now look as follows. As before, there are a number of important points relating to the layout, which are explained below.

SUNRISE LTD
BALANCE SHEET AS AT 31 DECEMBER 1995

Fixed assets

Machinery			2,200
Delivery van			6,000
			8,200

Current Assets

Stock		3,000	
Debtors		700	
Bank		500	
		4,200	

Current Liability

Creditors		400	
			3,800
			12,000

Long-term liability

Loan, repayable in five years			2,000
			£10,000

Share capital			£10,000

▶ The completed balance sheet must be headed by the name of the reporting entity and the date of the balance sheet. Remember that the balance sheet only reports the entity's state of affairs at a single moment.

▶ The division of liabilities into current and long term is done on the same basis as the split of assets into fixed and current. That is, current liabilities are those we expect to have cleared within a year, while long-term liabilities are those we expect to still owe one year from the date of the balance sheet.

▶ The reason why we originally inset the current assets should now be clearer. It was to provide a subtotal from which we could deduct the total of the current liabilities, and so identify the working capital (£3,800). We will consider the importance of working capital in more detail in Chapter 10. Note that if we had had more than one current liability, we would have had to inset those current liabilities into a third column, and carry the total out below the current assets subtotal.

▶ The terms 'current liability' and 'long-term liability' are the traditional ones, and may still be used for the balance sheets of sole traders and partnerships. However, for limited companies the correct terms are now the clumsier phrases 'Liabilities: amounts falling due within one year' and 'Liabilities: amounts falling due after more than one year', respectively. Unfortunately, these are the phrases you should use in company balance sheets in future.

▶ The net total of all assets less all liabilities (£10,000 in our case) is underlined in bold to denote that this is a final total. It marks the end of the first side of the balance sheet, and is called the 'net worth'. In principle, this is what the company is worth, ie what we would be left with if we sold all the assets and paid off the liabilities out of the proceeds.

What the balance sheet tells the user

Having now prepared a balance sheet, it is worth considering what it tells us. In other words, what does a balance sheet mean? We already know that it provides a list of assets and liabilities at a particular point in time, and you saw above that the total of the balance sheet represents, in principle, what the entity is worth. Knowing the state of affairs of an entity would obviously be a useful thing to know, but it is not necessarily true that this is what the balance sheet tells us.

ACTIVITY **2.7**

Look at the balance sheet for Sunrise Ltd, above.

1   We have included the delivery van at what we paid for it. List at least two other ways we could have valued it.
2   Note down one reason why the debtors may not actually result in a benefit to the business of £700.

Answer

Sorting out alternative valuations of assets, and indeed liabilities, is one of the major difficulties in financial accounting and reporting. As you have seen in the balance sheet above, the usual practice is to record assets at what the business paid for them. This is known as the *historical cost*. Nevertheless, alternatives are possible, and you could have listed any or all of the following:

▶   Historical cost less an allowance for wear and tear to date. Such an allowance is called depreciation, and is dealt with in more detail in Chapter 6. This valuation is, of course, still simply a refinement of the historical cost valuation.
▶   Selling price, ie what the van could be sold for. This is usually called the realisable value. Normal practice when considering realisable value is to deduct any costs of sale, such as advertising. In this case the net figure is known as the net realisable value, or NRV.
▶   Replacement cost, that is the cost of replacing the van if, for example, it were stolen this afternoon. In a perfect market, that is one of perfect competition and perfect knowledge of the market by all concerned, this should be the same as the realisable value.
▶   A refinement of the replacement cost approach would be to use the cost of replacing the asset, not with another identical one, but with something that will do the same job. This may be particularly relevant in times of rapidly changing technologies, such as computing.
▶   Finally, we could take a more complex view, and say that the van's value is the economic benefit that it will bring to the business. This is in line with the definition of an asset that we looked at earlier in this chapter. Arriving at this valuation will involve estimating the additional net revenues that the business will earn because of its use of the van. Such additional net revenues will be difficult to determine, but might be the profit on the orders that we only got because we were able to deliver directly and quickly to the customer. This is conceptually and practically the most difficult approach to valuation, and we will therefore examine it more thoroughly later in this chapter and in Chapter 12.

As far as the debtors are concerned, their balance sheet valuation will not turn out to be what they are worth if the debtor does not, in fact, pay us. We have, after all, previously defined the essence of an asset as being control of future economic benefit. If there is no payment, we will receive no economic benefit, and the debtor will therefore not turn out to be an asset. It should therefore not be shown as an asset in the balance sheet, but as an expense in the Profit and Loss Account, usually described as something like 'Bad Debt Written Off'. We will look at expenses in the Profit and Loss Account in more detail in Chapter 3.

Alternatively, the debtor may only be expected to pay us part of what is owed, perhaps £500 of the total £700. In this latter case it would seem to be sensible, and consistent with the definition of an asset, to value the debtor in the balance sheet at £500. The remaining £200 would then be written off as an expense.

Valuation in the balance sheet, especially of assets, is thus a problematic area of financial accounting and reporting. The final part of this chapter therefore considers each of the suggested methods of valuation in the balance sheet more fully.

The alternative valuation methods

We have seen that the obvious way to value an asset is at what we paid for it, that is at its historical cost. This is obviously simple and unambiguous as a method. In other words, it has the advantage of objectivity.

ACTIVITY **2.8**

List at least two disadvantages that you can see with the use of historical cost as a method of valuing an asset.

Answer

The most obvious problem with historical cost is that it will gradually become more and more out of date. It will describe the value of an asset as it was several years ago. This is inappropriate when we have already said that a balance sheet is supposed to give us a picture of the entity at today's date. Furthermore, the higher the level of inflation then the more inappropriate the historical cost valuation will become, as the difference between today's cost and the historical cost gets wider.

Second, and more subtly, adding together assets in the balance sheet which were bought at different dates is implicitly adding together items expressed in different £s, since the real value of the £ will fall during times of inflation. The meaning of the aggregate amount is then highly questionable.

If the deficiencies of historical cost stem from the fact that it becomes more and more out of date, perhaps we should use a current method of valuation. One possibility would be to value an asset at what it would cost today, that is its *current cost*. One way of looking at this is to say that we will value each asset at what it would cost if we were to buy it today, as a replacement for the existing asset. This is known as the replacement cost.

Which of the following statements about a method of valuing assets are true? Mark each with a T for true, or an F for false.

---

1   Replacement cost represents a current valuation of what the entity is worth

2   Replacement cost is usually simpler to determine than historical cost

3   Replacement cost is more objective than historical cost

4   Historical cost is the more true and fair valuation

5   Historical cost is a more useful method of valuation than replacement cost

---

Answer

Our suggested answer is set out below. Note that some of our answers are debatable, especially the last two. Whether historical cost is the more true and fair valuation or not depends on what we mean by true and fair. There is no agreed definition of this key phrase. Nevertheless, we think that replacement cost comes closer to providing a true and fair valuation, if only because it is a better representation of the position at the balance sheet date.

Similarly, question 5 depends on your definition of useful – an issue that we looked at in the previous chapter. This is a very contentious statement, and our answer depends on seeing objectivity as a very important quality of accounting. We think it is because it improves the comparability and the understandability of financial accounting, as well as its reliability. We have therefore marked this question as true. However, you could think that the more up-to-date nature of replacement cost makes that valuation method the more useful.

---

1   Replacement cost represents a current valuation of what the entity is worth   T

2   Replacement cost is usually simpler to determine than historical cost   F

3   Replacement cost is more objective than historical cost   F

4   Historical cost is the more true and fair valuation   F

5   Historical cost is a more useful method of valuation than replacement cost   T

Replacement cost is a current valuation, but it is not the only one. Net realisable value is also a current valuation, one that values an asset at what it could be sold for, rather than at what it could be bought for. You might expect these two valuations to be the same, or certainly very similar. In perfect market circumstances, that is where all buyers and sellers have the same information and competition is universal, you would be right. However, you should note that buying and selling costs, and imperfections in the market, for example through poor information being available to one party to the deal, will often mean that what we could sell for, net of selling costs, is not the same as what we could buy for.

Furthermore, you should note that using net realisable value could be held to be inappropriate to a business which has no intention of selling one or all of its assets. After all, selling all the assets would probably only be the case if the entity were being wound up. For an entity which is a going concern, replacement cost might be held to be more suitable as a method of valuation, although not all accountants would agree with this view. Going concern is a concept that we will return to in Chapter 4.

Finally, as we noted above, the economic value method is both conceptually and practically the most difficult method, and we will therefore leave a detailed exploration of that method until Chapter 12.

At this point you may be beginning to feel that there are no clear answers in accounting, and that it is not the straightforward process you thought it was. We know that this may be unsettling, and that you may be asking whether there is any point to accounting when the answer always seems to be 'it depends . . .'. Nevertheless, for better or worse, this is the position of UK accounting.

At anything above a very basic level, accounting is not a mechanistic exercise, because it has to reflect the uncertainties and complexities of the transactions it describes. We have deliberately started this book with a consideration of fundamental questions about the nature and purposes of accounting for two reasons. First, you can only learn to do good accounting if you understand why you are accounting in the way you are. Second, we think that sorting out these issues is one of the more interesting aspects of accounting.

To check your understanding of what we have covered in this chapter you should now attempt the following question. It brings together many of the points from Chapter 1 as well as this chapter, so you will help yourself if you attempt it seriously. We have provided an answer after the question, but try not to simply read through our answer.

ACTIVITY **2.10**

Dayspring Ltd undertakes the following activities in its first week of existence:

1   Starts its activities by raising £50,000 from the issue of 50,000 £1 shares, and putting this money into a new bank account.
2   Buys a workshop for £30,000, paying by cheque.
3   Buys two delivery vans for £8,000 each, paying by cheque.
4   Interviews and appoints two employees, to start work next week.
5   Borrows £10,000, agreeing to repay it in one lump sum, with interest, in two years' time. Puts the money into the bank account.
6   Buys machinery for £15,000 on credit from Hartford Supplies.
7   Decides that it does not need two delivery vans, and sells one of them on credit to Sunset Garages for £8,000.

Required
There are three questions for you to deal with:

1   Prepare the balance sheet at the end of the week. You could do this by preparing successive balance sheets after each relevant transaction, but this would be rather clumsy and time-consuming. For a fairly small set of transactions like this, it is probably better, therefore, to simply keep a rough

record of the balance of each item. The workshop, for example, starts at £30,000 and then does not change, and so will appear in your balance sheet at £30,000. The bank account will take more analysis.

You may find it helpful to use the Sunrise Ltd balance sheet (above) as a guide to the correct layout.

2 Justify your treatment of transaction (4).

3 Suggest two groups who would probably be particularly interested in the balance sheet you have prepared. Briefly note down why each would be interested.

Answer

Our suggested answers are set out below. Make sure you understand all parts of them before you leave this chapter.

1 **DAYSPRING LTD**
BALANCE SHEET AS AT END OF FIRST WEEK

Fixed assets

Workshop		30,000	
Machinery		15,000	
Delivery van		8,000	
		53,000	

Current assets

Debtors	8,000		
Bank	14,000		
	22,000		

Current liability

Creditors	15,000		
		7,000	
		60,000	

Long-term liability

Loan, repayable in five years		10,000	
		£50,000	

Share capital		£50,000

2 There are a number of reasons why the appointment of two employees should not be reflected in the balance sheet. If you have done some accounting before, you may have mentioned the accruals, or matching concept. In terms of what we have covered so far in this book, you could have justified the exclusion of transaction (4) by reference to the definitions of assets and liabilities.

We know that only assets and liabilities (including capital) appear in a balance sheet. Does the appointment of employees to start next week result in an asset or liability as defined? An employee will normally result in future economic benefit to the business, and will in principle, therefore, be an asset. However, quantifying this benefit with reasonable objectivity will usually be impossible. In these circumstances, an employee should therefore not be recognised as an asset in a balance sheet.

3   It is possible to make out a case for virtually any user group having some interest in the financial statements of any organisation. However, it is likely that the shareholders and the lender will be particularly interested in the balance sheet of Dayspring Ltd, since they have substantial sums at stake in the company. Additionally, you could have made out a good case for saying that Hartford Supplies would be especially interested, given that they have effectively lent Dayspring Ltd £15,000.

Summary
············

This chapter has been about the balance sheet. We have seen that it is essentially just a listing of assets and liabilities, though in a specified format. You have also prepared a simple balance sheet for yourself.

However, what ultimately determines the nature and usefulness of the balance sheet are the definitions of the assets and liabilities. These definitions are worth learning and remembering. Furthermore, we have explored the different bases on which assets and liabilities can be valued, and seen that the usual method – historical cost – is not necessarily the best basis.

In Chapter 3 we continue our review of the basic accounting statements with an exploration of the Profit and Loss Account.

Further study
·················

Most of the issues covered in this chapter can be found in any good basic text on financial accounting. Alternatively, there are now a number of computer-based learning packages available which cover the fundamentals of balance sheets, although many of them tend to focus on how to prepare them, rather than what they mean. Such packages can be expensive, but most institutions of higher education in the UK now have at least one such learning aid, and more are being developed. They can be particularly good for consolidating your knowledge, so try them out if you can.

SELF-
CHECK
QUESTION

Mortlake Ltd owned a building that had cost £42,000 just before the end of the current accounting year on 31 December, and a vehicle bought for £13,000 at the same time. A new access road was announced on the balance sheet date, perhaps making the building worth about £50,000 on the open market. Stock existing at the balance sheet date had been bought for £7,000, but had deteriorated in storage and was now valued at £6,000. Debtors and creditors at the balance sheet date were £4,000 and £5,000 respectively.

You are required to prepare the balance sheet, including the equity figure as the amount needed to make the balance sheet balance. For each item where there is a choice of valuation, you should briefly note down why you have chosen the valuation you have.

Answer

MORTLAKE LTD
BALANCE SHEET AS AT 31 DECEMBER
Fixed assets

Building		42,000
Vehicle		13,000
		55,000

Current assets

Stock	6,000	
Debtors	4,000	
	10,000	

**Creditors: amounts falling due within
        one year**

Creditors	5,000	
		5,000
		£60,000
Equity		£60,000

Notes:

1 The fixed assets have been valued at historical cost, rather than at the higher market value, since the market value is uncertain, and it is, in any case, more prudent (cautious) to apply the lower figure to the valuation. Prudence is a concept that we will look at in more detail in Chapter 4.
2 The stock has similarly been valued at the lower of the possible valuations. This is our best estimate of the economic benefit that it represents to Mortlake.
3 The equity can be taken as the balancing figure because the balance sheet equation defines equity as the difference between assets and liabilities, which is what the first half of the balance sheet has calculated.

Further review questions are available in a separate resource pack which is available to lecturers.

CHAPTER 3

The profit and loss account

Objectives:

By the end of this chapter you should be able to:

▶ List the main trading transactions.
▶ Prepare a simple profit and loss account, including the treatment of opening and closing stock.
▶ Explain and account for typical appropriations of profit.

Introduction

This chapter introduces the second of the main financial statements typically used in the UK, that is the profit and loss account. The balance sheet that we explored in the previous chapter tells us something about the state of affairs at a point in time, usually the last day of the accounting year. The profit and loss account tells us something about what happened during that year.

In its simplest form, the profit and loss account is just a list of the revenues and expenses which arose during a particular period. In practice, it can be complicated. This chapter looks first at the basics of profit and loss accounts, and then goes back to pick up some of the complications. In this way you should be able to grasp the essentials without being distracted by the intricacies.

It is important to be clear right from the start that the profit and loss account does not tell us about everything that happened during the year. First, it does not tell us about events that can not be objectively quantified. This exclusion is one that we have already come across in relation to the balance sheet. Secondly, it does not report anything other than trading transactions.

ACTIVITY 3.1

Note down at least three specific events that will therefore not usually be included in a Profit and Loss Account.

Answer

There are many examples that you could have chosen, but they should all be either events:

▶ the effect of which can not be quantified with reasonable certainty, such as the employment of a new manager, or the introduction of a new manufacturing process, or

▶ which do not relate to trading, such as the purchase of an asset, or the issue of new shares (both of these would, however, be reflected in the balance sheet instead).

The nature and content of the profit and loss account

So, what does go in the profit and loss account? We can approach an answer to this by first giving the profit and loss account its full title, that is 'The Trading and Profit and Loss and Appropriation Account'. In other words, there are technically three distinct elements to what is commonly called just the profit and loss account. We can then deal with each of these elements in turn.

The trading account

As the name suggests, the trading account details the core trading of an organisation. For a supermarket, for example, this would deduct the cost of purchasing the goods sold from the proceeds of the sales, and so calculate the profit on trading. This profit is more properly called the 'gross profit'.

ACTIVITY **3.2**
••••••••••••••

Mr Tate owns a supermarket, which trades as Lowprice Supermarkets. In June, Lowprice Supermarkets buys goods from its suppliers costing £220,000, and makes sales of £300,000. Prepare the trading account.

Answer

LOWPRICE SUPERMARKETS
TRADING ACCOUNT FOR THE MONTH ENDED 30 JUNE

Sales	300,000
Cost of goods sold	220,000
Gross profit	£80,000

You should note that the trading account is headed by the name of the entity, just as the balance sheet was in the previous chapter. It is also useful to head the trading account not only with the fact that it is a trading account, but also to specify which period it covers.

It is unlikely, of course, that the supermarket sells all the stock it has on its shelves. There will almost certainly be a closing stock of goods left over at the end of the month. This stock represents goods that have been bought, but not sold. If we are to compare the selling price of the goods sold with their cost, then we should deduct the cost of any goods not sold from the purchases cost. This net amount, which we then deduct from sales to calculate the gross profit, is called the 'cost of goods sold' or the 'cost of sales'. These are both good names, because they accurately describe exactly what this net figure represents, ie the cost to Lowprice of the goods it has sold to its customers.

If, for example, the supermarket staff do a stock take at the end of June – ie they physically count it – and find that there are goods left which cost Lowprice £55,000, then the trading account will look like this:

LOWPRICE SUPERMARKETS
TRADING ACCOUNT FOR THE MONTH ENDED 30 JUNE

Sales		300,000
Purchases	220,000	
Less: closing stock	55,000	
Cost of sales	————	165,000
Gross profit		£135,000

Notice the technique we used above of insetting a subsidiary calculation into a left-hand column, and carrying the total out into the main, right-hand column.

Before we move on to the profit and loss account, we should look at how we cope if there was stock at the beginning of June as well as at the end. If a stocktake at the start of June had shown an opening stock for the month of, say, £48,000, think what must have happened to this stock. Assuming it was neither lost nor stolen, then this stock must have been sold during the month. In other words, it is part of the cost of sales for June, and should therefore be added to the purchases in the trading account. True, some of it might still be stock as part of the £55,000 at the end of the month, but this does not change the fact that what has been sold should be added to the purchases.

ACTIVITY **3.3**

Use the opening stock figure of £48,000 to revise the trading account above.

Answer

LOWPRICE SUPERMARKETS
TRADING ACCOUNT FOR THE MONTH ENDED 30 JUNE

Sales		300,000
Opening stock	48,000	
Add: Purchases	220,000	
	268,000	
Less: Closing stock	55,000	
Cost of sales	————	213,000
Gross profit		£87,000

In our examples above we have put a bold line under the gross profit to indicate that that is the end of the financial statement. This is correct so long as we are only preparing a trading account. Usually, however, the user of the financial statements will also want information about other expenses, such as insurance, wages, rent and so on. Such information is provided by the Profit and Loss account.

The profit and loss account

The profit and loss account proper starts where the trading account left off, that is with the gross profit. There will then be no need to double underline the gross profit, since we will construct what will effectively then be a single finan-cial statement, the trading and profit and loss account.

At its simplest, the profit and loss account is a list of expenses to be deducted from the gross profit. What is therefore happening is that the trading account presents the 'raw' profit on direct trading, and the profit and loss account shows what expenses are then paid out of that profit. The net result is called the 'net profit'.

ACTIVITY **3.4**

Assume that the other expenses for June were wages of £32,000, insurance of £4,000, heat and light expenses amounting to £17,000, and telephone costs of £2,000. Draft the trading and profit and loss account for June. (You can use the same insetting technique that we saw above to provide a subtotal of the overhead expenses.)

Answer

LOWPRICE SUPERMARKETS
TRADING AND PROFIT AND LOSS ACCOUNT
FOR THE MONTH ENDED 30 JUNE

Sales		300,000
Opening stock	48,000	
Add: Purchases	220,000	
	268,000	
Less: Closing stock	55,000	
Cost of sales	———	213,000
Gross profit		87,000
Wages	32,000	
Insurance	4,000	
Heat and light	17,000	
Telephone	2,000	
	———	55,000
Net profit		£32,000

As we noted at the beginning of this chapter, this first look at the profit and loss account will avoid complications. We will pick up some of the more impor-tant ones later in this chapter, and others in later chapters, particularly in Chapters 7 and 8. Nevertheless, the trading and profit and loss account above is valid for non-company accounting, where the net profit is simply transferred to the owner's capital account. For limited companies, it only remains to consider what will happen to the £32,000 profit and to report those happenings. Such a report is the purpose of the appropriation account.

The appropriation account

As the name suggests, the appropriation account details the various appropria-tions of profit. In simpler language, it lists what has happened to the profit made by the entity in the past year. There are normally only three things that can happen to the profit.

ACTIVITY 3.5

Think about who is likely to be entitled to a share of a limited company's profit, and so suggest what these three appropriations will be.

Answer

You may have expressed your ideas in different ways, but your suggestions should have fallen into the following groups:

1   Tax. The Inland Revenue, or equivalent authority in other countries, will want the first slice of a limited company's profit. We will look at tax in more detail in Chapter 8.
2   Owners' share. In a limited company this share will be in the form of dividends – again we will look at dividends in more detail in Chapter 8. More generically, this slice of profit will more usually be called the distribution.
3   Retained profit. By default, this is the amount left over after the other appropriations. In a sole trader or partnership business, this amount will simply be added to the capital of the sole trader or shared out to the capitals of the partners. In a company the procedure is more formal, and the retained profit will be transferred to one or more 'reserves'. Once again, Chapter 8 will examine this transfer in greater detail.

The presentation of the appropriation account is relatively simple. All we need to do is list each appropriation in turn, in the order set out above. As each amount is deducted from the net profit it is usual to calculate a sub-total, so that the user can see what profit is left after each appropriation.

ACTIVITY 3.6

Assume that Lowprice Supermarkets is a limited company. It calculates its tax liability on the profit for June at £11,000. Mr Tate, the managing director, declares a dividend of £8,000 from the remaining profit after tax. Any retained profit is to be transferred to the company's reserves. Draft the appropriation account for June.

Answer

LOWPRICE SUPERMARKETS LTD
APPROPRIATION ACCOUNT
FOR THE MONTH ENDED 30 JUNE

Net profit before tax	32,000
Tax	11,000
Profit after tax	21,000
Dividends	8,000
Retained profit, transferred to reserves	£13,000

You have now seen all the elements of what is properly called the trading and profit and loss and appropriation account, and more commonly known as simply the profit and loss account. Most of the rest of this chapter will now explore some of the complications which typically arise in practice. Before we do this, however, you should try the following activity. It brings together all we have covered in this chapter, and is intended to consolidate your knowledge and understanding of the basics, before we go on to tackle the difficult bits.

ACTIVITY **3.7**

Suraya Ltd started in business on 1 January 1997. On 31 December 1997 the following balances were taken from the company's books, and from a final stocktake.

	£
Sales	296,483
Heat and light	26,730
Insurance	11,978
Wages	36,389
Opening stock	15,450
Closing stock	16,070
Purchases	175,962
Dividend	18,400
Rent	6,397

The tax liability on the profit for the year was estimated at £7,360. Any retained profit is to be transferred to the company's reserves.

Prepare the trading and profit and loss and appropriation account for the year ended 31 December 1997.

Answer

Your answer should look like the following. Check your answer against ours, noting not just the numbers, but also the narration in the title and in how each number is labelled. Accounting is about communication, and the words matter.

SURAYA LTD TRADING AND PROFIT AND LOSS AND APPROPRIATION ACCOUNT FOR THE YEAR ENDED 31 DECEMBER 1997

Sales		296,483
Cost of sales:		
Opening stock	15,450	
Purchases	175,962	
	191,412	
Closing stock	16,070	
		175,342
Gross profit		121,141
Heat and light	26,730	
Insurance	11,978	
Wages	36,389	
Rent	6,397	
		81,494
Net profit before tax		39,647
Tax		7,360
Profit after tax		32,287
Dividend		18,400
Retained profit, transferred to reserves		£13,887

The rest of this chapter is now concerned with three refinements which you need to be aware of before we leave the profit and loss account. These are stock valuation, non-trading organisations, and the particular presentation of profit and loss accounts for limited companies.

Stock valuation
....

We have seen how the purchases figure has to be adjusted by adding on the opening stock and deducting the closing stock to arrive at the cost of the sales figure. However, we have not yet given any thought to where the stock figure came from, other than to say it resulted from a stock-take.

A stock-take involves counting all the stock items that we hold at a particular time. While this will give us the number of each stock line we hold, it will not attach a value to that number. Counting the stock of bags of sugar held by Lowprice Supermarkets at the end of June, for example, will tell us that we have, say, 60 bags in stock, but not what each is worth. There are a number of different bases of valuation that we could use, such as:

▶ Historical cost, that is what Lowprice Supermarkets paid for each bag.
▶ Replacement cost, that is what it would cost Lowprice to buy the stock again today. This will often be more than the historical cost, especially when prices are rising quickly.
▶ Net realisable value, which is what Lowprice could sell each bag of sugar for, less any immediate costs of sale. In these circumstances, this would be the selling price on the shelf, and would normally be more than either cost above.

We shall see in Chapter 12 that there are other bases of valuation, and we will look at the relative merits of each in that chapter. For the moment we can take a pragmatic approach, and all we need to know is what Statement of Standard Accounting Practice (SSAP) 9 says. In Chapter 9 we shall examine the nature and purposes of such accounting standards, but note for now that their regulations should be followed when preparing financial statements. SSAP 9 is called 'Stocks and Long-Term Contracts' and specifies that stock should be valued 'at the lower of cost and net realisable value'.

As with the bags of sugar in Lowprice Supermarkets, the lower of these alternatives will normally be cost. Net realisable value will only be lower in relatively rare cases, such as when the stock has gone out of fashion, or is close to its sell-by date. In such circumstances the owner might be prepared to sell for less than he or she paid for it, in order to be able to sell it.

However, this is not the end of the matter, because identifying what we paid for the stock, that is its historical cost, is not always straightforward. Look, for example, at the following case.

Lowprice supermarkets had the following transactions in bags of sugar during June.

1st	Bought 300 bags from the supplier for 60p each
14th	Sold 160 bags for 95p each
19th	Bought 100 bags for 65p each
26th	Sold 200 bags for 95p each

If we now try to work out the profit on our trading in sugar, we must follow through the sales transactions. The first sale was of 160 bags at 95p, ie £152, and the cost of this sale is clearly 160 bags at the 60p we paid for them, ie £96. There was thus a gross profit of £56 on the first sale.

The sales value of the second batch of sales is also fairly easy to calculate, that is 200 bags at 95p, ie £190. However, the cost of these sales is problematic. Have we now sold the remaining 140 bags from those we bought on 1 June, and 60 from those bought on 19 June? If so, the cost of sales will be 140 at 60p plus 60 at 65p, ie £123.

Alternatively, have we sold all the 100 bought on 19 June and thus 100 from those left from the batch bought on 1 June? In this case, the cost of sales will be 100 at 65p plus 100 at 60p, ie £125. This is certainly not a large difference from the other calculation of £123, but replicated over all product lines in the supermarket it is clear that we potentially have a significantly different cost of sales figure, and hence a different gross profit reported.

One way to decide which batch of purchases are being sold for any given sale is to consider the physical reality. Normal supermarket practice would be to sell the older stock first, so that they are not left with stock past its sell-by date. In other words, the first stock that came in is the first to go out. This method is called 'first in, first out', usually abbreviated to 'FIFO'. In our example above, this is the first scenario, the one that resulted in a cost of sales of £123. It is widely used in practice, largely because it does reflect normal stock rotation practice.

DID YOU KNOW ...?
Valuation methods such as FIFO and LIFO are sometimes referred to as 'theoretical pricing models'.

Some traders, however, do not deal in stock which has a short sell-by date, but do have stock which is difficult to handle. An example would be a steel stockholder, dealing in girders, RSJs and so on. When a new delivery arrives from the steel mill, the stock holder is unlikely to move the existing stock to store the new delivery underneath the old. When he then sells to a customer, he will usually take the steel from the top of the pile, and will thus be selling the newer stock. In other words, the last stock that came in is the first to go out. A stock system that rests on this model is known as 'last in, first out', or 'LIFO'. This is the approach implicitly adopted by the second alternative in our example above, and resulted in a cost of sales of £125.

Notice that if we adopt a FIFO approach, any stock left over is assumed to be from the later delivery, while LIFO assumes that any such closing stock is drawn from the earlier delivery. This should become clearer if you work through an example for yourself.

ACTIVITY **3.8**

Anne, a trader, had the following dealings during August in her only item of stock. There was no opening stock.

1st	Bought 40 for £28 each
5th	Bought 25 for £30 each
10th	Sold 50 for £45 each
21st	Bought 30 for £32 each
27th	Sold 35 for £45 each

Draft the trading account for the month, assuming:

▶ a FIFO basis of stock valuation
▶ a LIFO basis of stock valuation.

Answer

We have used a tabular layout for our answer, which we think allows for a better comparison of the methods.

	FIFO		LIFO	
Sales		3,825		3,825
Purchases	2,830		2,830	
Closing stock	320		280	
Cost of sales		2,510		2,550
Gross profit		£1,315		£1,275

Notice that the sales and purchases figures do not alter. What gives the different gross profit figure is the different stock valuation. Under FIFO the remaining ten items are valued at £32, since the earlier stock has been sold and what is left as the closing stock is priced at what came in last. Under LIFO, the same ten items are valued at the earliest valuation, ie £28 each, since we assume that it is the latest stock which has been sold, so leaving the earliest.

There is one more possibility for our stock valuation. Consider the position of a garage that takes a new delivery of petrol into a tank already part full from a previous delivery. When a customer draws off a few gallons what she takes will be a mixture of the old and new stock. Neither FIFO nor LIFO will now be wholly appropriate – what we need is a mixture, to reflect the mixture that has been taken as the cost of sales. This third method is called average cost, abbreviated to AVCO, and calculated as follows.

Suppose customers in Lowprice Supermarkets could help themselves to sugar from the total stock, and took some of the old delivery and some of the new. The sales on 14 June must have been from the stock bought on 1 June for 60p, since we had no other stock at that time. The cost of sales must therefore have been 160 at 60p, ie £96 again. However, the sale on 26 June of 200 is now deemed to come partly from the 140 bags remaining from those delivered on 1 June (cost 60p), and partly from the 100 delivered on 19 June (cost 65p). The way to work out the average cost to Lowprice of the bags sold on 26 June is:

140 bags at 60p	=	84
100 bags at 65p	=	65
240		£149

The average cost of each bag sold on 26 June must therefore have been 149/240, ie 62p. This would then be the AVCO valuation of the remaining stock of 40 bags, so that the closing stock under AVCO would be shown in the trading account at 40 times 62p, ie £25, to the nearest £.

ACTIVITY **3.9**

Draft the trading account for Anne, using the same data as in the previous activity, but this time assuming an AVCO valuation base for stock.

Answer

Our answer is as follows:

Sales		3,825
Purchases	2,830	
Closing stock	309	
Cost of sales		2,521
Gross profit		£1,304

The closing stock is calculated like this:

Sale on 10 August

40 at £28	=	1,120
25 at £30	=	750
65		£1,870

Cost of sale = 50/65 x 1,870 = 1,438
Stock remaining = 15/65 x 1,870 = 432

Sale on 27

15 at average cost, as above =	432
30 at £32 =	960
45	1,392

Cost of sale = 35/45 × 1,392 = 1,083
Stock remaining = 10/45 × 1,392 = 309

Notice that AVCO occupies a mid-way position between FIFO and LIFO in terms of valuation, and hence results in a mid-position report of gross profit.

We thus have three bases on which we can arrive at a cost for our stock, and the question that should occur to you is which one is right? As you may be beginning to suspect by now, the answer is that there is no single right choice. It would seem reasonable to choose the method that best reflects our stock management in practice, using FIFO, for example, where strict stock rotation is a feature of our business. Many businesses do, in fact, use FIFO. However, it is important to note that many accountants would argue that the accounting treatment need not necessarily reflect the physical reality – certainly, there is no obligation for it to do so, either in law or in any accounting standard. Hence, there is no absolutely correct method, but bear in mind that SSAP 9 does not recommend the use of LIFO, as it argues that the stock value under this method is unlikely to bear a reasonable relationship to actual costs incurred in the period.

Non-trading organisations

So far in this chapter we have been looking at organisations whose aim is to trade for a profit. While this will be true of the great majority of organisations for whom accounts are prepared, it is not universal. Some organisations exist for more fundamental purposes. Examples are charities, social clubs and religious bodies.

DID YOU KNOW ...?
A receipts and payment account is just a summary of the club's bank account during the financial period.

Such organisations will not usually prepare a trading and profit and loss account, because they typically do not trade, and because a financial statement that reports on the profit or loss is inappropriate for bodies that do not aim at a profit. There are two possible alternatives to the profit and loss account for such bodies. These are the 'Receipts and Payments Account' and the 'Income and Expenditure Account'.

The receipts and payments account is, in fact, sometimes also used for reporting the activities of very small trading organisations, but is more often found in non-trading bodies. As the name suggests, it is simply a list of what money has been received and what has been paid out. In other words, at its simplest, it is just a summary of the bank account. There will thus be no stock adjustment, such as we have just looked at above for the trading account. Nor will there be any of the other adjustments that we will come across in Chapter 6, and which are involved in the preparation of a commercial profit and loss account.

The receipts and payments account for an athletics club might look like this:

MOORTOWN ATHLETICS CLUB
RECEIPTS AND PAYMENTS ACCOUNT
FOR THE MONTH ENDED 31 JANUARY

Subscriptions from members		120
Life memberships		45
		165
Rent of clubhouse	75	
Publicity	10	
Travel	20	
Furnishings	40	
		145
Excess of receipts over payments		£20

The 'subscriptions from members' is a typical source of funds for a non-profit-making organisation. It will usually cover the whole of the forthcoming year. 'Life memberships' may be a feature of some clubs. They represent lump sums paid by members which entitle them to life membership without paying any further subscriptions.

Notice also that the payments include a fixed asset, 'furnishings'. Everything, including capital expenditure (ie fixed assets) that would normally be shown separately in the balance sheet, is included in the receipts and payments account.

By contrast, an *income and expenditure account* is prepared using all the adjustments, such as the stock adjustment, that are used in preparing the profit and loss account. The difference between the income and expenditure account and the profit and loss account is one of terminology. The former title seems more appropriate than the latter when the statement is reporting on a non-profit-making organisation. In all other respects an income and expenditure account is identical to a profit and loss account.

If, for example, Moortown Athletics Club decides to prepare an income and expenditure account instead of a receipts and payments account, it will use exactly the same techniques that a commercial organisation would use to prepare a profit and loss account. It will therefore need to determine its debtors, creditors and stock, and to distinguish between capital and revenue items.

ACTIVITY **3.10**

Suppose that the subscriptions from members of the Moortown Athletics Club (see above) are for the year to 31 December, but were all received in January, and that the rent of the clubhouse was paid in January for the first three months of the calendar year. There is a stock of publicity materials left at the end of January valued at £5. Amend the receipts and payments account above to turn it into an income and expenditure account. To do this, you will need to adjust the cash flows by the amounts outstanding in order to arrive at the amount which relates to January alone. Life memberships are awkward because they relate to an uncertain future period, ie the lives of the relevant members. It will therefore often be regarded as acceptable for the club to account for these wholly in the period when they are received.

You may find this a difficult activity, but, as always, do try it before you look at the answer.

Answer

MOORTOWN ATHLETICS CLUB
INCOME AND EXPENDITURE ACCOUNT
FOR THE MONTH ENDED 31 JANUARY

Subscriptions from members (£120/12 months)		10
Life memberships		45
		55
Rent of clubhouse (75/3 months)	25	
Publicity (10–5)	5	
Travel	20	
Furnishings	40	
		90
Excess of expenditure over income		£35

Our answer above includes notes of the adjustments we have made. Make sure you at least understand the answer before you move on. Notice that the cash surplus reported by the receipts and payments account indicated a positive view of the club's finances, but the income and expenditure account gives a very different view of its financial health. This is primarily because the income and expenditure account allows for the fact that the subscriptions received in January will have to last the club for the whole year.

Limited companies

This is a topic that we will deal with more fully in Chapter 8. However, if you have seen any profit and loss accounts published by limited companies, you may have noticed that they do not look exactly like the one you prepared for Lowprice Supermarkets (see p. 29). This is because the Companies Act 1985 lays down very detailed rules about the layout of both the profit and loss account and the balance sheet.

The profit and loss account that we prepared earlier will be acceptable for sole trader and partnership businesses, but will only be acceptable for *internal* use by a limited company. For *external* published use, Schedule 4 to the Companies Act 1985 specifies that all expenses must be grouped, not by 'purpose' as we have done (cost of sales, heat and light, insurance, wages, rent), but by 'function'. The three broad functional areas that are specified in the Companies Act are:

▶ cost of sales
▶ selling and distribution expenses
▶ administration expenses.

There are other changes, as we will see in Chapter 8, but this regrouping of expenses is perhaps the most striking. For now, all you need to be aware of is the different presentation of the profit and loss account imposed by the law. Note that it is purely a matter of different presentation – the final net profit will be exactly the same, whichever method of presentation is used.

Summary

This chapter has introduced you to what is usually just called the profit and loss account. You have seen that it is actually made up of three parts, that is:

▶ the trading account
▶ the profit and loss account
▶ the appropriation account.

Each of these parts has been examined in turn, and you should now be able to prepare at least a simple profit and loss account, including a stock adjustment. Since you learnt how to draft a simple balance sheet in the previous chapter, you have now covered the essentials of financial reporting. The later part of this chapter has started our exploration of some of the complications that attach to the profit and loss account. In particular, we have looked at some of the problems surrounding the question of how to value stock, and you should now be able to distinguish between, and calculate, the FIFO, LIFO and AVCO bases.

One of the points that has hopefully struck you is that each of these bases results in a different profit figure. Furthermore, we saw in Chapter 2 that there are a number of different ways to value assets, and each results in a different balance sheet position being reported. There is obviously a problem looming here, which is the range of possible accounting results from given data. Before looking at any more of the techniques of accounting, we will therefore look in some detail at what theory of accounting has been developed to help us tackle this problem. The next chapter is therefore concerned with the concepts and characteristics of accounting.

Further study

As with the balance sheet in Chapter 2, most of the issues covered in this chapter can be found in any good basic text on financial accounting. If you want an alternative view of the issues, then browse your local library to find a text that you personally find readable. Alternatively, there are now a number of computer-based learning packages available which cover the profit and loss account. Probably the most widely available such package in UK universities is 'EQL'.

**SELF-
CHECK
QUESTION**

The following details relate to the trading activities of Anarkhi Ltd for its first year of trading, to 30 June:

	£
Purchases	531,946
Sales	794,062
Wages	218,470
Transport	54,475
Rent and insurance	30,775
Tax	3,900

All purchases may be considered as part of cost of sales. All other costs should be allocated 40% to cost of sales, 40% to selling and distribution expenses, and 20% to administration expenses.

Anarkhi Ltd uses the FIFO method of stock valuation. On 23 June there was no trading stock. During the last week of the year, stock transactions were:

5,000 units delivered at £12 each
2,000 units delivered at £13 each
3,000 units sold at £19 each

You are required to draft the trading and profit and loss and appropriation account for the year, adopting the Companies Act format as far as possible. You will need to calculate the value of the closing stock, and to allocate the expenses as listed above to their Companies Act categories before you can construct the profit and loss account.

Answer

Our answer starts with the calculation of closing stock, ie:

5,000 + 2,000 - 3,000 = 4,000 units in stock
Under FIFO, those sold are deemed to be from the first delivery, leaving 2,000 units at £12, and the other 2,000 units therefore being from the delivery at £13. The closing stock valuation is therefore:
(2,000 × 12) + (2,000 × 13) = 50,000.

We can now calculate the cost of sales, being purchases less closing stock – there is no opening stock to worry about in this case. The calculation is 531,946 – 50,000 = 481,946.

Next we need to allocate the expenses to their Companies Act categories. This is best set out as a table.

	Cost of sales	Selling	Administration
Cost of sales, as above	481,946		
Wages	87,388	87,388	43,694
Transport	21,790	21,790	10,895
Rent and insurance	12,310	12,310	6,155
	£603,434	£121,488	£60,744

Finally, we can put all the above together into our profit and loss account, as follows:

ANARKHI LTD
TRADING AND PROFIT AND LOSS AND APPROPRIATION ACCOUNT
FOR THE YEAR ENDED 31 DECEMBER

Sales		794,062
Cost of sales		603,434
Gross profit		190,628
Selling and distribution expenses	121,488	
Administration expenses	60,744	
		182,232
Net profit		8,396
Tax		3,900
Retained profit		£4,496

Further review questions are available in a separate resource pack which is available to lecturers.

CHAPTER 4

Concepts and characteristics

Objectives:

By the end of this chapter you should be able to:

▶ Outline the generally accepted concepts and conventions of financial accounting.

▶ Explain the four major characteristics of financial reporting.

Introduction

At this stage, it is worth taking stock of where we have got to. In Chapter 1 we explored the nature and uses of accounting, and then in Chapters 2 and 3 we looked at the two major statements conventionally used in financial accounting, that is the balance sheet and the profit and loss account. One of the points that should have struck you is that accounting is far from being the exact science many people believe it to be.

In particular, we have already seen how both the balance sheet and the profit and loss account can vary according to the basic assumptions we make about how and what we should measure. For example, balance sheets would look very different if all companies did what some football clubs currently do, and showed the value of their employees – the players, valued at their transfer fees – on the balance sheet. Again, we saw in the last chapter that the gross profit will vary if we change our assumptions about stock rotation, and use FIFO instead of LIFO as a basis of stock valuation. As you will see as we work through this book, there are many other examples.

What we seem to have in accounting is a situation where the balance sheet and the profit and loss account, taken together, present a different picture of the state of affairs and the performance of an entity, respectively, depending on what fundamental assumptions we make.

In other words, the economic health of an entity can apparently vary not only with the reality of economic changes, but also with how we choose to account for that reality. How, then, can any user place any reliance on the financial statements?

The approach that accountants in the UK have chosen as their way forward is a two-stage technique:

▶   to agree on explicit underlying assumptions, and then
▶   to develop accounting practices that are consistent with those generally accepted assumptions, and hence lead towards 'a true and fair view'.

We have come to accept this approach in the UK as being so obviously correct that it can be hard to think of any alternative. However, it is instructive to look at what, say, the French approach has been. The French approach is to specify in great detail exactly what sort of transactions go under each heading or account, and then to further specify how those accounts shall be presented. The set of rules that specify these headings and presentations is known as the *plan comptable* – the plan of accounts. There is thus, for example, no choice about whether to use FIFO or LIFO, since the single, 'correct' method is laid down in the *plan comptable*.

The French equivalent of the UK idea of a true and fair view is the *image fidèle*. A rough translation would be 'faithful picture', and it is notable that the French first specified the 'plan', as the way to produce accounts, and only subsequently imposed the aim of an *image fidèle*. In other words, the attainment of an *image fidèle* is not central to French accounting in the same way as the attainment of 'a true and fair view' is central to UK accounting.

ACTIVITY 4.1

Complete the following table, by making at least one entry under each heading. You may find it helpful to think in terms of the relative disadvantages of the UK system, rather than of the relative advantages of the French system. You will be addressing much the same issues.

	UK approach	French approach
Relative advantages		

Answer

Any answers to this activity will be a matter of debate, but our views are that the UK approach has advantages in terms of relevance. By allowing some choice of method, it can be argued that UK accounts can be prepared according to methods which are geared to the particular needs of the entity, rather than being geared to a mythical 'national average' entity. Furthermore, it may be that the need to consider the most appropriate treatment of a given accounting issue, rather than to simply follow the specified treatment, results in a more lively and participative accounting profession.

On the other hand, the French approach does have the key benefit of consistency. All entities will, in principle at least, treat the same item in the same way, so improving comparability between the accounts of different entities. In addition, the prescription of practice should result in less debate and therefore in faster preparation, and faster will mean cheaper.

You may have had your own, equally valid, ideas. We hope so, because, as you have just seen, accounting in the UK is ultimately determined by some minimum agreement on fundamental underlying assumptions. If you have no ideas then you can't engage in this fundamental debate. The rest of this chapter presents the current state of the more important parts of this debate. It is divided into two main sections. The first part, concepts, covers fairly well-established ideas. The second part, characteristics, deals with more recently developed thinking about what makes a set of financial statements 'good' – whatever that means.

Concepts
••••••••••••

To reiterate, concepts are the underlying ideas of accounting. They have usually been implicit and understood as a common culture of accounting, rather than being made explicit, even though we have seen above how important they are. Given that such underlying theoretical principles can radically change the view the financial statements give of an entity, it should be obvious that preparers and users of those statements should be very clear about the particular principles that have been applied to any given set of statements. Requiring such a recognition of the fundamental principles, and an explicit declaration of the accounting practices they result in for a given entity are the twin purposes of Statement of Standard Accounting Practice (SSAP) 2 'Disclosure of Accounting Policies'.

We will consider the nature and authority of accounting standards in more detail in Chapter 9, but for the moment you need only be aware that they are generally held to be effectively mandatory in almost all cases. At the heart of SSAP 2 is the assumption that all financial statements produced in the UK will be consistent with a few basic, specified principles, known as the concepts. As the standard itself expresses it, 'In the absence of a clear statement to the contrary, there is a presumption that the four fundamental concepts have been observed.'

The four that were set out in that standard in 1971 are known as prudence, accruals (sometimes called the matching concept), consistency and going concern. These four are the bedrock of accounting practice, and are worth looking at in some detail.

Prudence concept

When we have to choose between two or more accounting treatments of an economic event, prudence dictates that we should always choose the one that results in showing the lowest profit, and/or the lowest net worth. For example, we saw in Chapter 3 that stock is valued at the lower of cost and net realisable value, rather than at the normal selling price. The justification for this lower valuation is the prudence concept.

Accruals (or matching) concept

When preparing the profit and loss account, revenue and profits are matched with the associated costs and expenses incurred in earning them. This means that revenues and expenses are recognised when they are incurred, rather than when the related cash is received or paid. A sale will thus be accounted for when the contract is agreed, and not when the goods or services are paid for.

Consistency concept

There should be consistency of treatment of like items within each accounting period and from one period to the next. In other words, once you have chosen an accounting treatment, you should stick with it from one year to the next. The key reason for this is to promote comparability, that is it helps the user to make comparisons over time, and so to pick out useful trends. Having decided, for example, to value our buildings at historical cost, rather than at, say, replacement cost, consistency requires that we will normally continue to adopt historical cost for the buildings.

Going concern concept

There is an assumption that the business will continue to operate for the fore-seeable future. The application of this concept could make a difference, for example when we consider asset valuations. We have seen that the usual basis is historical cost, but if the entity is no longer a going concern and will be wound up, it is arguably more appropriate to value the assets at selling price, since they will soon be sold.

ACTIVITY 4.2
....

SSAP 2 sets out the above ideas in rather more formal terms. In the list below, four extracts are given from that standard. Identify which extract relates to which of the four concepts.

A This means in particular that the profit and loss account and balance sheet assume no intention or necessity to liquidate or curtail significantly the scale of operation.

B . . . accounting treatment of like items within each accounting period and from one period to the next.

C The profit and loss account reflects changes in the amount of net assets that arise out of the transactions of the relevant period (other than distributions or subscriptions of capital and unrealised surpluses arising on revaluation of fixed assets). Revenue and profits dealt with in the profit and loss account are matched with associated costs and expenses by including in the same account the costs incurred in earning them.

D Revenue and profits are not anticipated, but are recognised by inclusion in the profit and loss account only when realised in the form either of cash or of other assets the ultimate cash realisation of which can be assessed with reasonable certainty; provision is made for all known liabilities (expenses and losses) whether the amount of these is known with certainty or is a best estimate in the light of the information available.

Answer

The correct answer is that A is an extract from the definition of going concern, B from that for consistency, C from that for accruals, and D is taken from the definition of prudence.

In addition to these four well-established concepts, there are also a number of implicit ideas that are generally accepted. You will find that these are referred to both in books and, less commonly, in practice, so it is worth being aware of them.

Separate valuation

Separate valuation is probably the most important of this latter group because, along with the four basic concepts, it is specifically referred to in the Companies Act 1985. This Act includes extensive accounting rules, and requires that all UK financial statements will normally be based on the four concepts in SSAP 2, plus the concept of separate valuation. This concept is best explained by an example:

> Assume that A has sold goods on credit to B worth £600, so that, in A's books, B shows up as a debtor for £600. Meanwhile, B has sold goods on credit to A for £400. In A's books, B also therefore appears as a creditor for £400. No agreement has been made about setting off one amount against another. What should we show in A's balance sheet in relation to B?

You could argue that we should simply show the net debtor of £200 as a current asset. However, there is a counter-argument that holds that showing just the net debtor does not give a full picture of the total situation, and thus does not give a true and fair view. After all, in the absence of an explicit agreement between A and B to legally set off the £400 against the £600, the position is that B must pay the full £600. This being so, the correct presentation in A's balance sheet would be to show a debtor of £600 and a creditor of £400. In other words, the debtor and the creditor should be separately valued, and disclosed as such.

Business entity

We have come across this concept already, in relation to capital in the balance sheet. The business has an identity and existence distinct from the owners, so that the business can and should record an amount owing to its owner, ie the capital. Transactions of a business are recorded as they affect the business, not as they affect the owner.

Duality

Again, we have already seen this concept in action, when we looked at sources and applications of funds in Chapter 2. In relation to any one economic event, two aspects are recorded in the accounts, that is the source of funds and the related applications. The balance sheet equation is an application of the duality concept. In Chapter 5 we will see that it also underpins double entry bookkeeping.

Monetary measurement

Only those events and situations that can be reasonably objectively measured in money terms are recorded. This means, for example, that 'happy and skilled workforce' is not an asset that you will see on a balance sheet, even though most managements routinely say that their workforce is the company's greatest asset, and it may even be true. It does not appear because the value of this asset can't be objectively quantified.

Objectivity

This concept is obviously closely linked to money measurement. More generally, however, and more formally, it is a required attribute of accounting that competent individuals working independently should arrive at the same or very similar measures of given economic events or situations.

Historical cost

The usual method of arriving at an objectively agreeable quantification of an event is to value it at what the item in question cost. This is known as its historical cost. It has the huge advantage over any other system of being relatively objective, but we will see in Chapter 12 that it has its own problems in times of significant inflation.

Realisation

Revenue is recognised when it is capable of objective measurement and we are reasonably certain that the related transfer of resources will occur. We account for a sale, for example, in the period in which we agree the sale contract, even if we don't get paid until the next accounting period. It is thus related to the accruals concept.

Materiality

A very small mistake in the financial statements of an entity will not invalidate those statements. They should still be usable by anyone interested in the entity. However, the key issue is obviously what we mean by 'very small'. The concept of materiality applies the test of whether the financial statements still show a true and fair view. If the answer is yes, then the error is not material, and we need not spend time and resources trying to find and correct it. If, on the other hand, the mis-statement, or even the total omission, of an item would result in the financial statements as a whole not showing a true and fair view, then that item would be regarded as material. Such an error would have to be corrected if the statements are to comply with the Companies Act 1985 and show a true and fair view.

The materiality of an item is related to the size of the entity. The omission or mis-statement of a £10,000 item would probably not be material in the financial statements of ICI or Thorn-EMI, but would almost certainly be very material in the financial statements of a one-person business. Note that materiality can be measured against size, as suggested above, but occasionally it may be more appropriate to measure it against profits. If, for example, the profits of ICI were only £20,000, then a £10,000 item could, perhaps, be considered material.

ACTIVITY **4.3**

Sam and Louise had £800, out of which they purchased a second-hand van for £500. All their other assets are to be ignored. They estimated that the van will have a life of about another 20,000 miles. Sam and Louise started a light removals business, but were involved in an accident on their first day, and damaged a bicycle. Sam promised to pay for the damage and the rider said he thought the bike could be repaired for between £60 and £100.

At the end of their first day, Sam and Louise were offered £600 for the van. They were also paid £50 cash for a job they did in the morning and £70 for the afternoon's job, payable next week. During the day, they had travelled 50 miles.

List Sam and Louise's assets and liabilities at the start and end of the first day and hence say how much better, or worse, off they are since they started. More importantly, in doing so, clearly indicate which accounting concepts justify your calculations.

This is an important activity, drawing together much of what we have covered so far in this book, so try to do it, and do it conscientiously.

Answer

Given that the ideas involved in any answer to this question are so open ended, what follows should not be regarded as the definitive answer, but rather as a reasonable response that covers all the main points that should be made.

		Relevant concepts
Opening position		
Asset		
Cash	800	Money measurement
Liability		
Capital	800	Business entity
Closing position		
Assets		
Van	500	Historical cost, materiality, prudence
Debtor	70	Accruals
Cash	350	Money measurement
	920	
Liabilities		
Owing for bicycle	100	Accruals, prudence
	820	
Capital		
Opening position	800	Business entity
Increase in wealth	20	Going concern
	£820	

What our answer sets out is both the opening and closing balance sheets. Notice how the increase in wealth has been calculated by determining the difference between the opening capital position and what the net result of the assets and liabilities tells us must be the closing value of the business. Another way to view this increase in wealth is as the net income for the period. In other words, what we have done above is to calculate the net profit without preparing a profit and loss account. We do not have the detail about revenues and expenses that the profit and loss account provides, but it is an alternative way to calculate profit. This is an idea that we will return to in Chapter 12.

In terms of the concepts that we have listed above, there are a number of points to be made. First, both the opening and the closing cash positions depend on their validity as measures of wealth on the basic assumption that we can measure anything by attaching a number of £s to it. In other words, the whole exercise rests on the money measurement concept.

Second, the valuation of the van is more of a problem. The usual basis would be to value it according to what we paid for it, ie at its historical cost, but there are other possibilities. We could, for example, decide that a more relevant and useful valuation would be what we were offered for it, that is £600. Would this value be any less logical or reasonable than using the old cost? If not, the implication is that the conventional choice of historical cost is at least partly arbitrary. If, on the other hand, the choice of historical cost is more logical and reasonable than any other, we should be explicit about why we believe this. As we saw before, the great advantage historical cost has is its relative objectivity.

Third, this is not the only issue in relation to the valuation of the van, there is also the question of depreciation. This a topic that we will cover in more detail in Chapter 6, but note that if the van is going to be of benefit for 20,000 miles, the accruals concept would suggest that we should allocate some of the cost of £500 against the day's profits. The question of how much benefit can be answered by saying that we have presumably had 50/20,000ths of the benefit, since we have travelled 50 miles out of a total usable mileage of 20,000. Using the historical cost value of £500, this works out to a depreciation charge for the period of £1.25, which hardly seems worth bothering with. In more formal terms, we can invoke the convention of materiality to justify ignoring any charge for the using up of the value of the van, at least for one day.

Fourth, accruals and realisation could be used to justify the inclusion of the amount due for the afternoon's work, that is the debtor of £70.

Fifth, the adoption of prudence would guide our valuation of the creditor, since showing £100 as being outstanding is a more prudent treatment than only showing £60, or even a compromise of, say, £80. The amount has not yet been paid, but we conventionally allow for it since it relates to this accounting period. The formal justification for making such allowances is, of course, the accruals concept.

Sixth and finally, the net effect of applying all these concepts and conventions to the opening and closing valuations of Sam and Louise's business is to report an increase in wealth of £20. Unless they withdraw this profit, it will be carried forward to finance their business in future periods. The implication is that we are assuming that the business is a going concern.

This has been a discursive answer to a fairly short activity. However, we have been concerned to demonstrate how even simple accounting practice rests explicitly on fundamental assumptions, usually known as the concepts of accounting. If we change the concepts, we will get different accounting. To look in more detail at how the concepts work through into practical accounting, we need to consider what SSAP 2 calls the bases and policies.

Accounting bases and policies
....

In the conceptual framework set out by SSAP 2, bases build on the concepts, and policies then build on the bases. The standard explains bases and policies well in its paragraphs 3 and 4, so the best we can do is to reproduce those paragraphs below.

3 Accounting bases are the methods which have been developed for expressing or applying fundamental accounting concepts to financial transactions and items. By their nature accounting bases are more diverse and numerous than fundamental concepts, since they have evolved in response to the variety and complexity of types of business and business transactions, and for this reason there may justifiably exist more than one recognised accounting basis for dealing with particular items.

4 Accounting policies are the specific accounting bases judged by business enterprises to be most appropriate to their circumstances and adopted by them for the purpose of preparing their financial accounts.

DID YOU KNOW ...?
You can think of this in terms of an inverted pyramid, with broad concepts at the top, gradually narrowing down via accounting bases until a policy is appropriate to a specific company.

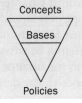

Concepts

Bases

Policies

In other words, those bases chosen by management, which are most suited to the particular business, become the accounting policies of that business. Accounting policies are the application of these principles to a particular set of accounts. To take our continuing example of stock valuation, we know that prudence is a key concept, and, as such, implies that we should choose the method that results in the lowest valuation. One basis for complying with prudence would be to value at historical cost, since this is likely to be less than the selling price, or, given inflation, the current price. Note, however, that the selling price of obsolete or unfashionable stock may actually be less than the original historical cost, so an alternative basis for stock accounting would be net realisable value, ie the selling price less any direct costs of sale.

The managers of the entity must then decide which of these bases, or some other basis, should be taken as the accounting policy for stock. In fact, the usual accounting policy for stock valuation is to combine the two bases we have looked at and value at the lower of cost and net realisable value, ie a prudent policy. It is worth noting that the accounting standard on stocks, SSAP 9, actually requires exactly this as standard practice. So notice what has happened. Not only has the concept – bases – policy framework been used to develop our own accounting practice, but it has also been used to develop standard national practice.

Accounting practice is thus determined by the policies the entity chooses. If it had chosen different policies then the practices would have been different, and the profit and loss account and balance sheet would present a different view of the entity. If users are to be able to make allowances for differing policies between entities they are looking at, then they must at least know what the policies are. Finally, therefore, SSAP 2 requires that the accounting policies 'followed for dealing with items which are judged material or critical in determining profit or loss for the year and in stating the financial position should be disclosed by way of note to the accounts'.

The 'Statement of Principles'

SSAP 2 was an early attempt at a conceptual framework for accounting. However, four concepts do not, in themselves, constitute a coherent theoretical underpinning for accounting. A more comprehensive attempt has recently been made, with the gradual publication of the 'Statement of Principles' by the Accounting Standards Board. This will ultimately have seven chapters, and will effectively have the same status as accounting standards, such as SSAP 2. The seven chapters are:

1 The objective of financial statements
2 The qualitative characteristics of financial statements
3 The elements of financial statements
4 The recognition of items in financial statements
5 Measurement in financial statements
6 Presentation of financial information
7 The reporting entity

We considered the objectives covered in Chapter 1 in our Chapter 1. The characteristics that are discussed in Chapter 2 form most of the rest of this chapter.

Chapter 3 identifies and defines the basic building blocks of financial accounting. These are identified as being assets, liabilities, equity, gains and losses, and contributions from, and distributions to, owners. These classifications will be familiar to you from our exploration of the balance sheet in Chapter 2. The significance of their formal declaration in Chapter 3 of the 'Statement of Principles' is that they now define the scope of financial accounting. All items that appear in financial statements must fall into one of the specified categories, as defined by the Chapter. The question of whether a key employee should be shown as an asset of the company in the balance sheet, for example, should be answered, at least partly, by reference to the definition of an asset in Chapter 3. In such a case, the issue would be whether the employee represents 'future economic benefit' to the company, since that phrase is the heart of the definition of an asset. Presumably, the answer would be yes, given that it is likely that the net revenues generated by such a key employee would exceed his or her wages cost. However, the question does not rest there, because Chapter 3 should be seen in conjunction with Chapter 4.

Chapter 4 is concerned with the circumstances in which these elements should be recognised in the financial statements. It should come as no surprise to find that it requires that items should only be recognised if they are elements as defined in Chapter 3. We have already accepted that our key employee probably fits the definition of an asset. However, Chapter 4 imposes the further condition that the element must also be capable of being objectively quantified. In other words, we need to be able to objectively quantify the 'future economic benefit' that our employee represents. One approach could be to sum the net revenues after wages costs that the employee will bring in over his or her time with the company.

Briefly, note down at least one practical problem that you foresee with such an approach to valuation. As always, you will learn more and faster if you think about the issue raised in the activity than if you simply skip ahead to the answer.

Answer

Our view is that the main problem is the uncertainty inherent in any estimate of future revenues and expenses. It would be highly questionable, for example, whether our guesses about the net revenues or the number of years the employee will stay with us will turn out to be accurate. If we can not objectively quantify an element, then Chapter 4 requires that we do not recognise it, that is we should not include it in the financial statements.

More subtly, such an approach to valuation is not historical cost, and we have already seen that historical cost is the most widely used and accepted method of valuation. If we use some estimate of future value for an employee, and historical cost for another asset, such as a building, it is hard to see what the total of the two assets represents or means. Valuation problems are a topic that we briefly looked at in our Chapter 2, and will return to in greater depth in our Chapter 12. In the meantime, Chapter 5 of the 'Statement of Principles' also addresses the issue of valuation.

Chapter 5 of the 'Statement of Principles' deals with the alternative bases on which we could quantify. So far we have only looked seriously at historical cost, but we will explore other possibilities in our Chapter 12. As you may be beginning to realise from the brief discussion above, valuation is a complex topic, and you need therefore only note here that Chapter 5 identifies an approach to valuation called 'Deprival Value' as its ideal.

Chapter 6 considers what information should be presented, and in what form. Briefly, it identifies four 'primary statements'. These are the profit and loss account, the balance sheet, the cash flow statement, and the statement of total recognised gains and losses. The first two should be reasonably familiar to you now. The cash flow statement will be covered fully in this book in Chapter 11, and the statement of total recognised gains and losses in our Chapter 12. Notice that what Chapter 6 of the 'Statement of Principles' effectively does is define the content of UK financial statements.

Finally, Chapter 7 of the 'Statement of Principles' is concerned with the principles and presentation of group accounts. Group accounts are a single set of accounts covering more than one company, where one or more companies are owned by another. Being under the same control, the argument is that they are effectively a single entity and should therefore have a single set of accounts to report on that total entity. Group accounts are a complex topic, and beyond the scope of this book.

In the rest of this chapter we will consider Chapter 2 in more detail, because it outlines the conventional wisdom on what constitutes good accounting. It therefore represents guidelines for everything else we do in this book.

The characteristics

Chapter 2 of the 'Statement of Principles' categorises the qualitative characteristics of good financial reporting into primary and secondary characteristics. The primary, ie the more important characteristics, are relevance and reliability. The less important characteristics are known as secondary, and are understandability and comparability.

ACTIVITY 4.5

Write two sentences of your own to define each of the characteristics, 'relevance' and 'reliability'. In other words, what do you think these words mean in accounting terms?

Answer

Our answer is based closely on Chapter 2 of the 'Statement of Principles', which says, first, that the relevance of financial information is related to its two roles, which are held to be predictive and confirmatory. The predictive role of financial information is its use for estimating future performance, eg the attempt by a potential investor to predict future profitability and dividend levels. The confirmatory role relates to the use of financial information to confirm past predictions, eg about returns on a particular capital project.

Second, in relation to reliability, Chapter 2 asserts that reliability of financial information is deemed to be achieved by producing information that has a series of characteristics. There are five of these, but most should already be familiar from your studies earlier in this book.

1 Faithful representation. This consists of valid description, free from error, although it should be taken together with a suitable 'choice of aspect', i.e. a decision of which properties of a transaction we should disclose.
2 Substance. It is regarded as a key characteristic that an event should be reported by reference to its substance rather than by reference to its form.
3 Neutrality. The information presented must be free from bias. There is a very close link here to the prior characteristic of objectivity.
4 Prudence. This fundamental principle is restated.
5 Completeness. The more complete the information is the better, but the benefits of completeness should be weighed against the costs of the time and money needed to prepare full information.

ACTIVITY 4.6

The secondary characteristics are comparability and understandability. Repeat the previous activity, this time jotting down a couple of your own sentences to define each of these terms.

Answer

Once again, our answer draws heavily on the points made in Chapter 2 of the 'Statement of Principles'. Specifically, the achievement of comparability implies the presentation of financial information in a consistent way from one year to the next, and between enterprises. One important feature of this will be the disclosure of and adherence to accounting policies. The presentation of comparative figures for the previous year will also help to achieve this characteristic.

Understandability requires a prior consideration of who the users of the information are held to be. The presentation of the information should then be such that those users will normally be able to make substantial use of that information. It will, however, be acceptable to assume that users are reasonably well-informed about basic accounting and economic matters.

Finally, Chapter 2 insists that all the above characteristics are subject to a minimum threshold of quality. The main consideration here is materiality, which provides a cut-off point for the disclosure or non-disclosure of particular events. Furthermore, you should bear in mind that everything in the 'Statement of Principles' is still subject to the over-riding legal requirement to show a true and fair view.

ACTIVITY **4.7**

Global Trading is currently preparing its annual report and accounts. As its name suggests, it is a very big enterprise, with very complex accounting procedures and reports. Currently, it publishes a profit and loss account and a balance sheet. The directors are considering a proposal to produce a more simplified set of financial statements, either in addition to, or even instead of, the usual, more complex statements. One possibility, for example, would be to produce simply a summary of monies in and out of the bank account.

Taking each of the four characteristics in turn, assess whether the proposal is sound. You may ignore any legal requirements.

Answer

As with many of the questions in this fundamental area of accounting, there is no single correct answer. However, we think the following suggested answer covers most of the main points.

Relevance

Chapter 2 of the 'Statement of Principles' says that relevance rests on whether the financial statements are of significant use for predicting or confirming economic events. Whether the proposal improves relevance depends on who the users are, and what they want to predict or confirm. A lender, for example, would probably find a summary of cash movements relevant, since he or she would be concerned about the ability of Global Trading to make repayments. A shareholder, on the other hand, would probably be most concerned about the profit made, and would accordingly find the profit and loss account more relevant, and the proposal would therefore not be as sound.

Reliability

This characteristic is to be judged according to faithful representation, substance over form, neutrality, prudence and completeness. These points seem to be as valid for either approach to accounting, but they at least do not suggest that the proposal should be rejected on the grounds of reliability. Indeed, in terms of neutrality (objectivity) the proposal could be seen as positive, in that the amounts passing through the bank account are a more objective measure of events than, say, the measure of profit. In terms of completeness, the provision of the suggested statement in addition to existing statements is likely to be positive. Note, however, that provision of an extra statement will take time, so delaying the publication of the statements and so making them more out of date.

Understandability

A summary of monies in and out of the bank account will probably be understandable to a wider group of users than will a conventionally complex set of financial statements. On these grounds the proposal seems sound. However, we need to balance this against the difficulties we have already noted in relation to relevance and reliability. If there is a conflict between, say, reliability and understandability, then Chapter 2 of the 'Statement of Principles' requires that we prefer reliability, since that is a primary characteristic, and understandability is only a secondary characteristic. In other words, it is more important that the accounts be 'right' than that they be understandable.

Comparability

This refers to a user's ability to make comparisons both with Global Trading's own accounts in previous years, and with the accounts of other similar companies. Comparability with previous years will be poor, unless the company retrospectively prepares a similar cash summary for those years. This is possible, but would be expensive. Comparability with other companies will only be possible if other companies produce a similar statement.

Overall, it is not possible to make a clear recommendation to the directors, without knowing more about the circumstances. What we can say is that the four characteristics seem to provide criteria by which we can start to judge the validity of both current and proposed accounting practices.

Summary

This chapter has dealt with two topics. First, we have looked at the concepts of accounting, the most important of which are set out in SSAP 2. We also examined how SSAP 2 sets up a structure of concepts – bases – policies for determining accounting practice in a reasonably coherent way. Second, we reviewed the 'Statement of Principles', concentrating on Chapter 2, which attempts a definition of what constitutes good accounting. In other words, it provides a target for all our accounting to aim at.

This chapter concludes the first part of this book. So far, we have explored the nature of accounting, looked at the two main statements by which accounting reports to the outside world, and started to look at some of the theoretical underpinning to accounting. We will return to the theory in Chapter 12. In the meantime, however, we should turn our attention to the everyday practicalities of accounting. Chapter 5 therefore starts our study of double entry bookkeeping.

Further study
••••••••••••••••

Most other introductory texts will include a section on concepts and conventions. However, the publication of the 'Statement of Principles' is changing both the nature and the authority of the theoretical underpinning of financial accounting in the UK. Our advice is therefore to read the 'Statement of Principles' itself. In particular, in relation to the topics covered in this chapter, you should concentrate on Chapter 2 of the Statement.

SELF-
CHECK
QUESTION

'The Accounting Standards Board (ASB) should spend less time on developing a vague set of principles and more time on specifying clear accounting practices.' To what extent do you agree with this statement?

As in the self-assessment question for Chapter 1, you should justify your response and construct your answer as an essay of 300 to 500 words, or as comprehensive notes for such an essay. Again, we have provided feedback as a list of points that you should have covered.

Answer

1   The essay should start with a consideration of the stated purposes of the ASB. Their own statement, that the Board exists to 'establish and improve standards of financial accounting and reporting', is widely accepted.
2   The key question is how to achieve this. One major method is the publication of accounting standards, that is by specifying clear accounting practices.
3   Some consideration could be given to whether existing standards actually do this, and, if not, why not.
4   One possible reason for perceived lack of clarity in the specification of accounting standards is arguably the lack of general agreement on fundamental questions, such as the purposes of financial accounting.
5   If this is accepted, then practical accounting standards can only be specified once such underlying issues have been largely resolved. In other words, the theoretical principles must be established in order to guide the determination of what practical standards should be specified.

Further review questions are available in a separate resource pack which is available to lecturers.

CHAPTER 5

The double entry system

Objectives:

By the end of this chapter you should be able to:

▶ Identify the need for a system of double entry.
▶ Relate the duality concept to this system.
▶ Prepare ledger accounts.
▶ Balance off ledger accounts.
▶ Extract a trial balance and understand its importance within the system.
▶ Prepare simple profit and loss accounts and balance sheets from a trial balance.

Introduction

This chapter is intended to introduce you to the basics of the double-entry bookkeeping system that was codified by Luca Pacioli in the 15th century. As an accountant you may not be involved in the actual recording within the double entry bookkeeping system as this is carried out by bookkeepers or indeed a computer. You must, however, understand the system as you, as an accountant, will be called on to ensure the system is operating effectively and to complete year end entries to enable relevant and reliable financial statements to be prepared for an organisation.

The need for a double entry system

You have seen in previous chapters that it is possible to construct a balance sheet, to show the position of a business at a point in time, and a profit and loss account, to identify the profitability of a business for a period of time. How did you do this? Refresh your memory with the following activity.

ACTIVITY **5.1**

Mr Bean intends to set up in business as an antique dealer. He places £20,000 of his own money into a business bank account then purchases items for resale for £12,000 and a van for £5,000. He rents a shop for £3,600 per annum paying the first monthly instalment of rent. At the end of his first month of trading he is able to identify the fact that he has sold for cash two items, one costing £2,000 for £3,500, and one costing £500 for £800.

Draw up the balance sheet for Mr Bean as at the end of the first month's trading and a profit and loss account for the period.

Answer

MR BEAN
BALANCE SHEET AS AT END OF FIRST MONTH

Fixed assets		
Van		5,000
Current assets		
Stock	9,500	
Bank	7,000	16,500
		£21,500
Capital		
Opening	20,000	
Profit	1,500	£21,500

MR BEAN
PROFIT AND LOSS ACCOUNT FOR THE
PERIOD ENDED FIRST MONTH

Sales	4,300
Cost of sales	2,500
Gross profit	1,800
Rent	300
Net profit	£1,500

How did you construct the above?

Probably by doing calculations on a piece of paper to arrive at sales, cost of sales, stock and bank figures.

Would the above have been as simple though if Mr Bean had made 100 sales during the month?

Obviously the answer is no. Thus you have identified that there is a need for a record of all Mr Bean's transactions that will enable a balance sheet and a profit and loss account to be drawn up at the end of any given period.

Double entry system – duality
....

You learnt in Chapter 4 about the concept of duality.

ACTIVITY **5.2**
....

Identify for Mr Bean the duality involved in the introduction of his capital into the business and the purchase of his van.

Answer

This was fairly straightforward. In the first case you created a liability of capital and the asset of bank, in the second you reduced the asset of bank and created an asset of van. There was a dual effect of each transaction to maintain the accounting equation:

ASSETS = CAPITAL + LIABILITIES

Double entry system – account
....

When you calculated the bank figure in Activity 5.1 you made a list of additions to and subtractions from the bank probably similar to the following:

Additions		**Subtractions**	
Capital	20,000	Van	5,000
Sale 1	3,500	Purchases	12,000
Sale 2	800	Rent	300
	£24,300		£17,300

Additions were sources of funds to the business and subtractions applications of those funds from the business.

The above can be represented as an Account in a double entry system as follows:

BANK ACCOUNT

Capital	20,000	Van	5,000
Sale 1	3,500	Purchases	12,000
Sale 2	800	Rent	300

The left-hand side of this account is referred to as the debit side (debit means 'to give' – I give (place) £20,000 to the bank account) the right-hand side as the credit side (credit means to receive – I receive £5,000 from the bank to buy a van.)

This bank account has enabled you to make a very neat recording of Mr Bean's dealings with the bank but has not recorded the *duality* of the above transactions. Looking at the transaction of purchasing the van, you have credited the bank account with £5,000, so to comply with duality it would seem reasonable to suggest that you should debit another account with £5,000.

Thus:

VAN ACCOUNT

Bank	5,000	

ACTIVITY **5.3**

Complete the duality for the other transactions in the bank account.

Answer

PURCHASES ACCOUNT

Bank	12,000		

RENT ACCOUNT

Bank	300		

SALES ACCOUNT

Bank sale 1	3,500		
Bank sale 2	800		

CAPITAL ACCOUNT

		Bank	20,000

The pattern of the above accounts is that of *double entry*. For each transaction we have made a debit and a credit entry for the same amount, the description (narrative) referring always to the other double entry account.

Using your knowledge of the duality concept, the accounting equation and with reference to the double entry accounts used above you should be able to complete the following activity without too much trouble.

ACTIVITY **5.4**

Complete the following table:-

Account	Transaction	Entry to account
Asset	Addition	Debit
Asset	Subtraction	(a)
Liability	Addition	(b)
Liability	(c)	Debit
Capital	(d)	Credit
Capital	Subtraction	(e)
Expense	Addition	(f)
Expense	Subtraction	(g)
Income	Addition	(h)
Income	(i)	Debit

Answer

The missing entries are as follows:

(a) Credit, (b) Credit, (c) Subtraction, (d) Addition, (e) Debit, (f) Debit, (g) Credit, (h) Credit, (i) Subtraction.

Fairly easy we know, but we hope you thought about the activity rather than just following the pattern.

Credit transactions
....

So far the transactions you have dealt with for Mr Bean have all involved cash as one side of the double entry.

A lot of business is carried out on credit. For example Mr Bean, when he acquired £12,000 of goods could well have paid only £5,000 immediately and bought the rest on credit.

We account for this in the double entry system as follows:

PURCHASES ACCOUNT

Cash	5,000	
Creditor	7,000	

CASH ACCOUNT

		Purchases	5,000

CREDITOR ACCOUNT

		Purchases	7,000

Similarly sales may be made on credit so a debtor account would be created. Note the creditor is a liability of the business and the debtor an asset. It is also customary to maintain separate accounts for each debtor and each creditor in the double entry system.

To help reinforce your understanding of the double entry system a full example is provided below for you to work through as a self-check of understanding. The suggested answer is provided at Activity 5.7 so if you feel fairly confident in respect of your understanding so far you could wait and complete Activities 5.5 and 5.7 together. By the way, it is normal in the double entry system to enter the date against each entry made. The places where double entry accounts are recorded are generally known as ledgers.

Worked example of double entry
....

ACTIVITY **5.5**
....

Enter the following transactions in the ledgers of A Bate, maintaining separate bank and cash accounts.

		£
March 3	Bate placed £20,000 in a business account	
3	Bought car for £8,000, paying cheque	3,000
4	Bought goods on credit from Hall	6,350
5	Paid cheque for office expenses	340
5	Paid cheque for car insurance	195
8	Cashed a cheque for cash	600
9	Cash received for sales	2,345
12	Sold goods on credit to White	1,645
14	Paid wages in cash	250

18	Cash received for sales	300
20	Banked excess cash	
24	Bought goods on credit from Dunn	1,895
25	Cheque received from White	850
26	Cash sales	400
27	Paid wages in cash	250
28	Sold goods on credit: White	600
	Black	750
29	Cash sales	250
30	Cheque sent: Hall	5,500
	Dunn	1,500
31	Paid all cash into bank	

Answer

The answer to the above is contained in the answer to Activity 5.7 but we suggest you carry out the exercise now and check your answer later.

Balancing off accounts

You have now learnt how to record business transactions in the books but you also need to know the following data at the end of a period:

▶ what the cash balance is
▶ what the total value of sales is that has been made
▶ how much is owed to the creditors
▶ how much debtors owe the business
▶ what the total of expenses is.

To do this we need to balance off the accounts. Looking back at the bank account on page 58 we had:

BANK ACCOUNT

Capital	20,000	Van	5,000
Sale 1	3,500	Purchases	12,000
Sale 2	800	Rent	300

The left-hand side of this account (the debit) totals £24,300 and the credit side (the right) £17,300. The difference is £7,000, the balance at the bank you identified at Activity 5.1, an asset. You should also have noticed that the van, another asset of the business, appeared in the double entry account on page 58 as a debit which implies that the asset of £7,000 at the bank has to appear as a debit.

The 'balancing off' takes place as follows:

BANK ACCOUNT

Capital	20,000	Van	5,000
Sale 1	3,500	Purchases	12,000

Sale 2	800	Rent	300
		Balance carried down	7,000
	£24,300		£24,300
Balance brought down	7,000		

To check whether you understand what we did to balance the bank account try the next activity.

ACTIVITY **5.6**

Identify the sequence that occurred to balance off the above bank account.

Answer

You should have identified a sequence similar to the following:

1 Add up both sides and identify the difference.
2 Enter the difference on the side with the smaller total (the credit side here).
3 Enter the totals for both sides – which are now identical.
4 Complete the double entry in respect of (2) by entering the same figure on the opposite side (in this case the debit side) below the totals.

This balance brought down of £7,000 debit is the balance of cash at bank, an asset of the business. Again it is normal to enter the date in the accounts when balancing off the accounts, the carried down date being that of the end of the period and the brought down date that of the start of the next period.

The rest of the accounts for Mr Bean are balanced as follows:

VAN ACCOUNT

| Bank | 5,000 | Balance carried down | 5,000 |
| Balance brought down | 5,000 | | |

PURCHASES ACCOUNT

| Bank | 12,000 | Balance carried down | 12,000 |
| Balance brought down | 12,000 | | |

RENT ACCOUNT

| Bank | 300 | Balance carried down | 300 |
| Balance brought down | 300 | | |

SALES ACCOUNT

		Bank	3,500
Balance carried down	4,300	Bank	800
	£4,300		£4,300
		Balance brought down	4,300

CAPITAL ACCOUNT

Balance carried down	20,000	Bank	20,000
		Balance brought down	20,000

Notice that when there is only one entry in an account there is no need to enter the total for each side. It is also customary to abbreviate brought down and carried down to b/d and c/d respectively. 'Balance' can also be abbreviated to 'bal'.

ACTIVITY **5.7**

Balance off all the accounts for Activity 5.5.

Answer

The answer below is that for Activity 5.5 and 5.7.

CAPITAL ACCOUNT

Bal c/d	20,000	Bank	20,000
		Bal b/d	20,000

OFFICE EXPENSE ACCOUNT

Bank	340	Bal c/d	340
Bal b/d	340		

CAR ACCOUNT

Bank/loan	8,000	Bal c/d	8,000
Bal b/d	8,000		

INSURANCE ACCOUNT

Bank	195	Bal c/d	195
Bal b/d	195		

LOAN ACCOUNT (note 2)

Bal c/d	5,000	Car	5,000
		Bal b/d	5,000

WAGES ACCOUNT

Cash	250		
Cash	250	Bal c/d	500
	£500		£500
Bal b/d	500		

PURCHASES ACCOUNT

Hall	6,350		
Dunn	1,895	Bal c/d	8,245
	£8,245		£8,245
Bal b/d	8,245		

SALES ACCOUNT

		Cash	2,345
		White	1,645
		Cash	300
		Cash	400
		White	600
		Black	750
Bal c/d	6,290	Cash	250
	£6,290		£6,290
		Bal b/d	6,290

DEBTOR – WHITE					DEBTOR – BLACK			
Sales	1,645	Bank	850	Sales	750	Bal c/d	750
Sales	600	Bal c/d	1,395	Bal b/d	750		
	£2,245		£2,245				
Bal b/d	1,395						

CREDITOR – HALL					CREDITOR – DUNN			
Bank	5,500	Purchases	6,350	Bank	1,500	Purchases	1,895
Bal c/d	850			Bal c/d	395		
	£6,350		£6,350		£1,895		£1,895
		Bal b/d	850			Bal b/d	395

BANK ACCOUNT					CASH ACCOUNT			
Capital	20,000	Car	3,000	Bank	600	Wages	250
Cash	2,995	Office	340	Sales	2,345	Bank (1)	2,995
White	850	Insurance	195	Sales	300	Wages	250
Cash	400	Cash	600	Sales	400	Bank (1)	400
		Hall	5,500	Sales	250		
		Dunn	1,500		£3,895		£3,895
		Bal c/d	13,110				
	£24,245		£24,245				
Bal b/d	13,110						

Note 1   At this point the cash account had to be totalled to identify the balance that was then paid into the bank.

Note 2   As the cost of the car was £8,000 but only £3,000 was paid in cash the remaining £5,000 is identified as a loan.

Trial balance

The double entry system follows the duality concept – for every debit there is an equal credit – thus if the system has been carried out correctly the *total debit balances* should equal the *total credit balances*. This check on the operation of the system is known as a trial balance.

TRIAL BALANCE FOR MR BEAN AS AT (PERIOD END DATE)

	Dr	Cr
Sales		4,300
Capital		20,000
Van	5,000	
Purchases	12,000	

Rent	300	
Bank	7,000	
	£24,300	£24,300

ACTIVITY **5.8**

Construct the trial balance in respect of Activity 5.5.

Answer

TRIAL BALANCE AS AT 31 MARCH

	Dr	Cr
Capital		20,000
Bank	13,110	
Office expenses	340	
Car insurance	195	
Car	8,000	
Wages	500	
Loan		5,000
Purchases	8,245	
Sales		6,290
Creditors: Hall		850
Dunn		395
Debtors: White	1,395	
Black	750	
	£32,535	£32,535

DID YOU KNOW ...?
The trial balance is simply a check on the arithmetical accuracy of the book-keeping entries. It is not part of the double entry system itself.

Use of trial balance

If the totals of the trial balance agree, it does not necessarily prove that the books are correct. What it will prove is that you have entered an equal debit for every credit and that the accounts have been added correctly, but there are several errors that could have been made that the trial balance will not identify.

ACTIVITY **5.9**

The following errors have been made in the books of Mr Bean. Identify those errors that the use of a trial balance will reveal and those it will not.

1 The sales account has been incorrectly added.
2 The purchase of goods on credit was entered in the relevant creditor account but not the purchases account.
3 Wages paid of £92 was debited as £92 to the wages account but as £29 credit to the bank account.
4 The sale of goods for £100 on credit was not entered in the books at all.
5 An electricity bill was correctly credited to the bank account but the debit entry was made to the office expenses account not the electricity account.
6 Goods for £50 were bought on credit and entered in the books as purchases account debit £5 creditor account credit £50. Sales made of £50 cash were

entered in the cash account as debit £50 but as £5 to the credit of the sales account.

7   A loan made to Mr Bean of £1,000 was debited to the loan account and credited to the bank account.

Answer

A little bit of thought and you should have been able to identify that the trial balance will reveal the following types of error.

▶   Incorrect additions in an account as per item 1.
▶   Posting (entering) one side only of the double entry as per item 2.
▶   Entering a different amount in the debit side than the credit side for example debit £92 credit £29 as per item 3 but will not reveal the following.
▶   An entry completely missed as per item 4.
▶   An entry in a wrong account but the double entry still maintained as per item 5.
▶   Where errors cancel each other as per item 6.
▶   Entries where the double entry is completely the wrong way round as per item 7.

Profit and loss account
· ·

At the very beginning of this chapter you were able to construct a profit and loss account and a balance sheet for Mr Bean (see Activity 5.1).

You did this by identifying the expenses to match with the income in the profit and loss account and identifying the assets and liabilities at the end of the period and recording these in the balance sheet. In effect you made use of the accounting equations:

PROFIT = INCOME − EXPENSES USED UP
ASSETS = CAPITAL + LIABILITIES + PROFIT

It is possible to treat the profit and loss account as part of the double entry system and transfer expenses and income to it maintaining the principles of double entry. We must be careful though that we only transfer that expense used up in generating the income – the accruals or matching concept. Refer back to Chapter 4 here to refresh your memory on the accruals concept. In particular we must be careful how much of the purchase expense we transfer.

Mr Bean, at Activity 5.1, had not sold all of the goods he bought, in fact he has only sold goods costing £2,500. He therefore has goods remaining of £9,500 which is not recorded as yet in the double entry system. This figure of stock could have been ascertained in one of two ways:

1   By counting the goods remaining in the shop and valuing them at the cost Mr Bean paid.
2   By reducing the figure of purchases, each time a sale is made, by the purchase price of that item sold.

When a business has several sales within a period the easiest method is to count stock at the end of the period (refer back to Chapter 3 for how we did this).

This stock figure is then entered in the books by the means of a closing stock account and the profit and loss account is used to calculate the cost of goods sold. The following demonstrates this.

SALES ACCOUNT

Profit and loss account	4,300	Bal b/d	4,300

PURCHASES ACCOUNT

Bal b/d	12,000	Profit and loss account	12,000

RENT ACCOUNT

Bal b/d	300	Profit and loss account	300

CLOSING STOCK ACCOUNT

Profit and loss account	9,500		

PROFIT AND LOSS ACCOUNT

Purchases	12,000	Sales	4,300
Gross profit c/d	1,800	Closing stock	9,500
	£13,800		£13,800
Rent	300	Gross profit b/d	1,800
Net profit c/d	1,500		
	£1,800		£1,800
		Net profit b/d	1,500

Did you understand what we did here?

ACTIVITY 5.10

Identify the sequence carried out above to arrive at the net profit figure of £1,500.

For example the sequence will start:

▶ Transfer balance on sales account to profit and loss account by debiting sales account and crediting profit and loss account.

Answer

Your sequence should have been similar to the following:

▶ Transfer balance on sales account to profit and loss account by debiting sales account and crediting profit and loss account.
▶ Transfer balance on purchases by crediting this account and debiting profit and loss account
▶ Enter closing stock in the ledgers by debiting closing stock account and crediting profit and loss account.
▶ Balance off the profit and loss account but call the balance *Gross Profit*, ie difference between sales and cost of goods sold.

▶ Transfer balance on rent account to profit and loss account
▶ Balance off profit and loss account again calling balance *Net Profit*.

Let us see if you can do all this now.

ACTIVITY **5.11**
• • • • • • • • • • • • • •

Given that the closing stock as at 31 March in Activity 5.8 is £4,500 draw up a profit and loss account for the month ended 31 March.

Answer

**PROFIT AND LOSS ACCOUNT
FOR THE MONTH ENDED 31 MARCH**

Purchases	8,245	Sales		6,290
Gross profit c/d	2,545	Closing stock		4,500
	£10,790			£10,790
Office expenses	340	Gross profit b/d		2,545
Car insurance	195			
Wages	500			
Net profit c/d	1,510			
	£2,545			£2,545
		Net profit b/d		1,510

Format profit and loss account
• .

In Chapter 3 we discussed the format of the profit and loss account. The above profit and loss would normally be written as follows:

	£	£
Sales		6,290
Purchases	8,245	
Less closing stock	4,500	3,745
Gross profit		2,545
Office expenses	340	
Car insurance	195	
Wages	500	1,035
Net profit		£1,510

This is known as a vertical profit and loss account. It is perceived as being easier for users to understand, and avoids the need to insert 'carried down' and 'brought down' figures.

Balances remaining in the books

Having constructed a profit and loss account for Mr Bean it is possible at this point to extract another trial balance as follows:

	Dr	Cr
Capital		20,000
Stock	9,500	
Van	5,000	
Bank	7,000	
Net profit		1,500
	£21,500	£21,500

Again just a minor leap in imagination and the above could be written as follows:

BALANCE SHEET AS AT ——
Fixed assets

Van		5,000
Current assets		
Stock	9,500	
Bank	7,000	16,500
		£21,500
Capital		20,000
Profit		1,500
		£21,500

Thus the balances remaining in the books, after having extracted a profit and loss account, form a balance sheet. The balance sheet records the position of the business at a specific point in time.

ACTIVITY **5.12**

Draw up the balance sheet for the information contained in Activity 5.8 after the extraction of the profit and loss account as at 31 March.

Answer

The balance sheet should look as follows:

BALANCE SHEET AS AT 31 MARCH

	£	£	£
Fixed assets			
Car			8,000
Current assets			
Stock		4,500	
Debtors: White	1,395		
Black	750	2,145	
Bank		13,110	
		19,755	
Creditors: Hall	850		
Dunn	395	1,245	18,510
			26,510
Loan			5,000
			£21,510
Capital			20,000
Profit			1,510
			£21,510

Summary
....

This chapter has introduced you to the double entry system of accounting. We identified the need for the system when a business has several transactions to account for and saw that it was based upon the concept of duality.

We have taken you through the workings of the ledgers, balanced them off, and extracted a trial balance. In addition you learnt that the profit and loss account was in fact part of the double entry system and that income and expense accounts were cleared by being transferred to the profit and loss account, recognising that the concept of matching must be applied.

We illustrated the matching concept within the context of cost of sales.

The remaining balances in the ledgers then formed a balance sheet at the end of the financial period. The two main statements extracted from all this double entry, the profit and loss account and the balance sheet, have also been written in what is regarded as a 'user friendly' manner, ie vertical format.

All this has been rather 'long winded' and the accounts take time to enter up. However, practice makes perfect, so we have provided another question below.

SELF-
CHECK
QUESTION

To complete your understanding of this section attempt the following self-test exercise. You will find the answer to this exercise at the end of the section.

On the 1.4.19X1 H Britton commenced a business dealing in subaqua equipment.

He paid £20,000 into the business bank account and the following transactions took place during the month of April.

		£
1st	From previous owner bought shop £8,000, fixtures and fittings £5,000 and stock £4,000 paying by cheque £17,000	
2nd	Withdrew cash from bank for shop use	500
	Paid for stationery and other incidentals	175
3rd	Sold goods for cash	450
4th	Sold goods on credit to A Britton	650
5th	Cash sales	250
	Wages paid in cash	160
8th	Bought goods for resale on credit from R Sevier	950
	A Britton returned faulty goods	100
9th	Cash sales	340
	Paid sundry expenses in cash	80
10th	Sold goods on credit to R Sewell	440
11th	Returned goods to R Sevier	230
12th	Cash sales	340
	Wages paid in cash	160
	Paid excess cash into bank	
15th	Sold goods on credit to S Boatman	260
16th	Bought goods for resale from P Ocean	1,500
17th	Paid cheque on account to R Sevier	500
	Received cheque on account from A Britton	400
18th	Cash sales	550
	Office expenses paid in cash	60
19th	Paid wages in cash	160
22nd	S Boatman paid on account by cheque	50
	Paid P Ocean by cheque	900
	Cash sales	850
24th	Wages paid in cash	160
	Office expenses paid in cash	50
	Withdrew cash for personal use	400
25th	Paid excess cash into bank account	

Stock on hand 30 April cost £2,000

Required

➤ Record the above transactions in the ledger accounts of H Britton maintaining separate cash and bank accounts and separate accounts for returned goods.

➤ Balance off the ledger accounts as at 30 April and extract a trial balance.

➤ Prepare the profit and loss account for the month ended 30 April and close off all revenue and expense accounts.

➤ Prepare a balance sheet as at 30 April.

Answer

CAPITAL ACCOUNT

30.4.	Bal c/d	£20,000	1.4.	Bank	£20,000
			1.5.	Bal b/d	20,000

BANK ACCOUNT

1.4.	Capital	20,000	1.4.	Premises etc	17,000
12.4.	Cash	1,305	2.4.	Cash	500
17.4.	A Britton	400	17.4.	R Sevier	500
22.4.	S Boatman	50	22.4.	P Ocean	900
25.4.	Cash	570	30.4.	Bal c/d	3,425
		£22,325			£22,325
1.5.	Bal b/d	3,425			

PREMISES ACCOUNT

1.4.	Bank	£8,000	30.4.	Bal c/d	£8,000
1.5.	Bal b/d	8,000			

CASH ACCOUNT

2.4	Bank	500	2.4.	Stationery	175
3.4.	Sales	450	5.4.	Wages	160
5.4.	Sales	250	9.4.	Sundries	80
9.4.	Sales	340	12.4.	Wages	160
12.4.	Sales	340	12.4.	Bank	1,305
18.4.	Sales	550	18.4	Sundries	60
22.4.	Sales	850	19.4	Wages	160
			24.4.	Wages	160
			24.4.	Sundries	50
			24.4.	Drawings	400
			25.4.	Bank	570
		£3,280			£3,280

DRAWINGS ACCOUNT

24.4.	Cash	£400	30.4.	Bal c/d	£400
1.5.	Bal b/d	400			

FIXTURES ACCOUNT

1.4.	Bank	£5,000	30.4.	Bal c/d	£5,000
1.5.	Bal b/d	5,000			

STOCK ACCOUNT

1.4.	Bank	£4,000	30.4.	Profit and loss	£4,000
30.4.	Profit and loss	£3,500	30.4.	Bal c/d	£3,500
1.5.	Bal b/d	3,500			

WAGES ACCOUNT

5.4.	Cash	160			
12.4.	Cash	160			
19.4	Cash	160			
24.4.	Cash	160	30.4.	Profit and loss	640
		£640			£640

PURCHASES ACCOUNT

8.4.	R Sevier	950			
16.4	P Ocean	1,500	30.4.	Profit and loss	2,450
		£2,450			£2,450

STATIONERY AND SUNDRIES ACCOUNT

2.4.	Cash	175			
9.4.	Cash	80			
18.4	Cash	60			
24.4.	Cash	50	30.4.	Profit and loss	365
		£365			£365

SALES ACCOUNT

			3.4.	Cash	450
			4.4.	A.Britton	650
			5.4.	Cash	250
			9.4.	Cash	340
			10.4	R Sewell	440
			12.4.	Cash	340
			15.4.	S Boatman	260
			18.4	Cash	550
30.4.	Profit and loss	4,130	22.4	Cash	850
		£4,130			£4,130

S BOATMAN ACCOUNT

15.4	Sales	260	22.4.	Bank	50
			30.4.	Bal c/d	210
		£260			£260
1.5.	Bal b/d	210			

P OCEAN ACCOUNT

22.4.	Bank	900	16.4.	Purchases	1,500
30.4.	Bal c/d	600			
		£1,500			£1,500
			1.5.	Bal b/d	600

A BRITTON ACCOUNT

4.4.	Sales	650	8.4.	Returns	100
			17.4.	Bank	400
			30.4.	Bal c/d	150
		£650			£650
1.5.	Bal b/d	150			

R SEVIER ACCOUNT

11.4.	Returns	230	8.4.	Purchases	950
17.4.	Bank	500			
30.4.	Bal c/d	220			
		£950			£950
			1.5.	Bal b/d	220

R SEWELL ACCOUNT

10.4.	Sales	£440	30.4.	Bal c/d	£440
1.5.	Bal b/d	440			

RETURNS INWARDS ACCOUNT

8.4.	A Britton	£100	30.4.	Profit and loss	£100

RETURNS OUTWARDS ACCOUNT

30.4.	Profit and loss	£230	11.4.	R Sevier	£230

TRIAL BALANCE AS AT 30.4.

	Dr	Cr
Capital		20,000
Premises	8,000	
Fixtures	5,000	
Stock	4,000	
Wages	640	
Purchases	2,450	
S Boatman	210	
A Britton	150	
P Ocean		600

Returns inwards	100	
Returns outwards		230
Bank	3,425	
Stationery	365	
Sales		4,130
R Sevier		220
R Sewell	440	
Drawings	400	
	£25,180	£25,180

PROFIT AND LOSS ACCOUNT FOR THE MONTH ENDED 30.4.

	£	£	£
Sales		4,130	
Less returns inwards		100	4,030
Opening stock		4,000	
Add purchases	2,450		
Less returns outwards	230	2,220	
		6,220	
Less closing stock		3,500	2,720
Gross profit			1,310
Wages		640	
Stationery		365	1,005
Net profit			£305

BALANCE SHEET AS AT 30.4.
Fixed assets

	£	£	£
Premises		8,000	
Fixtures		5,000	13,000
Current assets			
Stock		3,500	
Debtors: S Boatman	210		
A Britton	150		
R Sewell	440	800	
Bank		3,425	
		7,725	
Current liabilities			
Creditors: P Ocean	600		
R Sevier	220	820	6,905
			£19,905
Capital			20,000
Add net profit	305		
Less drawings	400		(95)
			£19,905

Further review questions are available in a separate resource pack which is available to lecturers.

CHAPTER 6

Adjustments, including entries in ledger accounts

Objectives:
················

By the end of this chapter you should be able to:

▶ Identify the need for adjustments to ledger accounts.
▶ Understand the nature of prepayments and accruals.
▶ Describe the necessity for adjustments for bad and doubtful debts.
▶ Define depreciation.
▶ Carry out the required ledger entries for depreciation.
▶ Balance off all ledger accounts after adjustments.
▶ Understand the nature of any balance remaining.

Introduction
················

Chapter 5 introduced you to the double entry system of bookkeeping. This chapter intends to build on that knowledge and expertise gained and also to further develop the concepts and conventions of accounting in relation to this double entry system.

So far we have assumed, with the exception of the stock adjustment that we looked at in Chapter 5, that all entries made in the ledger for assets, liabilities, expenses and income relate to the period for which you wish to extract a profit and loss account and balance sheet and that no items are missing. This is a wrong assumption!

Accruals and prepayments
····································

In the previous chapter all the expenses for Mr Bean's business entered the ledger accounts via the cash or bank account and the assumption was made that these related to sales, and were used up by Mr Bean in achieving those sales.

ˈ However, many expenses may be recorded as they are paid but may not relate, match, to the period in question. This was true in the case of purchases. Mr Bean may have purchased £12,000 of goods during a period but he did not

DID YOU KNOW ...?
The concept (convention) of accounting that you were using was that of accruals (matching).

use up all those purchases in achieving his sales. He had some purchases left, ie stock. We accounted for this by making an adjustment to the accounts. A stock account was debited with the amount of stock in the warehouse and the same figure was credited to the profit and loss account. The closing stock also appeared on the balance sheet as it was a balance remaining after extracting the profit and loss account at the period end. Closing stock is an example of a *prepayment*. We have acquired the stock but not yet used it up in generating revenues.

Identify whether the following payments made by Mr Bean during the period 1.1.95 to 31.12.95 actually relate (need to be matched) with any income achieved in that period and, if so, how much?

▶ Rent of £200 paid on 1.7.95 relating to the period 1.7.95 – 30.6.96.
▶ Electricity paid 14.12.95 relating to the period 1.9.95 – 30.11.95.
▶ Car insurance paid 1.4.95 relating to the annual premium for the car purchased on that date.

Answer

This was quite tricky if you gave a full answer to the question.

▶ The rent payment related to the year from 1.7.95 so some of this needs matching to the period in question – six months of it, ie £100. The other £100 will need matching to the income of the next year. Mr Bean has in fact *prepaid* his rent.
▶ The electricity amount paid does need matching to the period in question. A very interesting question is what about the electricity expense that was presumably used up in December. Mr Bean will not pay for this until after he receives his next quarterly bill – presumably in March 1996 – so there is no reference to this expense within the ledgers as yet. There should be if expenses are to be correctly matched. An *accrual* of one month's electricity charge is required.
▶ Only nine months of the insurance premium needs matching to the income for the period ended 31.12.95. The other three months will relate to next year's accounts. Again Mr Bean has prepaid part of his insurance.

The prepayments identified above, for insurance and rent, will need adjusting for in the ledger accounts of Mr Bean in order to correctly match expense with income achieved. The electricity account will also need an adjustment otherwise the 12 month expense for electricity will not be matched, only 11 months. For the electricity an accrual is required. Adjustments for accruals and prepayments are necessary to ensure compliance with the matching concept. The adjustments for accruals and prepayments within the ledger accounts can at first sight appear rather confusing but as long as you think very carefully about the *period* an expense relates to rather than its *payment date* you should find no difficulty with it.

Adjustment to ledger accounts

The following example shows the necessary ledger adjustments for accruals and prepayments. An activity then follows asking you to carry out some adjustments. Work through the example and activity carefully.

EXAMPLE **6.1**
••••••••••••••

Mr Carn has set up in business as a florist and the annual rental for shop premises is £2,000. This rental is paid by Mr Carn as follows:

▶ *£500 5.4.95*
▶ *£500 10.7.95*
▶ *£500 11.11.95*

The remaining £500 Mr Carn expects to pay sometime in January 1996.

The three rental payments above will have been entered into the ledger accounts when they are paid, by crediting the bank account and debiting the rent expense account. (See Chapter 5 if you need to refresh your memory on double entry.)

The rent account will appear as follows:

RENT ACCOUNT

5.4.	Bank	500
10.7.	Bank	500
11.11.	Bank	500

Mr Carn wishes to draw up a profit and loss account for the year ended 31.12.95. To do this you saw in Chapter 5 that the expense accounts were balanced off and the balance transferred to the profit and loss account – a double-entry account.

If the rent account as above is balanced off then the balance will be £1,500 and this will be transferred to the profit and loss account. However, this would not be the matched expense for rent for the year. An accrual of £500 needs to be made, ie the remainder of the rent that is due for the period but will not be paid until January 1996.

RENT ACCOUNT

5.4.	Bank	500			
10.7.	Bank	500			
11.11.	Bank	500			
31.12.	Accrual c/d	500	31.12.	Profit and loss	2,000
		£2,000			£2,000
			1.1	Accrual b/d	500

This account now shows that the expense transferred to the profit and loss account is the matched expense of £2,000 and that there is a balance on the account on the credit side of £500 as at 1 January. This arose because duality had to be maintained. An entry was made on the debit side of the account for the accrual of £500 and duality demands that an equal and opposite entry also be made – this is the credit entry below the balance on the account. This credit balance of £500 will appear in the balance sheet as at 31.12.95 as a liability, as it is an amount that is owed in respect of the period.

Mr Carn has also made a payment of £600 on 1.4.95 for his annual car insurance premium.

This again will be entered into the ledger via the bank account and the car insurance account will appear as follows:

CAR INSURANCE ACCOUNT

1.4.	Bank	600			

However, only part of this premium relates to the period for which we wish to draw up the profit and loss account. There is a prepayment of £150. This is reflected in the ledger accounts as follows:

CAR INSURANCE ACCOUNT

1.4.	Bank	600	31.12	Prepaid c/d	150
			31.12.	Profit and loss	450
		£600			£600
1.1.	Prepaid b/d	150			

The duality concept again gives rise to a balance on the account but this time it is a debit balance b/d as £150 has been paid in advance. This prepayment will form an expense of the next period and will appear on the balance sheet at 31.12.95 under current assets.

ACTIVITY **6.2**
••••••••••••••

Tom, a greengrocer, wishes to prepare his profit and loss account for the year ended 31.10.95 and balance sheet as at that date.

During the year he has made the following payments:

▶ Rent £1,200 for the period 1.1.95 to 31.12.95.
▶ Wages £1,020, £20 owing as at 31.10.95.
▶ General expenses £470, £50 owing as at 31.10.95.
▶ Electricity for three quarters £900.
▶ Telephone rental, quarterly in advance, £18 paid 1.11.94, 1.2.95, 1.5.95, 1.8.95, and 28.10.95.
▶ Telephone calls, quarterly in arrears, £55 1.2.95, £65 1.5.95, £60 1.8.95.

Show the ledger accounts for all these payments and balance them off at the year end, 31.10.95. Clearly show the matched transfer to the profit and loss account for the period and identify where balances, if any, on these ledger accounts will appear in the balance sheet.

Answer

RENT ACCOUNT

31.10.95	Bank	1,200	31.10.95	Profit and loss	1,000
			31.10.95	Bal c/d	200
		£1,200			£1,200
1.11.95	Bal b/d	200			

WAGES ACCOUNT

31.10.95	Bank	1,020	31.10.95	Profit and loss	1,040
31.10.95	Bal c/d	20			
		£1,040			£1,040
			1.11.95	Bal b/d	20

GENERAL EXPENSES ACCOUNT

31.10.95	Bank	470				
31.10.95	Bal c/d	50	31.10.95	Profit and loss	520
		£520			£520
			1.11.95	Bal b/d	50

TELEPHONE RENTAL ACCOUNT

1.11.94	Bank	18			
1.2.95	Bank	18			
1.5.95	Bank	18			
1.8.95	Bank	18	31.10.95	Profit and loss	72
28.10.95	Bank	18	31.10.95	Bal c/d	18
		£90			£90
1.11.95	Bal b/d	18			

TELEPHONE CALLS ACCOUNT

1.2.95	Bank	55			
1.5.95	Bank	65			
1.8.95	Bank	60			
31.10.95	Bal c/d	60	31.10.95	Profit and loss	240
		£240			£240
			1.11.95	Bal b/d	60

BALANCE SHEET EXTRACT AS AT 31.10.95

	£
Current assets	
Prepayments: Rent	200
Telephone rentals	18
	218
Current liabilities	
Accruals: Wages	20
General	50
Telephone calls	60
	130

Note that the accruals and prepayments b/d will appear as the first item on the ledger account for the next period and will automatically adjust the accounts for the next period. These accrual and prepayment balances must never be ignored! They exist as a liability or asset in the books in the same way as a creditor or a fixed asset. If you ignore them your trial balance will not balance nor will your balance sheet. The final activity within this section involves you in providing definitions in your own words for accruals and prepayments.

ACTIVITY 6.3

In your own words provide a definition for an 'accrual' and a 'prepayment'.

Answer

Your definitions should have been similar to the following:

▶ Accrual – the addition necessary to the cash paid to ensure that all expense used up in generating revenue is matched with that revenue. The accrual will be a liability, an amount owing at the end of the period.
▶ Prepayment – the reduction necessary to the cash paid when payments have been made in advance but the expense has not been used up in generating revenue. The prepayment will appear as an asset at the end of the period.

You must also note at this point that accruals and prepayments can also occur in respect of items of income. For example, a business may own some property, an asset, which it rents to another business. This rent receivable will be income to the business owner but could be cash paid in arrears or in advance. If in *arrears* then at the end of the period an adjustment will be made to accrue the rent receivable, if in *advance* an adjustment of a prepayment will be required.

A simple example follows to illustrate this

EXAMPLE 6.2

A Flower rents part of his business premises, which he owns, to A Carn at an annual rental of £2,400. This rental is payable quarterly in arrears commencing 1.4.95.

Show the ledger account for rents receivable in A Flower's books with the year end adjustments necessary for the year ended 31.12.95 assuming all payments are received on their due dates.

RENTS RECEIVABLE ACCOUNT

			1.4.95	Bank	600
			1.7.95	Bank	600
			1.10.95	Bank	600
31.12.95	Profit and loss	2,400	31.12.95	Accrued c/d	600
		£2,400			£2,400
1.1.96	Accrued b/d	600			

One further point to note is that the main item of revenue for a business, sales income, has already had any revenue owing accrued in the books by the introduction of debtors into the system. So neither accruals nor prepayment adjustments are usually necessary for sales income.

However, other adjustments are required in respect of debtors.

Adjustments for bad and doubtful debts

The point at which you have recognised sales in the business books, generally at the point of delivery or invoicing of the goods, rather than the point at which cash is received gives rise to the next lot of adjustments to the year end accounts.

Recognising sales before cash has been received has introduced debtors into the books but there may be a possibility that some of these debtors may not pay the amounts due. Under the concept of prudence an allowance for this possibility must be made, but how much does this allowance need to be? This problem can be broken down into two parts.

Bad debts

Some debts can be identified as bad debts, that is the debtor will never pay what he owes as he has been declared bankrupt or cannot be traced. These bad debts are a normal part of business today and like all other expenses of a business must be charged as an expense to the profit and loss account.

See if you can complete the following activity without an example first.

ACTIVITY **6.4**

A Flower has several debtor accounts within his books. Two of these debtors, A Carn and P Rose, who owe respectively £250 and £130, have both been declared bankrupt and there is no possibility that these debts will be paid. Show the adjustments necessary in the accounts of A Flower as at the year end, 31.12.95, to deal with these bad debts.

Answer

A CARN ACCOUNT

31.12.95	Bal	£250	31.12.95	Bad debts	£250

P ROSE ACCOUNT

31.12.95	Bal	£130	31.12.95	Bad debts	£130

BAD DEBTS ACCOUNT

31.12.95	A Carn	250			
31.12.95	P Rose	130	31.12.95	Profit and loss	380
		£380			£380

As you can see, a bad debt account is set up to which the bad debts are transferred at the year end. This bad debt account is then cleared to the profit and loss account as it is an expense of trading.

Sometimes it is possible to find a situation where part of a debt will be paid and the remainder will be declared bad. This quite often occurs in bankruptcy situations where debtors receive a proportion of what they are owed. For example, it could have been the case that P Rose was able to pay 50p in the pound in respect of his debts, in which case P Rose's account would have been adjusted as follows:

P ROSE ACCOUNT

31.12.95	Bal b/d	130	31.12.95	Bad debts	65
			31.12.95	Balance c/d	65
		£130			£130
1.1.96	Bal b/d	65			

The balance of £65 will remain as a collectable debt on P Rose's account as it is expected he will pay this amount in the future.

Provision for bad debts

In addition to adjusting for debts that you know are bad a provision in respect of amounts owing that may turn out to be bad is also required. This is to accord with prudence and ensure that assets are not over stated in the balance sheet.

DID YOU KNOW...?

Businesses generally assess the amount of debts that may turn out to be bad by looking at the length of time a debt has been outstanding and making an estimate based on past experience of the probability of a debt turning bad.

The problem is, how does the business assess the amount of debts that may turn out to be bad; how much provision do they need to make?

By doing this a trader could arrive at the conclusion that of the balance of debtors at the year end there is a probability that 2% could turn out bad. A provision will then be made for this amount of 2% but the debtors' balances will not be reduced as the trader still hopes to recover the debts. He is just being prudent by making a provision for any bad debts that could occur.

Let's see how this works in the books.

EXAMPLE **6.3**

A Flower has a total debtors balance of £11,600 at the year end after writing off the bad debts. From past experience he estimates that 2% of these debtors may be bad. He therefore needs to make a provision for bad debts of £232. Note that the provision is calculated after taking account of bad debts! To make this provision the accounting entries necessary are:

▶ *Credit provision for bad debts account.*
▶ *Debit profit and loss account.*

PROVISION FOR BAD DEBTS ACCOUNT

31.12.95	Bal c/d	232	31.12.95	Profit and loss	232
		£232			£232
			1.1.96	Bal b/d	232

You must note that this provision for bad debts account will have a balance on it at the year end and this must be shown, as all other balances, on the balance sheet. It is customary to show this provision together with the debtors balance as follows:

A FLOWER BALANCE SHEET EXTRACT AS AT 31.12.95

Current Assets	£	£
Debtors	11,600	
Less provision for bad debts	232	11,368

Provision for bad debts after the first year

This provision for bad debts of £232 will form part of the ledgers for the following year of A Flower, and at the end of the next year a further estimate for bad debts will be made.

Suppose that at 31.12.96 A Flower has a debtors balance of £12,400 after writing off bad debts, and estimates that 2% of these debtors may not pay, ie £248.

In the ledgers there is already a provision for £232 from the previous year and therefore the only adjustment necessary at 31.12.96 is to increase this provision to £248 by crediting the provision account and debiting profit and loss with £16.

PROVISION FOR BAD DEBTS ACCOUNT

31.12.96	bal c/d	248	1.1.96	Bal b/d		232
			31.12.96	Profit and loss		16
		£248				£248
			1.1.97	Bal b/d		248

Depreciation
....

Another adjustment that is required at the year end is depreciation. But what is depreciation?

In Chapter 5 Mr Bean purchased a van for £5,000 for use in his business. This van was regarded as an asset of the business and was shown on the balance sheet as a fixed asset at the amount it was purchased for. If this van is not sold by Mr Bean, then after several years, unless an adjustment is made in the accounts, it will still be shown on the balance sheet as an asset of £5,000, but it may in fact be quite useless if it has come to the end of its useful life. In other words fixed assets generally have a finite life and are therefore used up in the business. An estimate of the amount of this use in each year must be made and charged to the profit and loss account for the year in the same way as all other expenses that are used up are matched to the revenue they generate. This estimate of usage of fixed assets is known as *depreciation*.

ACTIVITY **6.4**
....

Provide a definition for the term 'depreciation' as it is used in accounting.

Answer

Depreciation is an assessment of the amount of a fixed asset used up in a period by a business as it earns revenue.

Depreciation estimate

How is the estimate of depreciation arrived at?

ACTIVITY **6.5**

Identify two factors that you think will influence the estimate of depreciation to be charged in a period.

Answer

There are several factors that you could have chosen from:

▶ Original cost of asset – the amount used up will obviously depend on the amount originally paid for the asset. The expense of depreciation will be greater for a more expensive van.

▶ Life of the asset – the longer the use of the asset in the business then the lower the depreciation charge in each period.

▶ Residual value of asset at the end of its useful life – the total amount of the asset used up in the business will be the original cost less any resale value at the end of its useful life.

▶ Method of use of the asset – the charge for each period will depend upon how the asset is used in each period. For example the asset may be used up more in the first period than the second. This will need reflecting in the depreciation charge.

The business has to combine all these factors in order to arrive at the depreciation charge. The method of combination may well be different for each business as each business will use the asset in a unique way. Thus there are no rules which state how each type of asset should be depreciated. Within accounting practice there are two methods of combining these factors which are quite popular – straight line and reducing balance, but there are others.

Straight line method

This method assumes that the asset is used evenly throughout its useful life and allocates cost less residual value over the useful life of the asset providing an estimate of depreciation that is the same for each period of use.

ACTIVITY **6.6**

An asset was purchased for £10,000 on 1.1.90 and has an estimated residual value of £1,500 at the end of its useful life of five years. Calculate the depreciation charge for each year assuming the straight line method.

Answer

$$\text{Depreciation} = £(10,000 - 1,500)/5$$
$$= £1,700 \text{ per annum}$$

Reducing balance method

This method assumes that more of the asset is used up in the first period than the next and so on. It is calculated by applying a fixed percentage to the reducing balance of the asset. This is easiest to explain by the use of an example.

EXAMPLE **6.4**

An asset is purchased for £8,000 and is estimated to have a residual value of £2,000 at the end of its useful life of four years. The percentage charge for depreciation will be 30% applied to the reducing balance of the asset as follows:

Cost at beginning of Year 1	8,000
Depreciation charge Year 1, 30% × 8,000,	2,400
Reducing balance Year 2, 8,000 – 2,400,	5,600
Depreciation charge Year 2, 30% × 5,600,	1,680
Reducing balance Year 3	3,920
Depreciation charge Year 3, 30% × 3,920,	1,176
Reducing balance Year 4	2,744
Depreciation charge Year 4, 30% × 2,744,	823
Reducing balance end of Year 4	£1,921

The reducing balance at the end of Year 4 should have equated to the residual value of £2,000. It didn't as the percentage depreciation figure used was rounded for ease of calculation. The percentage charge for reducing balance depreciation is calculated from the following formula:-

$$r = 1 - n\sqrt{s/c}$$

where:

r = percentage	$r = 1 - 4\sqrt{2,000/8,000}$
n = useful life	$r = 1 - 4\sqrt{.25}$
s = residual value	$r = 1 - .707107$
c = original cost	$r = 29.2893\%$

There are other methods of calculating depreciation but the two identified above will suffice for your studies at this stage.

Ledger entries for depreciation

Having identified a figure for depreciation this must now be entered in the ledger accounts as a period end adjustment so as to charge depreciation as an expense to the profit and loss account for the period.

ACTIVITY **6.7**

If the depreciation estimate is debited to the profit and loss account in a period identify where the equal and opposite credit entry will be made. Show the entries in the accounts for the period ending 31.12.90 and 31.12.91 for the straight line example used in Activity 6.6

Answer

You need to identify another provision account here as you did for provision for bad debts. A provision for depreciation account is created and credited with the provision.

ASSET ACCOUNT

1.1.90	Bank	£10,000	31.12.90	Bal c/d	£10,000
1.1.91	Bal b/d	£10,000	31.12.91	Bal c/d	£10,000
1.1.92	Bal b/d	10,000			

PROVISION FOR DEPRECIATION ACCOUNT

31.12.90	Balance c/d	£1,700	31.12.90	Profit and loss	£1,700
			1.1.91	Bal b/d	1,700
31.12.91	Balance c/d	3,400	31.12.91	Profit and loss	1,700
		£3,400			£3,400
			1.1.92	Balance b/d	3,400

Note how the asset account remains at its original amount in the ledgers and that the provision for depreciation account increases each period as further charges are made to the profit and loss accounts.

These two accounts will be reflected in the balance sheet as at 31.12.90 and 31.12.91 as follows:

BALANCE SHEET EXTRACT AS AT 31.12.90

	£
Asset	10,000
Depreciation	1,700
Net book value	8,300

BALANCE SHEET EXTRACT AS AT 31.12.91

	£
Asset	10,000
Depreciation	3,400
Net book value	6,600

The above is quite often written in columnar form as follows:

	Cost	Depreciation	Net book value
	£	£	£
Fixed asset	10,000	3,400	6,600

Sale of fixed assets

The last adjustment to be considered in this chapter is that for the sale of a fixed asset.

When a fixed asset is sold the proceeds will, of course, be debited to the bank account as would all other income received. But where will the corresponding credit appear? The accounting answer is to credit a *sale of fixed asset account*. At this stage though, the ledger accounts will still include the asset account showing the original cost of the asset and a provision for depreciation account which has been built up over the period of use of the asset before its sale. These accounts need deleting from the books otherwise an asset will be recorded in the balance sheet which no longer belongs to nor is controlled by the business. These ledger accounts are deleted through the sale of asset account. We will return to this again in Chapter 12 when we look at the sale of the revalued assets.

ACTIVITY **6.8**

An asset is purchased for £12,000 on 1.1.90 and is estimated to have a useful life of four years with a residual value at the end of its useful life of £2,000. Its method of use is assumed to be straight line. On the 1.5.92 the asset is sold for £5,400. Assume a charge for depreciation is made in the year of purchase but not in the year of sale. Show the ledger entries required for all three years and identify what the balance is on the sale of asset account at 31.12.92.

Answer

ASSET ACCOUNT

1.1.90	Bank	£12,000	31.12.90	Bal c/d	£12,000
1.1.91	Bal b/d	£12,000	31.12.91	Bal c/d	£12,000
1.1.92	Bal b/d	£12,000	31.12.92	Sale of asset	£12,000

PROVISION FOR DEPRECIATION ACCOUNT

31.12.90	Bal c/d	£2,500	31.12.90	Profit and loss	£2,500
			1.1.91	Bal b/d	2,500
31.12.91	Bal c/d	5,000	31.12.91	Profit and loss	2,500
		£5,000			£5,000
31.12.92	Sale of asset	£5,000	1.1.92	Bal b/d	£5,000

SALE OF ASSET ACCOUNT

31.12.92	Asset	12,000	1.5.92	Bank	5,400
			31.12.92	Depreciation	5,000
			31.12.92	Bal c/d	1,600
		£12,000			£12,000
31.12.92	Bal b/d	1,600			

Note how the asset account and the depreciation account have been cleared to the sale of asset account. The balance on the sale account is the difference between what was paid for the asset, the amount of the asset estimated to have been used up in the business and the amount received on its sale. It is a loss on sale and will be charged to the profit and loss account as are all other expenses of the business.

SALE OF ASSET ACCOUNT

31.12.92	Bal b/d	£1,600	31.12.92	Profit and loss	£1,600

Summary
....

This chapter has introduced you to several adjustments that have to be made to the ledger accounts at the end of a period in order to draw up the profit and loss account and balance sheet in accordance with accounting concepts and conventions. The concepts and conventions used were mainly accruals (matching) and prudence. Adjustments were made for accruals and prepayments both for expense and revenue, bad debts and provision for bad debts and provision for depreciation. Depreciation is perhaps the hardest adjustment to get to grips with as it is an attempt to measure the use of the asset within the business, not an attempt to reduce the asset to its realisable (sale) value at any point in time. You must ensure that you are very clear on this fact.

This chapter concludes with several exercises involving these adjustments.

Further study
....

All introductory texts on bookkeeping or accounting will include the above material and several exercises for you to work through in addition to the ones we have provided.

Three books that you may like to reference are:

▶ *Business Accounting 1,* Frank Wood, Chapters 20, 21, 22, and 23, Pitman, 1996.
▶ *Foundations of Business Accounting,* Roy Dodge, Chapter 6, Chapman and Hall, 1993.
▶ *Accounting Practice,* 4th edition, Glautier and Underdown, Chapters 3 and 5, Pitman, 1994.

These books also make reference to an 'extended' trial balance which is a working paper used to speed up the preparation of the year end financial statements. Note that the use of this extended trial balance does not alleviate the necessity to adjust the ledger accounts in the books of the business. You may, however, find it a useful tool and we will look at it in the next chapter.

SELF-
CHECK
QUESTIONS

Accruals and prepayments

1   The following adjustments are required to be made to the ledger accounts for Mr Cog for the year ended 31.12.95:
▶   Stationery expenses paid in 1995 £450, amount owing as at 31.12.95 £50.
▶   Building insurance paid in 1995 £600 for the period 1.7.95 to 30.6.96 – note: the building was purchased 1.7.95.

▶   Motor expenses paid in 1995 £550, amount owing 31.12.94 £70, amount owing 31.12.95 £90.

▶   Rents paid in 1995 £1,500 for the period 1.7.95 to 30.6.96, £1,200 had been paid last year for the period 1.7.94 to 30.6.95

▶   Rents receivable during the year should be £50 per month. Only £500 has been received as at 31.12.95.

Show the ledger accounts for the above, the amounts transferred to the profit and loss account and any balances carried down.

2   Answer TRUE or FALSE in respect of the following and fully explain your choice:

▶   If an accrued expense is ignored at the year end the profit will be understated.

▶   If an accrued expense from the previous period is not carried forward into the current year the profit for the current year will be understated.

▶   An accrued expense is an expense that has been paid but not used up in generating revenue.

▶   A prepayment is an expense that has been paid but not used up in generating revenue.

▶   When adjusting a ledger account for an accrued expense, you debit the account with the accrual before balancing and bring down a credit balance.

▶   An accrued expense is an asset.

▶   An accrued revenue item is an asset.

Bad debts and provision for bad debts

3   Creating a provision for bad debts uses which accounting concept? Explain your choice.

4   When bad debts are eliminated from accounts a provision for bad debts is no longer necessary. Discuss.

5   As at the year end 31.12.95 the following debts out of a total debtors' figure of £54,500 are found to be bad:

A Bloggs   £780
B Swift   £320
P Trent   £1,500 – 50p in the £ is payable.

The balance sheet as at 31.12.94 showed a provision for bad debts for the business of £2,100. The provision for bad debts as at 31.12.95 is estimated to be 5% of debtors balances. Show the bad debts account, provision for bad debts account and the balance sheet as at 31.12.95.

Depreciation

6   Identify the factors involved in the calculation of depreciation for a fixed asset.

7   Are the following statements TRUE or FALSE? Explain your answer fully.

▶   Depreciation is the amount necessary to reduce the asset to its net realisable value at the year end.

▶ Depreciation is the assessment of the amount of an asset used up in generating revenue for a period.

▶ The amount of depreciation charged by two businesses using an identical asset will be the same.

▶ Motor vehicles are always depreciated using the reducing balance method and buildings using the straight line method.

▶ The straight line method of depreciation allocates an equal charge for depreciation to each period of use.

▶ If depreciation is omitted from the accounts, profit for the year will be overstated.

8   The following fixed assets are bought by C Brewer for use in his business on 1.1.90.

	Cost	Estimated useful life	Estimated residual value at end of useful life
	£	Years	£
Building	60,000	50	10,000
Vehicle	12,000	10	300
Equipment	9,000	10	800

Buildings and equipment are to be depreciated using the straight line method, vehicles reducing balance of 25%.

The vehicle is sold for £6,500 on the 1.12.92 and an item of equipment costing £1,500 for £1,200 on the same date. Assume that the residual value of the item of equipment sold was estimated to be £100 at its date of purchase. Assume a full year's depreciation in the year of purchase and none in the year of sale.

Show the asset accounts, provision for depreciation accounts, sale of asset accounts and extracts from the profit and loss account and balance sheet in respect of these assets for the years ended 31.12.90, 31.12.91, 31.12.92, 31.12.93.

Answers

1

STATIONERY ACCOUNT

1995	Cash	450			
31.12.95	Bal c/d	50	31.12.95	Profit and loss	500
		£500			£500
			1.1.96	Bal b/d	50

INSURANCE ACCOUNT

1995	Cash	600	31.12.95	Profit and loss	300
			31.12.95	Bal c/d	300
		£600			£600
1.1.96	Bal b/d	300			

MOTOR EXPENSES ACCOUNT

1995	Cash	550	1.1.94	Bal b/d	70
31.12.95	Bal c/d	90	31.12.95	Profit and loss	570
		£640			£640
			1.1.96	Bal b/d	90

RENTS PAID ACCOUNT

1.1.95	Bal b/d	600	31.12.95	Profit and loss	1,350
1995	Cash	1,500	31.12.95	Bal c/d	750
		£2,100			£2,100
1.1.96	Bal b/d	750			

RENTS RECEIVABLE ACCOUNT

31.12.95	Profit and loss	600	1995	Cash	500
			31.12.95	Bal c/d	100
		£600			£600
1.1.96	Bal b/d	100			

2 ▶ False. An accrued expense will increase the charge for expenses to the profit and loss account so if it is ignored the profit will be overstated.

▶ True. An accrued expense brought forward from a previous period will reduce the charge to the profit and loss account in the current year so if this is ignored the charge will be increased and profit understated.

▶ False. An accrued expense has not been paid but has been used up in generating revenue.

▶ True. Refer to rents paid above.

▶ True. Refer to stationery above.

▶ False. An accrued expense has not been paid therefore is a liability.

▶ True. This is income due in the period and therefore a form of debtor.

3 Prudence concept. This is to ensure that assets – debtors – are not overstated in the balance sheet.

4 False. There is still a possibility that further debts could turn bad.

5

BAD DEBTS ACCOUNT

A Bloggs	780			
B Swift	320			
P Trent	750	Profit and loss	1,850
	£1,850		£1,850

PROVISION FOR BAD DEBTS ACCOUNT

		Profit and loss	2,595

Calculation of required provision:

	£
Debtors	54,500
Bad debts written off	1,850
	52,650
Less debt to be paid	750
	51,900
Provision at 5%	2,595

Balance sheet extract:

	£	£
Debtors	52,650	
Less provision	2,595	50,055

6 Cost of the asset, estimate of useful life to the business, estimate of residual value at the end of that useful life at current prices, assessment of method of use of asset in the business.

7 ▶ False. Depreciation is the measure of the use of the asset in generating revenues. This may or may not equate to net realisable value.

▶ True.

▶ False. They may use the asset differently therefore the method will be different and also residual value and estimated life may be different.

▶ False. The method used should equate to how the asset is *used,* not the *type* of asset. However, in many businesses vehicles are depreciated by reducing balance and buildings by straight line.

▶ True. Depreciation is an expense so if omitted expenses will be understated and therefore profit overstated.

8

BUILDINGS ACCOUNT

		£			£
1.1.90	Bank	£60,000	31.12.90	Bal c/d	£60,000
1.1.91	Bal b/d	£60,000	31.12.91	Bal c/d	£60,000
1.1.92	Bal b/d	£60,000	31.12.92	Bal c/d	£60,000

VEHICLES ACCOUNT

		£			£
1.1.90	Bank	£12,000	31.12.90	Bal c/d	£12,000
1.1.91	Bal b/d	£12,000	31.12.91	Bal c/d	£12,000
1.1.92	Bal b/d	£12,000	1.12.92	Sale	£12,000

EQUIPMENT ACCOUNT

		£			£
1.1.90	Bank	£9,000	31.12.90	Bal c/d	£9,000
1.1.91	Bal b/d	£9,000	31.12.91	Bal c/d	£9,000
1.1.92	Bal b/d	9,000	1.1.92	Sale	1,500
			31.12.92	Bal c/d	7,500
		£9,000			£9,000

PROVISION FOR DEPRECIATION OF BUILDINGS ACCOUNT

31.12.90	Bal c/d	£1,000	31.12.90	Profit and loss	£1,000
			1.1.90	Bal b/d	1,000
31.12.91	Bal c/d	2,000	31.12.91	Profit and loss	1,000
		£2,000			£2,000
			1.1.92	Bal b/d	2,000
31.12.92	Bal c/d	3,000	31.12.92	Profit and loss	1,000
		£3,000			£3,000

PROVISION FOR DEPRECIATION OF VEHICLES ACCOUNT

31.12.90	Bal c/d	£3,000	31.12.90	Profit and loss	£3,000
			1.1.91	Bal b/d	3,000
31.12.91	Bal c/d	5,250	31.12.91	Profit and loss	2,250
		£5,250			£5,250
1.12.92	Sale	5,250	1.1.92	Bal b/d	5,250

PROVISION FOR DEPRECIATION OF EQUIPMENT ACCOUNT

31.12.90	Bal c/d	£820	31.12.90	Profit and loss	£820
			1.1.91	Bal b/d	820
31.12.91	Bal c/d	1,640	31.12.91	Profit and loss	820
		£1,640			£1,640
1.12.92	Sale	280	1.1.92	Bal b/d	1,640
31.12.92	Bal c/d	2,040	31.12.92	Profit and loss	680
		£2,320			£2,320

SALE OF VEHICLES ACCOUNT

1.12.92	Asset	12,000	1.12.92	Cash	6,500
			1.12.92	Depreciation	5,250
			31.12.92	Profit and loss	250
		£12,000			£12,000

SALE OF EQUIPMENT ACCOUNT

1.12.92	Asset	1,500	1.12.92	Cash	1,200
			1.12.92	Depreciation	280
			31.12.92	Profit and loss	20
		£1,500			£1,500

PROFIT AND LOSS ACCOUNT FOR THE YEAR ENDED 31.12.92

	£
Depreciation of buildings	1,000
Depreciation of equipment	680
Loss on sale of vehicles	250
Loss on sale of equipment	20

BALANCE SHEET AS AT 31.12.92

	Cost	Depreciation	Net book value
Buildings	60,000	3,000	57,000
Equipment	7,500	2,040	5,460
	£67,500	£5,040	£62,460

Further review questions are available in a separate resource pack which is available to lecturers.

CHAPTER 7

Preparation of profit and loss account and balance sheet from trial balance and adjustments

Objectives:

By the end of this chapter you should be able to:

▶ Prepare a profit and loss account from a trial balance after taking account of several adjustments.

▶ Prepare a balance sheet from a trial balance after several adjustments.

Introduction

This chapter aims to bring together your knowledge of Chapters 5 and 6 so that you can prepare profit and loss accounts and balance sheets at the period end of a business after taking account of all the period-end adjustments necessary to the ledger accounts. These period-end adjustments will ensure that the final statements prepared will be in accordance with concepts and conventions of accounting that were identified in Chapter 4.

Use will be made of the extended trial balance technique in compiling these final statements.

First, though, a recap on Chapters 5 and 6:

▶ Ledger accounts are required for all assets, liabilities, expenses and income within a business.

▶ These ledger accounts are written up using double entry – the duality concept.

▶ At a period end ledger accounts are balanced.

▶ Expense and income accounts are transferred to the profit and loss account which is a double entry account.

▶ Any other balances remaining in the ledgers are shown on a balance sheet.

▶ To prepare accounts in accordance with accounting concepts and conventions several adjustments need to be made to the ledger accounts before transfers are made to the profit and loss account.

▶ These adjustments take account of accruals and prepayments so that expenses used up are matched to the revenue they generate.

▶ Adjustments are required for bad debts and provision for bad debts to comply with prudence.

▶ A depreciation adjustment for fixed assets that are used up in generating revenue is also required.

This chapter will consist of an example that will demonstrate adjustments required to the ledgers at the period end, the extraction of a trial balance at this stage, and the preparation of a profit and loss account and balance sheet for the period. Work through this example carefully as you will then be expected to complete a similar activity yourself. Our example will conclude with a technique called an extended trial balance, which is a working paper from which the adjustments to the double entry accounts will be made. This speeds up the process of producing a profit and loss account and balance sheet without having to wait for all the ledger accounts to be adjusted. This can be a useful technique for students in examinations. Note that the ledgers will eventually have to be amended for the period-end adjustments whether or not we use an extended trial balance.

EXAMPLE **7.1**

The following trial balance was extracted from the ledgers of a sole trader, Mai Wong, as at 31.12.95:

	Dr	Cr
Sales		45,000
Purchases	15,000	
Stock 1.1.95	2,300	
Wages	5,200	
Office expenses	900	
Heating and lighting	850	
Telephone	450	
Rent	2,200	
Fixtures and fittings	7,550	
Vehicles	8,500	
Provision for depreciation 1.1.95		
Fixtures and fittings		755
Capital		8,805
Debtors	1,300	
Creditors		1,150
Insurance	650	
Motor expenses	210	
Drawings	10,400	
Bank and cash	200	
	£55,710	£55,710

The following period end adjustments are required:

▸ *Office expenses to be accrued, £50.*
▸ *Heating and lighting to be accrued, £150.*
▸ *Rent paid in advance, £200.*
▸ *Insurance paid in advance, £80.*
▸ *Fixtures and fittings to be depreciated at 10% of cost and vehicles 20% of cost.*
▸ *An item of fixtures was sold during the year for £90. The item had been bought on 1.1.93 for £120. The sale proceeds were credited to the sales account.*
▸ *Closing stock is valued at £1,950*
▸ *£90 of the motor expenses relates to items for Mai Wong's own use.*

Show the adjustments necessary to the ledger accounts to account for the above and the transfers to the profit and loss account for the year.

OFFICE EXPENSES ACCOUNT

31.12.95	Bal b/d	900				
31.12.95	Bal c/d (1)	50	31.12.95	Profit and loss (2)		950
		£950				£950
			1.1.96	Bal b/d (1)		50

Entry 1 is the accrual of £50 for the year and the corresponding carry down of the balance to the following year.

Entry 2 shows the charge to the profit and loss account for the year which is the £900 cash paid plus £50 accrual. This accrual is to ensure matching of expenses used up to the revenue generated.

HEATING AND LIGHTING ACCOUNT

31.12.95	Bal b/d	850			
31.12.95	Bal c/d	150	31.12.95	Profit and loss	1,000
		£1,000			£1,000
			1.1.96	Bal b/d	150

RENT ACCOUNT

31.12.95	Bal b/d	2,200	31.12.95	Profit and loss	2,000
			31.12.95	Bal c/d	200
		£2,200			£2,200
1.1.96	Bal b/d	200			

INSURANCE ACCOUNT

31.12.95	Bal b/d	650	31.12.95	Profit and loss	570
			31.12.95	Bal c/d	80
		£650			£650
1.1.95	Bal b/d	80			

The above three accounts show similar entries to those for office expenses.

FIXTURES AND FITTINGS ACCOUNT

31.12.95	Bal b/d	7,550	31.12.95	Sale	120
			31.12.95	Bal c/d	7,430
		£7,550			£7,550
1.1.96	Bal b/d	7,430			

Here we have shown the 'write out' from the asset account of the fixtures sold. The corresponding debit entry will be shown in the sale of fixtures account. A similar *write out needs to be made in the provision for depreciation account for fixtures and fittings. The depreciation previously provided on the fixtures sold will have been £120 × 10% for two years, that is £24.*

PROVISION FOR DEPRECIATION OF FIXTURES ACCOUNT

31.12.95	Sale	24	31.12.95	Bal c/d	755
31.12.95	Bal c/d	1,474	31.12.95	Profit and loss (1)	743
		£1,498			£1,498
			1.1.96	Bal b/d	1,474

Entry 1 is the depreciation for the current year calculated on the remaining assets of £7,430 after the sale of £120. A corresponding entry will be made in the profit and loss account.

The sale of fixtures account will appear as follows.

SALE OF FIXTURES ACCOUNT

31.12.95	Fixtures	120	31.12.95	Depreciation	24
			31.12.95	Sales (1)	90
			31.12.95	Profit and loss	6
		£120			£120

Entry 1 is the transfer of the sale proceeds of the fixtures which had been included in the sales account. The transfer of £6 to the profit and loss account represents a loss on sale of the asset. The sales account will need amending as follows:

SALES ACCOUNT

31.12.95	Sale of fixtures	90	31.12.95	Bal b/d	45,000
31.12.95	Profit and loss	44,910			
		£45,000			£45,000

The charge for depreciation on the vehicles also needs calculating and entering into the accounts: depreciation for the year 20% × £8,500 = £1,700

PROVISION FOR DEPRECIATION OF VEHICLES ACCOUNT

31.12.95	Bal c/d	£1,700	31.12.95	Profit and loss	£1,700
			1.1.96	Bal b/d	1,700

The motor expenses account also needs amending as £90 of these expenses related to Mai Wong's own use.

MOTOR EXPENSES ACCOUNT

31.12.95	Bal b/d	210	31.12.95	Drawings	90
			31.12.95	Profit and loss	120
		£210			£210

The accounts for purchases, stock 1.1.95, wages and telephone will all be transferred to the profit and loss account and an account for closing stock opened as follows:

CLOSING STOCK ACCOUNT

31.12.95	Profit and loss	£1,950

The profit and loss account will now appear as follows:

PROFIT AND LOSS ACCOUNT FOR THE YEAR ENDED 31.12.95

Sales		44,910
Opening Stock	2,300	
Add purchases	15,000	
	17,300	
Less closing stock	1,950	15,350
Gross profit		29,560
Wages	5,200	
Office expenses	950	
Heating and lighting	1,000	
Rent	2,000	
Insurance	570	
Depreciation: Fixtures	743	
Vehicles	1,700	
Telephone	450	
Motor expenses	120	
Loss on sale	6	12,739
Net profit		£16,821

All balances now remaining in the ledgers are entered in the balance sheet as follows:

BALANCE SHEET AS AT 31.12.95

	Cost	Depreciation	Net book value
Fixed Assets			
Fixtures and fittings	7,430	1,474	5,956
Vehicles	8,500	1,700	6,800
	15,930	3,174	12,756
Current Assets			
Stock		1,950	
Debtors		1,300	
Rent prepaid		200	
Insurance prepaid		80	
Bank and cash		200	
		3,730	

Current liabilities

Creditors	1,150		
Office expenses accrued	50		
Heat and light accrued	150	1,350	2,380
			£15,136
Capital			8,805
Add profit		16,821	
Less drawings		10,490	6,331
			£15,136

Adjusting the ledger accounts as shown above is very time consuming but has to be done by a business if it keeps double entry records. Many businesses will use computerised ledgers. We will look at these in Chapter 14. The process of adjusting the ledgers for both computerised and manual systems can be controlled by the use of an extended trial balance – a worksheet. The worksheet for the example above would appear as follows:

	Trial balance		Adjustments		Profit and Loss		Balance Sheet	
	Dr	Cr	Dr	Cr	Dr	Cr	Dr	Cr
Sales		45,000	90			44,910		
Purchases	15,000				15,000			
Stock	2,300				2,300			
Wages	5,200				5,200			
Office	900		50		950			
Heating and lighting	850		150		1,000			
Telephone	450				450			
Rent	2,200			200	2,000			
Fixtures and fittings	7,550			120			7,430	
Vehicles	8,500						8,500	
Depreciation, furniture and fittings		755	24	743				1,474
Capital		8,805						8,805
Debtors	1,300						1,300	
Creditors		1,150						1,150
Insurance	650			80	570			
Motor	210			90	120			
Drawings	10,400		90				10,490	
Bank	200						200	
	£55,710	£55,710						
Accruals				200				200
Prepayments			280				280	

Depreciation, furniture and fittings	743		743		
Depreciation, vehicle	1,700		1,700		
Profit on sale	6		6		
Provision for depreciation, vehicle		1,700			1,700
Closing stock	1,950			1,950	
Profit and loss		1,950	1,950		
Net profit			16,821		16,821
	£5,083	£5,083	£46,860	£46,860	£30,150	£30,150

Look at this extended trial balance carefully and follow all the adjustments made and the entries into the profit and loss account and balance sheet. You may find this method of drawing up the final accounts useful for examinations. The extended trial balance technique lends itself to computer spreadsheet applications.

Summary

This chapter has combined your learning from Chapters 5 and 6. You can now prepare a profit and loss account and balance sheet from a trial balance after making several adjustments at the period end to this trial balance. We also illustrated the technique of an extended trial balance which is, in fact, a work sheet to control the adjustments within the ledger accounts. It can, however, be a useful tool to use in an examination.

We have only provided one further example in this chapter as you will find plenty of practice in preparing profit and loss accounts and balance sheets in Chapter 8. You may like to attempt to do the exercise at the end of the Chapter using an extended trial balance but note that we have not provided the answer in that way.

Further study

The text books previously referred to will all provide you with further study and examples in the area covered by this chapter. In particular Dodge (*Foundation of Business Accounting*, 1993, Chapman and Hall) covers the extended trial balance technique.

SELF-
CHECK
QUESTION

The following trial balance was extracted from the books of Rodney, a sole trader, as at 31.12.95

	Dr	Cr
Capital 1.1.95		15,500
Drawings	4,660	
Debtors and creditors	6,530	5,210
Sales		71,230
Purchases	29,760	
Stock 1.1.95	4,340	
Rates	800	
Heat and light	2,650	
Wages	8,250	
Bad debts	230	
Provision for bad debts		280
General expenses	2,340	
Motor expenses	3,240	
Premises at cost	30,000	
Fixtures and fittings	8,000	
Vehicles	12,000	
Provision for depreciation 1.1.95		
Premises		2,400
Fixtures and fittings		1,600
Vehicles		5,400
Bank	820	
Loan		12,000
	£113,620	£113,620

The following matters have not been taken into account in the preparation of the above trial balance:

▶ Stock 31.12.95 £4,870.
▶ Light and heat due 31.12.95 £120, general expenses due £80.
▶ Depreciation is to be provided for the year as follows:
  premises – 2% on cost
  fixtures and fittings – 10% on cost
  vehicles – 20% reducing balance.
▶ A further bad debt of £130 is to be written off and the bad debts provision is to be at 5% of debtors after the write off.
▶ The loan interest of £600 has not been paid for the year.

You are required to prepare a profit and loss account for the year ended 31.12.95 and a balance sheet as at that date.

Answer

PROFIT AND LOSS ACCOUNT FOR THE YEAR ENDED 31.12.95 FOR RODNEY

Sales		71,230
Opening stock	4,340	
Purchases	29,760	
	34,100	

Less closing stock	4,870	29,230
Gross profit		42,000
Rates	800	
Heat and light	2,770	
General expenses	2,420	
Motor expenses	3,240	
Wages	8,250	
Bad debts	360	
Depreciation: Premises	600	
Fixtures and fittings	800	
Vehicles	1,320	
Provision for bad debts	40	
Loan interest	600	21,200
Net profit		£20,800

BALANCE SHEET AS AT 31.12.95 FOR RODNEY

	Cost	Depreciation	Net book value
Fixed assets			
Premises	30,000	3,000	27,000
Fixtures and fittings	8,000	2,400	5,600
Vehicles	12,000	6,720	5,280
	50,000	12,120	37,880
Current assets			
Stock		4,870	
Debtors	6,400		
Less bad debts provision	320	6,080	
Bank		820	
		11,770	
Current liabilities			
Creditors	5,210		
Accruals	800	6,010	5,760
			43,640
Long term liabilities			
Loan			12,000
			£31,640
Capital			15,500
Add net profit		20,800	
Less drawings		4,660	16,140
			£31,640

Workings for answer to self-check question

1 The following adjustments are required to the trial balance as given:

	£	£
Debit heat and light account	120	
Credit accruals account		120
Debit expenses account	80	
Credit accruals account		80
Debit loan interest account	600	
Credit accruals account		600

2 The depreciation charges are calculated as follows:

Premises £30,000 × 2% = £600
Fixtures and fittings £8,000 × 10% = £800
Vehicles £(12,000 – 5,400) × 20% = £1,320

3 The adjustment for bad debts is as follows:

Debit bad debts account	130	
Credit debtors account		130

The debtors balance now becomes:

£6,530 – 130 = £6,400

The provision for bad debts is required to be set at:

5% × £6,400 = £320

The provision already in the trial balance is £280 therefore an additional provision of £40 is required.

Further review questions are available in a separate resource pack which is available to lecturers.

Accounts of limited companies

The need for companies

. . . .

In previous chapters we have assumed a business is that of a sole trader. This is where an individual invests his capital in a business and trades with the intention of earning profit that will belong to him to do with as he chooses. However, this type of business has several drawbacks.

ACTIVITY **8.1**
. . . .

Identify two drawbacks of sole trader businesses.

Answer

You should have chosen two from the following list. However, this list is not exhaustive and you may have come up with drawbacks that we have not mentioned. You should be able to explain whether your drawbacks are reasonable.

▶ A sole trader has limited resources available – the capital he is able to invest in the business – limited specialist and management skills.
▶ For a business to grow, more resources are required in terms of capital and expertise.
▶ The sole trader is personally liable for all debts of the business – creditors can claim on the personal assets of the sole trader.
▶ The sole trader business is dependant upon the owner.

Establishing the business as a limited company can overcome all the above drawbacks. Capital resources are available from more than one person and in addition the company has easier access to loan funds. Specialist and management skills can be brought into the business by widening the number of owners. A company provides what is known as limited liability to the owners. Owners of the business can change without there being any effect on the business.

The company

A company has two notions as its basis

▶   Corporate entity.
▶   Limited liability.

The notion of corporate entity means that several people can band together as owners of a business, by investing capital in the business, and the business will be a legal entity separate from the owners. It also means that the owners, the investors of capital, can change without the need to change the legal entity of the company.

The notion of limited liability limits the claim on the owners of the business from any of its creditors to the capital these owners invested. It also means that a creditor has to sue the company, not the owners, for payment of any debts due to him, and these creditors could indeed force the winding up, liquidation, of the company.

DID YOU KNOW ...?
There are several hundred thousand companies in the United Kingdom, many of them large conglomerates such as British Telecom, Guinness and ICI.

The law in relation to companies was established by the first Companies Act of 1844 which fused these two notions of corporate entity and limited liability, and any confusion in respect of the two notions was put to rest by the judgement in the case of *Salomon* v *Salomon & Co. Ltd. 1897*. The judgement handed down by The House of Lords stated that the company was a separate legal entity distinct from the owners and that creditors could not claim on the personal assets of the owners, only on the assets of the company. From this it can be seen that creditors trade with a limited company at their own risk. Thus it is advisable for creditors to investigate the financial stability of a company before they trade with it.

Formation of a company

Further detail in respect of the formation of a company will be found in a company law course but it is worthwhile identifying the main points here.

▶   All companies must be registered with the Registrar of Companies by the submission of a number of legal documents. This marks the legal birth of a company.
▶   The two most important documents to be filed are the Memorandum of Association and the Articles of Association
▶   The Memorandum of Association defines the relationship between the company and any external parties and states the objectives of the company, that is what sort of trade it will undertake. It also identifies the maximum capital to be invested in the company by the owners, known as the Share Capital.

▶ The Articles of Association define the rights of shareholders, the rules of operation of the company and the rights and duties of owners and employees of the company.

▶ Companies are registered as either public limited companies (plcs) or private companies. Essentially the distinction is that plcs can, if they wish, raise capital by selling shares to the general public. They must have a minimum allotted (ie issued to shareholders) share capital of £50,000. Many plcs are quoted on the London Stock Exchange thus anyone who wants to can become an owner of the company as long as they have the necessary capital to invest. Private companies have restricted ownership.

▶ There must be at least two shareholders in any company but there is no maximum number.

▶ The day-to-day business of the company is generally not carried out by the owners but by directors who are appointed by the owners. The directors report to the owners through the facility of an Annual General Meeting.

Company capital

The capital of a company is divided into shares. Investors purchase however many of these shares they are able, and want, to buy. For example, a company could be registered with a maximum share capital of 100,000 £1 shares. The maximum capital of the company would therefore be £100,000. A company, not the same one, could also be registered with a share capital of say 50,000 £3 shares – a maximum capital of £150,000. The pound value attached to a share is known as its nominal (or par) value and a company can decide on the nominal value and total number of shares it wishes to issue. The decision will depend on how much capital the company needs to commence its operations.

Once a company has made the initial issue of the shares, further trading in these shares can take place in what is known as the share market – for many plcs this is the stock exchange. Company shares may well be bought and sold every day on the stock exchange but the company will make no reference to this in the ledger accounts as it will not be a transaction between the corporate entity and the buyer but between the separate shareholder and the buyer. Thus we are differentiating again between the entity of a company and the individual. The company will need to keep a list of who owns shares in the company so that it can pay over any return from the trading of the company due to the shareholders.

Companies are also able to vary the rights of shareholders within a company by issuing different types of shares.

ACTIVITY **8.2**

Obtain a set of company financial statements. This can be done by accessing library facilities or by using the Annual Reports Service offered in the *Financial Times* – read the small print at the end of the daily stock exchange listings to see how this is done. Identify the types of shares in issue for your chosen company from the financial statements and notes.

Answer

Your company almost certainly has in issue ordinary shares. These are the most important type of share and are those most commonly traded on the stock exchange. They carry voting rights in proportion to the number of shares held. These voting rights give control over the operations of the company to the shareholders through the right to appoint the directors.

Preference shares may also have been issued by the company. The main feature of preference shares is that they usually carry a specific rate of return to the holder from the company's profits. For example 5% £1 preference shares would require a payment to the shareholders every year of 5p for every share held. A holder of £10,000 of these preference shares would receive £500.

Preference shares can also be termed *cumulative*. This means that if the company does not make enough profit in any one year to pay out the amount due to the preference shareholders, it carries over to the next year and accumulates until the company does have enough profit to pay out the amount due – the dividend.

The preference shares may also be *redeemable*, giving the company the right to repay the capital to the preference shareholders at a determined future date.

Shares can also be issued by a company at a value above the nominal value declared in the Memorandum of Association. This is known as issuing shares at a *premium*.

ACTIVITY **8.3**

Explain why a company may wish to issue shares at a premium.

Answer

A company may wish to raise additional capital. To issue £1 ordinary shares at a price of £1 to new investors would be unfair to the initial investors in the company. The following example illustrates this point.

A company was initially formed by the issue of 100 £1 ordinary shares. The balance sheet of the company at its formation can be summarised as follows:

	£
Bank	100
Capital 100 £1 ordinary shares	100

The company trades for a number of years earning profits of £250 in total. Its balance sheet will then appear as follows:

Assets	£350
Capital 100 £1 ordinary shares	100
Profit	250
	£350

From this balance sheet we can conclude that each share now has a book value of £3.50. It is also feasible that if these ordinary shares were traded on the stock exchange they would probably sell at a price in excess of £1. The company at this stage now wishes to raise more capital, £140, so that it can expand by the purchase of further assets. If it issues more £1 ordinary shares at their nominal value then this will be unfair to the original shareholders as the balance sheet would now be:

Assets	£490
Capital 240 £1 ordinary shares	240
Profit	250
	£490

Now each share has a book value of £2.04. The original shareholders have lost £1.46 on each share!

To ensure equity (fairness) between old and new shareholders the new shares will be issued at a premium. In this case the shares of £1 nominal value will be issued at £3.50 and the number issued will be 40.

The balance sheet will now be:

Assets	£490
Capital 140 £1 ordinary shares	140
Share premium	100
Profit	250
	£490

Now each share has a book value of £3.50.

Note that the premium paid on the shares is entered in a separate ledger account known as share premium.

ACTIVITY **8.4**

A company is formed with a total authorised (authorised by its inclusion in the Memorandum of Association) share capital of £500,000, consisting of 300,000 £1 ordinary shares and 100,000 5% £2 preference shares. If the company wishes to raise £400,000 in capital, identify the number of shares of each type it should issue to minimise the preference dividend payment in each of the following circumstances:

1   All shares are to be issued at par.
2   Ordinary shares are to be issued at a premium of 25p and preference shares at a premium of 50p.

Answer

1   300,000 £1 ordinary shares and 50,000 £2 5% preference shares. Preference dividend payment £5,000.
2   300,000 £1 ordinary shares at £1.25 raises £375,000, the further £25,000 required is raised by issuing 10,000 £2 5% preference shares at £2.50. Preference dividend payment £1,000. Issuing the minimum number of preference shares in each case ensures that the preference dividend payment will be minimised. Note that the preference dividend is only calculated on the nominal value of shares issued not the premium.

Other forms of capital

When considering the business of a sole trader you saw that the owner could increase the funds available in the business not only by investing more money himself but perhaps by acquiring a loan from a bank. Companies can also raise extra finance in a similar way. However, they are also able to raise loan capital by the issue of *debentures* which can be traded in the market in the same way as a share.

The debenture document sets out the capital value, the interest rate payable, the date the loan is redeemable and any security for the loan. The capital value of the debenture is expressed in nominal value terms, usually in multiples of £100. The interest rate payable on the debenture is set at a fixed percentage of this nominal value. The only difficulty with debentures is that they are often issued at a value above or below nominal value. Thus a £100 debenture could be issued at £99. This means that on issue the cash received by the company will only be £99; that is the debenture has been issued at a discount of £1. It is important to remember, though, that the amount payable by the company on redemption, repayment, of the loan will be £100. In the same way that shares are entered into the company's ledger accounts at nominal value so are the debentures. The question to answer is 'How do we account for the £1 discount on issue?'

ACTIVITY **8.5**
....

A company makes an issue of £10,000 6% debentures at £99. Show the entries in the ledger accounts, including cash, to account for this issue.

Answer

The debenture account is used to record the nominal value of the debentures issued as for share capital.

6% DEBENTURES ACCOUNT

		Issue	10,000

CASH ACCOUNT

Debentures	9,900	

The above entries do not maintain duality. A debit of £100 is required to be made somewhere in the ledgers.

This £100 discount on issue can be considered as an expense of making the debenture issue. Therefore we have:

DEBENTURE DISCOUNT ACCOUNT

	£	
Issue	100	

Like all other expenses this debenture discount should be written off to the profit and loss account by debiting the profit and loss account.

DEBENTURE DISCOUNT ACCOUNT

Issue	100	Profit and loss	100

There is also another possibility for the write-off of this discount on issue which is permitted by the Companies Act and that is to charge it against the share premium account if there is one.

Return on shares and debentures

Any investment is made with the expectation of some form of return. For the sole trader this return was in the form of profits that he was free to withdraw from the business. In the same way the profits of a company belong to the shareholders and they will expect some return on their capital invested. This return is made in the form of a dividend payment. These dividend payments are usually made in two instalments, the interim dividend and the final dividend.

ACTIVITY **8.6**

From your set of company accounts identify the interim and final dividend payments made.

Answer

The dividends identified were probably expressed as so many pence per share. For example, if the dividend was declared as 6p per share and there were 100,000 £1 shares in issue then the total dividend payment made would be £6,000. Note the dividend is calculated by reference to the nominal value of shares issued.

The interim dividend is generally paid half way through the financial period and the final dividend, an additional payment, is proposed at the year end. This means that the shareholders will vote at the annual general meeting on the payment of this final dividend as proposed by the directors and after a vote in favour, the dividend will be paid. Note that this means that all final, proposed, dividends are unpaid at the year end and will therefore need to appear in the year end accounts as a current liability.

The return made to the debenture holder is in the form of interest at the rate specified on the debenture. In the example at Activity 8.5 the interest payable was 6% on a nominal debenture value of £10,000. Thus the company will be required to pay £600 in interest.

ACTIVITY **8.7**

Is the interest payable on the debenture an expense of trading for the company?
Is the dividend payable to the shareholders an expense of trading for the company?

Answer

For the debenture interest the answer is yes. This interest is treated in exactly the same way as the interest on a loan for a sole trader, as an expense of trading.

The dividend payable, though, is not an expense. Remember the drawings of a sole trader were not an expense but an extraction of capital invested.

For a company the dividend payment is shown as an appropriation of profit, as the following example demonstrates.

EXAMPLE **8.1**
·············

Alpha Ltd made a net profit before the payment of interest and the appropriation of dividends of £35,000. There were £10,000 6% debentures in issue and 100,000 £1 ordinary shares. The interim dividend declared was 3p per share and the final pro-posed dividend 4p per share. The interest and dividend payments are shown in the profit and loss account, as follows.

PROFIT AND LOSS ACCOUNT FOR ALPHA LTD

Profit		35,000
Interest on debentures 6%		600
Net profit		34,400
Appropriations		
Interim dividend 3p	3,000	
Final dividend 4p	4,000	7,000
Retained profit for the year		£27,400

Taxation in company accounts

If you look at the profit and loss account in your set of company accounts you will notice that there is another item that did not appear in the profit and loss account of a sole trader, and that is taxation.

Companies are separate legal entities, unlike a sole trader, and are subject to taxation, corporation tax, which will be shown in the profit and loss account. A sole trader did not show taxation in his accounts as the taxation authorities view the earnings of the business of the sole trader as his personal income and tax accordingly. The calculation of corporation tax is complicated and based on taxable profits, which is not the same as accounting profits. At this level of study you will be given a figure to use as the taxation charge for the year. This tax will not be payable, though, until nine months after the end of the accounting year, so will be shown as a liability in the year end accounts.

Reserves

If you look at the balance sheet in your set of company accounts you will notice that the share capital is entered under the heading, Capital and Reserves. Reserves consist of retained profits of the business, that is profits which have not been extracted from the business by the shareholders but have been left as further investment, and share premium which was an initial investment by shareholders. These reserves are further classified into capital or revenue reserves. Share premium is an example of a capital reserve, initial capital invested by shareholders. Retained profit is an example of a revenue reserve, capital earned from the trading of the business. Another distinction between capital and revenue reserves is that revenue reserves can be distributed in the form of dividends, capital reserves must be retained within the business and cannot be distributed in the form of dividends. This is to protect creditors.

The following activity brings together various issues that you have come across in your studies so far.

ACTIVITY **8.8**
••••••••••••

The trial balance of Beta Ltd as at 31.12.95, before adjustment for any of the items listed in the notes, is as follows:

	Dr	Cr
Issued £1 ordinary shares		50,000
Share premium		5,000
Buildings (cost)	55,000	
Fixtures and fittings (cost)	27,000	
Vehicles (cost)	15,000	
Depreciation as at 1.1 95		
Buildings		3,300
Fixtures and fittings		6,750
Vehicles		5,400
Sales		111,000
Purchases	75,000	
Wages and salaries	12,000	
Other expenses	8,000	
Stock 1.1 95	2,500	
6% debentures		30,000
Debenture interest paid	900	
Interim dividend paid	2,000	
Debtors and creditors	28,000	15,000
Retained profits 1.1.95		9,500
Cash	10,550	
	£235,950	£235,950

The following notes are to be taken into account:

1 Stock as at 31.12.95 is £3,400 valued at cost.
2 A final dividend of 5p per share is proposed.
3 Depreciation is to be provided for as follows:
    – buildings 2% per annum straight line
    – fixtures and fittings 25% straight line
    – vehicles 20% reducing balance.
4 Corporation tax for the year is estimated at £3,500.
5 Fittings originally costing £2,400 on which depreciation of £1,200 had been provided were sold on 31.12.95 for £950. No entries have been made in the accounts for the sale nor has any cash been received.

Prepare the profit and loss account and balance sheet for Beta Ltd for the year ended 31.12.95.

Answer

BETA LTD
PROFIT AND LOSS ACCOUNT FOR
THE YEAR ENDED 31.12.95

Sales			111,000
Opening stock		2,500	
Purchases		75,000	
		77,500	
Closing stock		3,400	74,100
Gross profit			36,900
Wages and salaries		12,000	
Office expenses		8,000	
Debenture interest		1,800	
Depreciation:			
Buildings	1,100		
Fixtures and fittings	6,150		
Vehicles	1,920	9,170	
Loss on sale		250	31,220
Profit before tax			5,680
Taxation			3,500
Profit after tax			2,180
Retained profit b/f			9,500
			11,680
Dividends: Interim		2,000	
Proposed		2,500	4,500
Retained profit c/f			£7,180

BETA LTD
BALANCE SHEET AS AT 31.12.95

	Cost	Depreciation	Net book value
Fixed assets			
Buildings	55,000	4,400	50,600
Fixtures and fittings	24,600	11,700	12,900
Vehicles	15,000	7,320	7,680
	94,600	23,420	71,180
Current assets			
Stock		3,400	
Debtors		28,000	
Debtors (fixtures)		950	
Cash		10,550	
		42,900	

Current liabilities

Creditors	15,000		
Taxation	3,500		
Debenture interest	900		
Dividends	2,500	21,900	21,000
			92,180

Long-Term liabilities

6% Debentures	30,000
	£62,180

Capital and reserves

Ordinary shares of £1	50,000
Share premium	5,000
Retained profits	7,180
	£62,180

Format presentation

As you have been looking at your set of company accounts you may have noticed that the presentation of the profit and loss account and balance sheet is slightly different to the one we have used so far. The Companies Act actually specifies four formats that can be used for the presentation of the profit and loss account of a company and two for the balance sheet. The formats that are most frequently used are reproduced below:

PROFIT AND LOSS ACCOUNT FOR THE YEAR ENDED 19YZ

Turnover		X
Cost of sales		(X)
Gross profit		X
Distribution costs	X	
Administration costs	X	(X)
Operating profit		X
Income from investments		X
Interest paid and similar charges		(X)
Profit on ordinary activities before tax		X
Tax on ordinary activities		(X)
Profit on ordinary activities after tax		X
Extraordinary charges	X	
Tax	(X)	(X)
Profit for year		X
Dividends		(X)
Retained profit for year		X
Profit b/f previous years		X
		£X

This presentation of the profit and loss account requires the analysis of expenses under three headings: cost of sales, distribution and administration. Wages and salaries will have to be analysed across these three headings as will depreciation.

BALANCE SHEET AS AT 19YZ
Fixed assets

Intangible assets			X
Tangible assets			X
Investments			X
			X
Current assets			
Stock		X	
Debtors		X	
Cash at bank and in hand		X	
		X	
Creditors due within one year			
Creditors	(X)		
Other	(X)	(X)	
Net current assets			X
Total assets less current liabilities			X
Creditors Due After One Year			(X)
			£X
Capital and reserves			
Called up share capital			X
Share premium account			X
Revaluation reserve			X
Other reserves			X
Retained profit			X
			£X

Summary

This chapter has introduced you to the accounts of a limited company. We identified the concept of legal entity of a company, the differences between a company and a sole trader and noted that the capital of a company was issued in the form of shares. We also noted that companies were subject to taxation which was accounted for as a deduction from the profit of the company.

Lastly we identified the fact that companies are required to publish their final accounts in a specified format. However, the preparation of the profit and loss account and balance sheet of the company required the same techniques as those used for a sole trader.

At the end of this chapter there are several exercises for you that will test your knowledge and understanding of accounting for companies and also the preparation of final accounts in accordance with the specified formats.

Further study

·················

Business Accounting, Wood and *Foundations of Business Accounting*, Dodge will again provide you with further study in the area covered by this chapter.

SELF-
CHECK
QUESTIONS

1 Answer the following questions for both sole traders and companies:
   ▶ Is there any statutory regulation governing them?
   ▶ Who owns the business?
   ▶ Who manages the business?
   ▶ Is the business a separate legal entity?
   ▶ Does the business end when its owners change?
   ▶ Is taxation an expense of the business?
   ▶ How do owners extract profits from the business for their own use?
   ▶ Is the business quoted on the stock exchange?

2 The directors of Britton plc wish to raise additional capital. They currently have in issue one million £1 ordinary shares and no long-term loans. What options do they have available to raise extra capital and which would you advise them to choose.

3 The following is an extract from the balance sheet of Comp plc as at 31.3.96:

	£m
Ordinary shares £1	20
Share premium account	5
Retained profits	12
5% debentures £1	8

   ▶ What is the par value of each share and the book value of each share?
   ▶ What is the interest payable per annum on the debentures?
   ▶ If the interest rate in the market for debentures similar to those of Comp plc was higher than 5% would the market price of Comp's debentures in the market place be higher or lower than £1?

4 The following trial balance was extracted from the books of Cuddly Toy Ltd as at 31.12.95

	Dr	Cr
	£000	£000
Sales		1,562
Stock 1.1.95	660	
Purchases	885	
Land	1,010	
Buildings	980	
Equipment	55	
Vehicles	72	
Depreciation: Buildings		390
Equipment		18
Vehicles		25
Debtors and creditors	180	235
Bank	121	
£1 ordinary shares		900

Share premium		350
Distribution expenses	98	
Administration expenses	24	
Retained profits 1.1.95		185
5% debentures		420
	£4,085	£4,085

The following information has not yet been accounted for:

▶ Closing stock 31.12.95 is valued at £560,000.
▶ Depreciation is to be charged as follows:
   – 2% straight line on buildings
   – 20% straight line on equipment
   – 25% reducing balance on vehicles.
▶ Assets are used as follows:
   – buildings: 50% cost of sales, 25% distribution and 25% administration
   – equipment: all cost of sales
   – vehicles: all distribution.
▶ Taxation to be charged for the year is estimated at £200,000.
▶ No interim dividend has been paid but a final dividend of 6p per share is proposed.

Prepare the published profit and loss account and balance sheet for the company as at 31.12.95.

5 You are required to prepare the profit and loss account for the year ended 31.3.96 and the balance sheet as at that date for internal purposes for the following company:

TRIAL BALANCE OF GERRY LTD AS AT 31.3.96

	Dr	Cr
Ordinary shares £1		100,000
6% preference shares £1		20,000
8% debentures		30,000
Share premium		9,500
Revaluation reserve		10,000
General reserve		12,000
Retained profit b/f 1.4.95		976
Fixed assets (cost £210,000)	191,000	
Stock 1.4.95	14,167	
Debtors and creditors	11,000	7,500
Provision for doubtful debts		324
Bank	9,731	
Purchases and sales	186,000	271,700
Wages and salaries	31,862	
General expenses	15,840	
Debenture interest	1,200	
Preference dividend	1,200	
	£462,000	£462,000

You are also given the following information:

▶ Stock 31.3.96 £23,483.
▶ Depreciation of fixed assets is to be provided at the rate of 10% per annum on cost.
▶ The provision for doubtful debts is to be at 5% of debtors.
▶ £1,200 of debenture interest and £1,437 of general expenses are to be accrued.
▶ £925 of general expenses have been paid in advance.
▶ Provision is to be made for taxation on this year's profits of £9,700.
▶ Provision is to be made for an ordinary dividend of 10%.
▶ The directors have decided to increase the general reserve by a further £3,000.

6 The trial balance of Hobo Ltd as at 30.9.96 was as follows:

	Dr	Cr
Audit fee	1,200	
Bad debts	5,320	
Debtors and creditors	92,360	111,450
Delivery expenses	22,060	
Productive wages	32,300	
Warehouse wages	30,200	
Administrative salaries	15,200	
Purchases and sales	426,500	623,300
Administration expenses	5,600	
Rents administration	12,600	
Stock 1.10.95	18,950	
Ordinary 50p shares		100,000
Share premium account		50,000
Retained profits 1.10.95		26,000
Premises	275,000	
Vehicles	18,500	
Equipment	12,000	
Depreciation as at 1.10.95		
Premises		3,750
Equipment		3,600
Vehicles		6,500
7% debentures		95,000
Bank	51,810	
	£1,019,600	£1,019,600

The following additional information is available:

▶ Stock as at 30.9.96 was valued at £20,650.
▶ Premises and equipment are used at 50% production and 50% distribution, and are to be depreciated at the rate of 1% and 10% straight line respectively.
▶ Vehicles are only used for distribution, and are depreciated at 20% reducing balance.
▶ A provision for bad debts of 5% is to be allowed for.

▶ Final dividend of 15p per share is proposed.

▶ £500 was prepaid for rent and £600 is owing for production wages as at 30.9.96.

▶ Taxation for the year is estimated at £22,680.

Prepare the profit and loss account and balance sheet for Hobo Ltd as at 30.9.96 in a form suitable for publication.

Answers

1   *Sole trader*   *Company*

▶ No   Yes – company acts

▶ The sole trader   The shareholders

▶ The sole trader   The directors appointed
                             by the shareholders

▶ No   Yes

▶ Yes   No

▶ No   Yes

▶ Drawings   Dividends

▶ No   Possible if a plc

2   Options available:

▶ issue of further share capital either ordinary or preference.

▶ issue of long-term loans for example debentures.

The company, given there are no long-term loans in existence, would probably find it relatively easy to raise further capital by the issue of debentures.

3   ▶ Par value is £1.

▶ Book value is 37/20 = £1.85.

▶ Interest payable on the debentures is 5% that is £400,000.

▶ Lower.

4   Cuddly Toy Ltd published profit and loss account for the year ended 31.12.95.

		£000
Turnover		1,562
Cost of sales		1,005.8
Gross profit		556.2
Distribution expenses (98 + 4.9 + 11.75)	114.65	
Administration expenses (24 + 4.9)	28.9	143.55
Operating profit		412.65
Interest		21
Profit before taxation		391.65
Taxation		200
Profit after taxation		191.65
Dividends proposed		54
Retained profits for the year		137.65
Retained profits b/f		185
		£322.65

Cost of sales calculation:

Opening stock		660
Purchases		885
		1,545
Less closing stock		560
		985
Depreciation: Equipment	11	
Premises	9.8	20.8
		£1,005.8

BALANCE SHEET AS AT 31.12.95

	£000 Cost	*£000* Depreciation	*£000* Net book value
Fixed assets			
Land	1,010		1,010
Buildings	980	409.6	570.4
Equipment	55	29	26
Vehicles	72	36.75	35.25
	£2,117	£475.55	£1,641.65
Current assets			
Stock		560	
Debtors		180	
Bank		121	
		861	
Creditors due within one year			
Creditors	235		
Taxation	200		
Debenture interest	21		
Proposed dividends	54	510	351
Total assets less current liabilities			1,992.65
Creditors Due After One Year			
5% debentures			420
			£1,572.65
Capital and reserves			
Ordinary £1 shares			900
Share premium			350
Retained profits			322.65
			£1,572.65

5   **GERRY LTD PROFIT AND LOSS ACCOUNT**
    FOR THE YEAR ENDED 31.3.96

Sales		271,700
Opening stock	14,167	
Purchases	186,000	
	200,167	
Closing stock	23,483	
Cost of sales		176,684
Gross profit		95,016
Depreciation	21,000	
Provision for bad debts	226	
General expenses (15840 + 1437–925)	16,352	
Wages and salaries	31,862	69,440
		25,576
Debenture interest		2,400
Net profit before taxation		23,176
Taxation		9,700
Net profit after taxation		13,476
Dividends: Preference paid	1,200	
Ordinary proposed	10,000	11,200
Retained profit for the year		2,276
Retained profit b/f		976
		3,252
Transfer to general reserve		3,000
Retained profit c/f		£252

BALANCE SHEET AS AT 31.3.96

	Cost	Depreciation	Net book value
Fixed assets	210,000	40,000	170,000
Current assets			
Stock		23,483	
Debtors		10,450	
Prepayments		925	
Bank		9,731	
		44,589	
Creditors due within one year			
Creditors	7,500		
Accruals	2,637		
Taxation	9,700		
Dividend	10,000	29,837	14,752
			184,752

Creditors due after one year

8% debentures	30,000
	£154,752

Capital and reserves

Ordinary shares of £1	100,000
6% preference shares	20,000
Share premium	9,500
Revaluation reserve	10,000
General reserve	15,000
Retained profit	252
	£154,752

6   Hobo Ltd:

PROFIT AND LOSS ACCOUNT FOR THE YEAR ENDED 30.9.96

Turnover		623,300
Cost of sales		459,675
Gross profit		163,625
Distribution expenses	56,635	
Administration expenses	44,038	100,673
Operating profit		62,952
Interest		6,650
Profit before taxation		56,302
Taxation		22,680
Profit after taxation		33,622
Dividends proposed		30,000
Retained profit for the year		3,622
Retained profit b/f 1.10.95		26,000
		£29,622

CALCULATIONS

Administration expenses:

Audit fee	1,200
Bad debts	5,320
Provision of bad debts	4,618
Salaries	15,200
Rents	12,100
Other	5,600
	£44,038

Cost of sales:

Opening stock	18,950
Purchases	426,500
	445,450

Less closing stock		20,650
		424,800
Production wages	32,900	
Depreciation: Buildings	1,375	
Equipment	600	34,875
		£459,675

Distribution expenses:		
Warehouse wages		30,200
Delivery expenses		22,060
Depreciation buildings		1,375
Equipment		600
Vehicles		2,400
		£56,635

BALANCE SHEET AS AT 30.9.96

	Cost	Depreciation	Net book value
Fixed assets			
Premises	275,000	6,500	268,500
Equipment	12,000	4,800	7,200
Vehicles	18,500	8,900	9,600
	305,500	20,200	285,300
Current assets			
Stock		20,650	
Debtors		87,742	
Prepayments		500	
Bank		51,810	
		160,702	
Creditors due within one year			
Creditors	111,450		
Taxation	22,680		
Debenture interest	6,650		
Dividends	30,000		
Accruals	600	171,380	(10,678)
Total assets less current liabilities			274,622
Creditors due after one year			
7% debentures			95,000
			£179,622
Capital and reserves			
Ordinary 50p shares			100,000
Share premium			50,000
Retained profits			29,622
			£179,622

Further review questions are available in a separate resource pack which is available to lecturers.

CHAPTER 9

Regulatory framework in the UK compared with European examples

Objectives:
··············

By the end of this chapter you should be able to:

▶ Describe the regulatory framework of accounting in the UK.

▶ Describe regulatory framework of accounting in other European countries.

▶ Compare and contrast the regulatory framework of accounting in the UK with those of other European countries.

Introduction
················

The regulatory framework of accounting in the UK has been shaped by various factors, many of which are historical. The same is true of other European countries. Several countries have a framework similar to that of the UK due to the influence of the UK in these countries at some point in history. Others have a framework very different to that of the UK. Attempts have been made to harmonise accounting across the European Union, the initial steps in this being taken by the issue of EU Directives. The Fourth Directive issued by the EU requires all EU members to prepare their financial statements in accordance with a true and fair view. In fact the Fourth Directive can be said to have exported the true and fair view from the UK to the rest of Europe and imported formatted presentation of accounts to the UK.

This chapter is intended to provide you with a brief introduction to, and flavour of, European accounting, as well as identifying the framework of accounting within the UK.

We hope it will encourage you to develop your studies in the area of European accounting at a later stage. Remember the world is getting ever smaller due to the improvements in communication networks, and it is essential to know something about how the rest of the world operates, particularly mainland Europe.

UK legal framework
···························

In Chapter 8 we referred to the legal framework in respect of limited companies. This legal framework consists of case law and Companies Acts.

Identify the case law that is at the base of corporate organisations in the UK.

Answer

A simple bit of revision here for you.

The case law was *Salomon* v *Salomon & Co Ltd 1897*. This case, after a ruling handed down by the House of Lords, clearly identified the fact that a limited company is a separate legal entity from its shareholders.

The Companies Acts detail numerous requirements for the preparation of published accounts. We have touched on the main requirements at various points within this text. A summary of these is provided below:

▶ Directors must prepare a balance sheet and profit and loss account for each financial year.
▶ Notes, as prescribed, to the accounts must also be provided.
▶ The balance sheet and profit and loss account must be prepared to a prescribed format.
▶ The balance sheet and profit and loss account must give a true and fair view of the state of affairs of the company.
▶ Accounting rules and principles are identified. These are consistent with those identified in Chapters 1 and 4.

This, then, identifies the legal framework within which accountants must work in the UK. However, there was and is a need for more than just a legal framework.

The need for a regulatory framework

The accounting concepts and conventions were identified in Chapter 4.

Identify the five principle accounting concepts.

Answer

▶ Going concern.
▶ Consistency.
▶ Prudence.
▶ Accruals/matching.
▶ Separate valuation of asset and liability.

These five principles are also contained in the legal framework – the Companies Acts. However, the faithful application of these principles can still result in different judgements being made which will lead to different profit and loss and balance sheet figures. For example:

▶ Does the prudence concept require us to account for all possible liabilities even those we believe have only a remote chance of occurring?

▶ Does the matching concept require us to delay charging advertising and research expenditure within the profit and loss account until we account for the income it has generated, if any?

ACTIVITY **9.3**
· · · · · · · · · · · · ·

Boss Ltd identifies a profit of £110,000 for the year before accounting for the following items:

▶ There is a law suit pending against Boss Ltd for which the amount of damages could be £200,000 if the case is lost.

▶ Expenditure on research for the year was £150,000. This was in respect of the development of new products. It is probable that a half of this expenditure will lead to a viable product in two years.

Identify two different accounting treatments for each of the above items both of which are in accordance with accounting concepts and conventions.

Answer

▶ The concept of prudence would suggest that we should take account of this potential liability for damages of £200,000. If a provision is made for all of the liability then the profit for the year will be reduced to a £90,000 loss!

Does prudence require us to provide for this liability no matter how remote the possibility of the damages becoming payable? Prudence should be about making judgements with a degree of caution, not about the deliberate overstatement of liabilities, which may not result in a true and fair view being presented. Perhaps a more reliable view to take would be to obtain an assessment of the likelihood of the damages becoming a liability. Therefore the profit for the company could be declared as anywhere from a £90,000 loss to a £110,000 profit.

▶ Accounting concepts require us to charge all expenses in the year of payment – prudence – unless they can be matched with the generation of future revenue, and if there is a conflict between prudence and matching then prudence should prevail. Note that we use this idea of prudence and matching in accounting for prepayments and depreciation. The research expenditure of £75,000 will be charged against the profit for the year as there is no possibility of future matching – the profit is therefore £35,000. The other £75,000 could either be written off in the year under prudence or carried forward to be matched with future income which looks very probable as it is stated there is a viable product. Therefore the profit is either £35,000 or a loss of £40,000.

Accounting for these two transactions together gives a profit figure of either £240,000 loss or a profit of £35,000, or indeed any figure in between.

The above activity clearly demonstrates the effects on profits of applying different judgements permitted within the faithful application of accounting principles as identified within the Companies Acts. These differences were highlighted in the 1960s and led to the necessity to introduce a regulatory framework of accounting as well as a legal framework.

One publicised case in the 1960s, demonstrating the above, was that of the takeover of Associated Electrical Industries Ltd (AEI) by General Electric Company Ltd (GEC). Before the takeover AEI published forecast profits of £10 million for 1967; after the bid the actual results showed a loss of £4.5 million. The majority of this difference of nearly £15 million was attributed to the difference in application of accounting concepts and conventions by the two companies.

Regulatory framework

The regulatory framework in the UK has its roots in the 1940s, when the Institute of Chartered Accountants in England and Wales (ICAEW) issued a series of Recommendations on Accounting Principles. These were little more than general summaries of existing practice and by the late 1960s, as we have seen above, something more was required. In 1971 the Accounting Standards Steering Committee was established by the ICAEW. In 1976 this became the Accounting Standards Committee (ASC), which was responsible for preparing standards of accounting under the auspices of the Consultative Committee of Accounting Bodies (CCAB). The CCAB comprises the six accounting bodies ICAEW, ICAS, ICAI, ACCA, CIMA and CIPFA.

The aims of the ASC were to narrow the areas of difference in accounting practice and to require full disclosure of all accounting bases. The ASC attempted to achieve these aims by issuing Statements of Standard Accounting Practice (SSAPs), for example SSAP 12 Accounting for Depreciation.

By the middle of the 1980s the ASC was facing a barrage of criticism because:

▶ it had no legal power to force companies to follow the standards
▶ the standards issued by the ASC allowed alternative treatments and were essentially of a general nature rather than detailed
▶ the time taken to issue a standard was often several years.

ACTIVITY **9.4**

Why did the ASC have no legal power to enforce standards?

Answer

The ASC was a function of the professional accounting bodies. Directors are responsible for accounts and may or may not be accountants. The ASC had no power to force directors to follow SSAPs, which were not legal requirements. It was possible to view them as an interpretation of the true and fair view, though.

As a result of the criticism of the ASC another committee was established in 1987 – the Dearing Committee – with the task of reviewing the accounting standard setting process within the UK. Dearing reported in 1988, proposing several radical changes to the process which resulted in the current regulatory framework.

Current regulatory framework

This is now a two-tier structure. First, the Financial Reporting Council (FRC) was established as the body responsible for overseeing accounting policy and direction.

Second, the Accounting Standards Board (ASB) was established under the auspices of the FRC with the power to issue accounting standards without the prior approval of the CCAB. To date the ASB has issued eight Financial Reporting Standards (FRSs), covering issues such as cash flow, FRS1, reporting financial performance, FRS3, and has also adopted all of the statements issued by the ASC.

ACTIVITY **9.5**

Find a copy of FRS1. This should be available in your library in a text of accounting standards, or may even be available on your computer network. (We will do more work on FRS1 in Chapter 11.) Identify the main sections of this accounting standard.

Answer

Summary of the main requirements of the standard:

▶ Objectives of the standard.
▶ Definitions of terms used.
▶ Statement of standard accounting practice covering scope, detailed requirements and the date from which effective.
▶ Reference to compliance with International Accounting Standards.
▶ Explanation of why the standard was needed.
▶ Illustrative examples.
▶ History of the development of the standard.

DID YOU KNOW ...?
The Review Panel reviews on average about 50 plcs each year.

As you can see from the above activity the FRSs are detailed and comprehensive, covering in addition to the actual accounting practice required the logic and reasoning behind the issue of the standard. Keep your notes in respect of this activity for further study at Chapter 11.

In addition to this two-tier structure the Financial Reporting Review Panel (FRRP) was formed under the FRC with the remit to review compliance with accounting standards by individual companies. The panel advises companies when their accounts do not appear to be in accordance with standards and/or a true and fair view, and can request the company to re-draft their accounts. In addition the panel has the facility to apply to the law courts for a declaration that the annual accounts do not comply with standards, and if this is given the company will be legally required to change its accounts. This then provides some legal backing for accounting standards, although just applying to the courts does not guarantee a judgement in the Review Panel's favour. A QC has issued a statement to the effect that compliance with accounting standards would constitute a true and fair view. Court cases are also a very expensive activity and for this reason the FRRP is provided with a 'fighting fund'. To date no court cases have occurred so the FRRP seems to have been successful in persuading companies to alter their accounts where they did not agree with standards.

ACTIVITY **9.6**

Identify any other reasons that you can think of why no court cases have occured.

Answer

▶ Companies may be preparing accounts in accordance with accounting concepts and conventions. However, this may still lead to the possibility of different profit figures being declared from the same set of information.

▶ Differences in profit figures may be allowed/permitted by the ASB. This is actually the case. The ASB was only established in 1990, has only issued eight FRSs and has not completed the review of all other standards that it took over from the old ASC.

The ASB has another body to assist it in meeting its objectives, the Urgent Issue Task Force (UITF). The UITF deals very quickly with emerging issues that require an immediate method of treatment. For example, the UITF has issued advice on the presentation of long-term debtors in current assets.

ACTIVITY **9.7**

Draw a diagram to show the relationships between the bodies governing the regulatory framework.

Answer

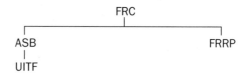

Determinants of the accounting framework

Many factors have determined the legal and regulatory framework of accounting in the UK. Accounts are prepared ostensibly for their usefulness to users, therefore the first determinant should be users' needs. Looking back over the history of accounting in the UK we can see that providers of finance, shareholders, have influenced the framework, notably the establishment of the ASC and then the ASB. Looking further back in history we can see that as companies were established, and owners passed the running of the company to directors, owners required information on stewardship (ie the management of the company's assets) which led to the establishment of the legal framework. The accounting profession is a determinant of the framework, the ICAEW was successful in promoting the idea of the true and fair view in the 1940s.The economic environment also has an effect on the framework. For example, the high levels of inflation suffered in the UK in the 1970s led to a consideration of alternatives to historic cost accounts, to reflect changing values.

The tradition of law within a country also has an effect on the framework. The UK has a common law system, that is our laws are about broad principles, for example Companies Acts, with the detail being left to case law or other forms of regulation, for example FRSs. Countries with a tradition of Roman law, that is detailed rules and regulations, will probably have a more codified set of rules for accounting regulation.

The framework of accounting in one country can also be influenced by another country. For example, many British Commonwealth countries have a system of regulation derived from the UK.

ACTIVITY **9.8**

List five possible determinants of a country's regulatory framework of accounting.

Answer

- ▶ Providers of finance.
- ▶ Accounting profession.
- ▶ Economic environment.
- ▶ System of law.
- ▶ Other country influences.

These are not the only determinants but are the main ones and will help in understanding why the framework of accounting in other European countries is different to that of the UK. We cannot look at all countries in Europe so we have chosen three, Germany, France and the Netherlands. The consideration of these three countries will be brief but we hope it stimulates your interest to study international accounting further.

Accounting framework in Germany – the determinants

The providers of finance in Germany were traditionally not so much individual shareholders but large banks. These banks were able to force companies to provide financial information to their requirements thus there was no pressure for full public disclosure. Germany has a tradition of Roman law and a strong tradition of central authority imposed by the government. One interesting element within German law is in relation to taxation; benefits given under tax law can only be claimed if reflected in the accounts. This is known in Germany as *Massgeblichkeitsprinzip* – principle of bindingness – it binds tax and accounting rules together. In the UK tax laws are, by and large, separate from accounting legislation. The strength of Germany as a world power has enabled it to resist influences from other countries so far.

ACTIVITY **9.9**

Given the information above suggest in one sentence what type of accounting framework Germany may have.

Answer

Law and Government prescription are prevalent in Germany, therefore one might expect a system of detailed instruction dominated by tax law.

Germany's accounting framework is indeed dominated by legislation. Companies acts and tax law identify the legal framework and a uniform chart of accounts is also prescribed. There is no official institution for the setting of binding accounting standards as they are all prescribed by law, particularly tax law. There is a strong accounting profession but it is one geared towards carrying out the letter of the law, not developing Generally Accepted Accounting Principles (GAAP). The majority of accounting decisions are formulated by the Supreme Tax Court.

However, Germany as a member of the EU is subject to EU Directives and has had to introduce into its law the concept of a true and fair view but this is not treated as an override as in the UK. Accounts are still prepared in accordance with law, which according to German law will provide a true and fair view. An interesting way of interpreting true and fair!

German law also identifies the concepts of going concern, consistency, accruals, prudence and individual determination (separate valuation of assets).

Accounting framework in France – the determinants

Providers of finance in France have traditionally been the government or banks. The accounting profession is government controlled as is the economic environment. The law is Roman law and one of the main influences on accounting in modern times has come from Germany. During the occupation of France in the Second World War Germany introduced a General Accounting Plan which was an accounting guide detailing valuation and measurement rules, definitions of accounting terms and structured financial statements. This plan was retained by France after the liberation as it provided the government with a means of control when rebuilding French industry. This plan – Plan Comptable – was referred to in Chapter 4.

ACTIVITY **9.10**

Suggest in one sentence what type of accounting framework France may have.

Answer

Government control is at the centre of these determinants, therefore the accounting framework will be one of detailed prescription by law.

The accounting framework is dominated by legislation. Accounting regulations and Charts of Accounts are drawn up by the *Conseil National de la Comptabilité (CNC)*, a body closely linked to the Finance Ministry.

The Legal framework is dominated by the General Accounting Plan which identifies the accounting concepts of accruals, consistency, individual determination, prudence and going concern. The EU Fourth Directive also introduced the principle of *Image Fidèle* – true and fair view – to French accounting.

Accounting framework in the Netherlands – the determinants

Providers of finance are traditionally shareholders and in addition the Netherlands is home to some of the world's major multinational enterprises.

There is a strong independent accounting profession founded in 1895 which focused attention on the development of accounting theory, particularly replacement value theory.

Economic environment is one dominated by the concept of economic value, that is businesses must ensure availability of resources to replace used inputs. Law is Roman but a distinction is made between accounting and tax law.

ACTIVITY **9.11**

Suggest in one sentence what type of accounting the Netherlands may have.

Answer

The Netherlands law is Roman but not dominant and as providers of finance are shareholders and there is a strong accounting profession then the accounting framework could well be similar to that in the UK.

The Netherlands system is basically similar to that of the UK but there are notable differences. One is that the Netherlands places emphasis on economic value not historic cost. Legal provisions tend to identify the general rules of accounting and the concept of true and fair was incorporated into Dutch law in 1970 prior to the EU Fourth Directive. Generally Accepted Accounting Principles (GAAP) is in the hands of the accounting profession, the Council for Annual Reporting, which has representatives from employers, employees and professional accountants. Standards produced by the council tend to be flexible and are not legally binding although would provide evidence as to the true and fair view. In 1970 a law was enacted to establish an Enterprise Chamber – a court of law – to consider cases where companies failed to comply with accounting standards. This chamber can order the issue of revised accounts. The general concepts of accounting are going concern, consistency, accruals and prudence.

ACTIVITY **9.12**

Complete the following table – the UK entries have already been made for you.

	UK	Germany	France	Netherlands
Type of law	Common			
Role of profession	Forceful			
Providers of finance	Shareholders			
Source of accounting regulation	Companies Acts, professional standards			

Answer

	UK	Germany	France	Netherlands
Type of law	Common	Roman	Roman	Roman
Role of profession	Forceful	Compliance	Minor	Forceful
Providers of finance	Shareholders	Banks	Banks Government	Shareholders
Source of accounting regulation	Companies Acts, professional standards	Legal Tax Binding	Legal plans	Companies Acts and standards

It is interesting to note that despite the differences above all four countries use the concepts of going concern, consistency, accruals and prudence and that the EU has adopted the principle of the true and fair view although this is of differing importance in each country, with Germany paying little regard to it.

DID YOU KNOW ...?
The international expansion of the UK accounting profession during the 19th century saw the development of what are now amongst the world's largest accounting, auditing and management consultancy firms, including Price Waterhouse, Coopers and Lybrand and KPMG.

Summary
. . . .

This chapter has identified the accounting framework within the UK, both legally and regulatory. It has also given you a flavour of accounting in three other European countries, and compared and contrasted those to that of the UK. The study of accounting in the international arena is, we believe, both interesting and essential as we move to the twenty-first century. We hope this chapter has stimulated your interest in this area.

Further study
. . . .

There are several texts available in this area, many specific to one country. If you wish to further your reading in this area we would suggest the following:

▶ *European Accounting*, Blake and Amat, Pitman, 1993.
▶ *Comparative International Accounting*, Nobes and Parker, Prentice Hall, 1991.

SELF-
CHECK
QUESTIONS

1 Identify the reasons for differences in financial accounting practices within Europe.
2 Do all European countries adopt the principle of the true and fair view?

Answers

1 The determinants of accounting practice tend to be:
  ▶ providers of finance
  ▶ accounting profession
  ▶ economic environment
  ▶ type of law – common or codified
  ▶ other country's influences
2 Only those countries that are members of the EU are required by the EU Fourth Directive to incorporate the concept of true and fair into their legislation. The interpretation placed on this phrase may be different in each country. Given the difficulty we have in understanding this phrase in the UK translating it into another language will increase those difficulties.

Further review questions are available in a separate resource pack which is available to lecturers.

CHAPTER 10

Interpretation, including ratio analysis and consideration of additional information required

Objectives:

By the end of this chapter you should be able to:

▶ Identify the needs and objectives of users of accounting information.
▶ Explain the standards by which a particular set of accounts can be judged.
▶ Understand the technique of ratio analysis and calculate ratios.
▶ Explain what the ratios mean and their limitations.
▶ Identify additional information that users may require.

Accounting information and users

Throughout the previous chapters you have learnt how to collect information about a company and how that culminates in its published financial statements. For a sole trader you have also seen that the production of a profit and loss account and balance sheet in respect of his business is very important even though it is not required to be published.

These financial statements therefore provide valuable information for both the owners of the business and for any potential owners/investors. It is therefore important that we learn how to analyse the information provided and make informed decisions by interpreting this analysis.

In Chapter 1 you identified the users of accounting information.

ACTIVITY **10.1**

Identify the users of accounting information. Note that your list could be wider than that identified in Chapter 1 if you refer to your studies in other areas such as economics.

Answer

You should have included the following in your list:

▶ Trade debtors – customers.
▶ Trade creditors – suppliers.
▶ Employees and their representatives.
▶ Taxation authorities.
▶ Financial analysts and stockbrokers.
▶ Other government departments – those concerned with the economy and environment.
▶ Those considering investing in the business – potential investors or purchasers of the business.
▶ The public, particularly environmental pressure groups and those who live close to the location of the business.

The above is not an exhaustive list and you may have thought of others which are not on our list.

Needs and objectives of users

Each of the users we have listed may well want to know different things about the business; they will have different needs and objectives. We must identify these needs and objectives so that the correct information is abstracted for them.

ACTIVITY **10.2**

Complete the following table:

User	Needs/objectives
Investors/owners	
Suppliers	
Customers	
Lenders	
Employees	

Answer

▶ Investors/owners – could their resources earn more if invested elsewhere, should they invest even more money in the business? Is the business likely to become insolvent, ie bankrupt, and thus the owners may not receive their investment back?

▶ Suppliers – is the business able to pay for the goods bought on credit? Will the business wish to purchase more goods from the supplier?

▶ Customers – do the customers receive the goods they want when they want them? Will the business continue in operation so that guarantees on goods purchased will be met?

▶ Lenders – is there adequate security for the loan made? Is the business able to make the interest payments on the loan when they fall due? Can the business redeem the loan on its due date.

▶ Employees – Does the business make sufficient profit and have enough cash available to make the necessary payments to employees? Will the business continue in operation at its current level so that employees have secure employment?

From the above answer to Activity 10.2 you should be able to identify three general areas of interest in which users' needs and objectives may lie.

ACTIVITY **10.3**

Identify the three general areas of interest for users of financial statements.

Answer

1 Performance – how successful is the business? Is it making a reasonable profit? Is it utilising its assets to the fullest? Is it, in fact, *profitable* and *efficient*?
2 Investment – is the business a suitable investment for shareholders or would returns be greater if they invested elsewhere? Is it a *good investment*?
3 Financial status – can the business pay its way? Is it in fact *liquid*?

Standards

The three questions posed above are subjective not objective. For instance, how do we define a 'reasonable profit'? We have to do so by comparing current profit to profit made in previous years and to profit made by other businesses. We need benchmarks against which we can compare current performance, financial status and investment potential. However, we need to take care with this comparison against benchmarks otherwise our comparison will not be valid.

Consider, for example, your opinion of a movie you recently watched. You may think it was the best movie you have seen; your friend may think it was the worst movie he or she has seen. This is because the experiences/benchmarks you each have are different and you are making a subjective judgement on how the movie compares with those you have previously seen. Thus, in setting benchmarks against which we can compare a company, we must be aware of the subjectivity that could be involved in these benchmarks.

First we need to identify benchmarks/indicators we can use, then we can consider their limitations.

Four possible benchmarks are:

▸ Past period achievements.
▸ Budgeted achievements.
▸ Other businesses' achievements.
▸ Averages of business achievements in the same area.

ACTIVITY **10.4**

Complete the following table:

Indicator	Uses of indicator	Limitations of indicator
Past periods		
Budgets		
Other business		
Industry averages		

Answer

Indicator	Uses of indicators	Limitations of indicator
Past periods	Is current activity better or worse than previous periods?	External factors may have influenced activity levels, eg public awareness of environmental issues may have necessitated a change in manufacturing process leading to increased costs
Budgets	Has current activity matched that planned?	The budget may not have been a valid standard of performance, eg underlying assumptions may have been unrealistic or set at too high a level
Other business	Is our business performing as well as another?	Businesses may not be truly comparable with regard to size and type, eg grocer sole trader compared to hairdresser, grocer sole trader compared to supermarket. External factors may affect one business, eg a lengthy strike. Accounting policies, bases on which accounting information is prepared, maybe different, eg stock valuations, depreciation
Industry averages	As other business	As other business

Technique of ratio analysis
....

From the study of previous chapters you now have enough knowledge to be able to pick out certain figures such as profit before tax, gross profit, total of fixed assets, net current assets, etc, from a set of financial statements. But what do these figures mean? For example, the financial statements for a record company may show profit before tax is £8 million but is this a good profit? It may, for example, be more than a computer company's profit but does it mean the record company is performing better? Consider the following example:

> You have £5,600 to invest, and discover that Type 1 investment will provide interest of £315 per annum and Type 2 investment, £1,500 after five years. Which investment would you choose assuming no compound interest and no change in the value of the pound?

The return on Type 1 investment is 315/5,600 = 5.625% per annum. The return on Type 2 investment is 300/5,600 = 5.36% per annum. Thus Type 1 investment provides the highest return. To reach this conclusion we compared the return with the amount invested and expressed the figures in the same units – interest per annum.

In evaluating the financial status, performance, and investment potential of a business we first need to identify which figures in a set of financial statements we need to have regard to and which other figures to compare these with. We will use the financial statements of Rodann Ltd, which are reproduced below to demonstrate this process.

RODANN LTD PROFIT AND LOSS ACCOUNTS

Year ended (£000s)	31.12.94		31.12.95	
Sales		150		250
Opening stock	8		12	
Purchases	104		180	
	112		192	
Closing stock	12		16	
		100		176
Gross profit		50		74
Wages and salaries	20		26	
Depreciation	4		8	
Debenture interest	–		2	
Other expenses	14		16	
		38		52
Net profit before tax		12		22
Taxation		4		10
Net profit after tax		8		12
Proposed dividend		4		6
Retained profit for year		£4		£6

RODANN LTD BALANCE SHEET AS AT

(£000s)	31.12.94		31.12.95	
Fixed assets		72		110
Current assets				
Stock	12		16	
Debtors	18		40	
Bank	10		4	
	40		60	
Creditors due for payment within one year				
Creditors	10		28	
Taxation	4		10	
Proposed dividends	4		6	
	18		44	
Net current assets		22		16
		94		126
Creditors due for payment after more than one year				
10% debentures		–		20
		£94		£106
Share capital and reserves				
Ordinary share capital		70		76
Retained profits		24		30
		£94		£106

ACTIVITY **10.5**
• • • • • • • • • • • • • • •

Compare and contrast each item on the balance sheet and profit and loss of Rodann with the figure for the previous year. Note seven points of interest from this comparison.

Answer

The points of interest were as follows:

▶ Sales increased in 1995.
▶ Cost of sales has increased.
▶ Expenses have increased.
▶ Profit after tax has increased by 50%.
▶ Fixed assets have increased by 50%.
▶ Net current assets have reduced.
▶ Shares and debentures have increased in 1995.

Having gained a 'pen picture' of what has occurred in the company from last year to this we can now carry out a ratio analysis which will help us to 'fill in' this pen picture with more detail.

Performance
••••••••••••••••

Performance is generally assessed by the return on capital employed ratio, ROCE.

$$\text{ROCE} = \frac{\text{profit before taxation and long-term loan interest}}{\text{net assets (capital employed including long-term loans)}}$$

This ratio identifies how much profit the business has made from the capital invested in it. It will also identify whether the owners would be better off placing their money in a bank deposit account rather than leaving it invested in the company.

ACTIVITY 10.6
•••••••••••••••

Calculate the ROCE for Rodann Ltd for 1994 and 1995.

Answer

ROCE   *1994*   *1995*
       12/94 = 12.77%   24/126 = 19.05%

This ratio has increased from 1994 to 1995 indicating an increase in profitability of the business from the increased investment. But where has this increased profitability come from? Is it because the business has increased sale prices or reduced expenses, that is increased net profit margins, or is it because the business has increased the volume of trade compared to the capital employed?
These two questions can be expressed as ratios as follows:

$$\text{Net profit margin} = \frac{\text{Profit before tax and long-term interest}}{\text{Sales}}$$

$$\text{Volume of trade} = \frac{\text{Sales}}{\text{Capital employed}}$$

Calculating these two ratios for Rodann Ltd:

Net profit margin   *1994*   *1995*
                    12/150 = 8%   24/250 = 9.6%

The net profit margin has increased indicating benefit gained from control of expenses or increased sale prices.

Volume of trade   *1994*   *1995*
                      150/94 = 1.6 times   250/126 = 1.98 times

Indicating that Rodann Ltd is earning more sales per £ of net assets or capital employed in 1995 than 1994.

These three ratios have the following relationship

ROCE = Margin × Volume
NP/CE = NP/S × S/CE
Where NP = Profit before interest and tax, CE = Capital employed, and S = Sales

This relationship can be shown as a family tree as follows:

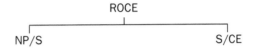

This family tree can be expanded and will provide a framework for ratio analysis.

For example:

NP/S = GP/S – E/S.
Where GP = Gross Profit and E = Expenses

If we invert first to CE/S, S/CE can then be expanded as:

FA/S + NCA/S
Where FA = Fixed Assets and NCA = Net Current Assets

We invert again and calculate S/FA and S/NCA.

ACTIVITY **10.7**   Calculate these four ratios for Rodann Ltd and interpret them.

Answer

Gross profit margin   *1994*   *1995*
                        50/150 = 33.3%   74/250 = 29.6%

This shows a reduction in gross profit probably due to a decrease in sale prices which has generated more sales or an increase in the cost of goods sold.

Expenses/sales   *1994*   *1995*
                    38/150 = 25.3%   50/250 = 20%

This has decreased from 1994 to 1995 indicating a better control of expenses.

           1994   *1995*
S/FA   150/72 = 2.08   250/110 = 2.27

Fixed assets have generated 2.08 times their value in sales in 1994 and 2.27 times their value in sales in 1995. Fixed assets are earning more sales in 1995 than 1994.

	1994	*1995*
S/NCA	150/22 = 6.82	250/16 = 15.6

Net current assets are also earning more sales in 1995 than 1994.

The family tree of ratios now looks like this:

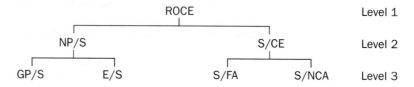

ROCE		Level 1
NP/S S/CE		Level 2
GP/S E/S S/FA S/NCA		Level 3

The pyramid can be extended to a fourth level by comparing individual expenses to sales and breaking down the fixed assets and net current assets into their constituent parts:

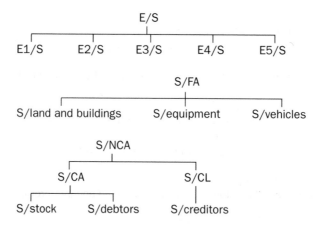

E/S

E1/S   E2/S   E3/S   E4/S   E5/S

S/FA

S/land and buildings   S/equipment   S/vehicles

S/NCA

S/CA   S/CL

S/stock   S/debtors   S/creditors

However, as stock is recorded at cost not selling price then a more appropriate ratio than S/stock would be, cost of goods sold/stock, and as creditors relates to goods purchased on credit, credit purchases/creditors. Lastly S/debtors would be more appropriate as credit sales/debtors. Example 10.1 demonstrates the calculation and interpretation of these Level 4 ratios.

EXAMPLE 10.1

The following information is provided for Anne Ltd as at 31.12.94:

	£000
Cost of goods sold	110
Average stock	25

Trade creditors	43
Credit purchases	108
Trade debtors	48
Credit sales	142

Cost of goods sold/stock = 110/25 = 4.4, that is 4.4 times the average stock level has been used in the cost of goods for the year. This could be written much simpler as stock is turned over every 83 days, ie 365/4.4 = 83 days.
The ratio is therefore:

$$\frac{\text{Average stock}}{\text{Cost of goods sold}} \times 365$$

The debtors and creditors ratio is written as:

$$\frac{\text{Trade debtors}}{\text{Credit purchases}} \times 365$$

which will tell us on average how long it takes debtors to pay:

$$\frac{\text{Trade creditors}}{\text{Credit purchases}} \times 365$$

which will tell us how long on average it takes the business to pay its creditors.
Total sales and total purchases will have to be used in lieu of credit sales and credit purchases in this example.

Debtors period = 48 × 365/142 = 123 days
Creditors period = 43 × 365/108 = 145 days

Whether or not these Level 4 ratios should be calculated when carrying out a ratio analysis will depend upon the information produced at previous levels. For example, when considering Rodann Ltd we noted a marked improvement in the efficiency of net current assets, therefore calculating the Level 4 ratios may tell us where this improvement came from.

ACTIVITY **10.8**

Calculate stock, debtor and creditor turnover periods for Rodann Ltd and interpret them.

Answer

	1994	1995
Stock turnover =	(8 + 12)/2 × 365/100	(16 + 12)/2 × 365/176
=	36.5 days	29 days

Thus stock is being turned over quicker in 1995, demonstrating greater efficiency.

	1994	*1995*
Debtors turnover period	$18/150 \times 365$	$40/250 \times 365$
	= 44 days	= 58 days

Thus debtors have been allowed 14 more days in 1995 than 1994 in which to pay their debts to the business. This could possibly indicate that Rodann Ltd is losing control of its debtor collection or that it has purposely allowed debtors more time to pay so as to encourage more sales.

	1994	*1995*
Creditors turnover period	$10/104 \times 365$	$28/180 \times 365$
	= 35 days	= 57 days

(Note that cost of goods sold could be used as a substitute for purchases if the financial statements do not provide a figure for purchases.) This indicates Rodann Ltd is taking longer to pay its suppliers – 22 days longer. This may damage relations with suppliers if Rodann does not take care, but also shows how Rodann is using creditors to finance its business operations. A balance has to be struck within this dichotomy.

Within the analysis of Rodann Ltd at Level 3 there was also a benefit gained from control of expenses. Therefore Level 4 analysis is required here.

ACTIVITY **10.9**

Calculate ratios of wages, depreciation and other expenses to sales and interpret them for Rodann Ltd.

Answer

	1994	*1995*
Wages/sales	20/150 = 13.3%	26/250 = 10.4%

Indicating that the amount of wages expended to generate one £ of sales has been reduced.

Depreciation/sales   4/150 = 2.7%   8/250 = 3.2%

Depreciation has marginally increased as a proportion of sales, which may be due to an increase in assets.

Other expenses/sales   14/150 = 9.3%   16/250 = 6.4%

Other expenses have also been controlled as a percentage of sales.

These three ratios, as we saw earlier, when combined gave an increase in profit margin – increased *profitability*. The pyramid also demonstrates that the ratios on the left-hand side show profitability and those on the right efficiency in the use of assets.

Let us look again at the first ratio on the pyramid – ROCE. Capital employed consists of shareholder funds, that is share capital and reserves, and long-term debt, for example debentures. In the example of Rodann Ltd ROCE was:

1994   12.77%
1995   19.05%

The debentures in 1995 only required a return to be paid to the holders of 10% even though the capital invested, £10,000, earned 19.05%. The earnings over and above the 10% will therefore accrue to the shareholders and their return will be increased beyond the 19.05% that the total capital earned. If we calculate another ratio, return on shareholders' funds, we can demonstrate the above quite easily. Return on shareholders' funds or owners' equity (ROOE) =

$$\frac{\text{Profit before tax but after long-term debt interest}}{\text{Shareholders' capital}}$$

1994	*1995*
12/94 = 12.77%	22/106 = 20.75%

The shareholders have increased their earnings in the business partly due to the benefit gained by borrowing at a lower rate of return than the business is earning. However, the converse can also occur! Note that ROCE and ROSHF were exactly the same in 1994 as there was no long-term debt.

ACTIVITY **10.10**

Given the following information calculate ROCE and ROOE for Ricmar Ltd for 1994 and 1995:

	1994	*1995*
	£	£
Profit before tax	80	85
Interest charged	10	10
Capital employed	1,250	1,280
Long-term debt	100	100

Answer

	1994	*1995*
ROCE	90/1250 = 7.2%	95/1280 = 7.4%

	1994	*1995*
ROOE	80/1150 = 7%	85/1180 = 7.2%

The return made in each year is 7.2% and 7.4% but the return payable to the long-term debt holders is 10% in both years, therefore the return available to the shareholders reduces to 7% and 7.2%

Investment potential

Before looking in detail at investment ratios it is useful to carry out some practical research.

ACTIVITY 10.11

Obtain a fairly recent copy of the Financial Times. Look up the London share information service found in the *FT* and make a note of the data provided for each company. Also read the 'UK company news' either in the *FT* or any other quality newspaper and note down any ratios or indicators used to evaluate the companies.

Answer

Your list possibly included the following:

▶ Book value per share compared with market value per share.
▶ Net dividend.
▶ Dividend cover.
▶ Earnings per share.
▶ Gross dividend yield.
▶ Price earnings ratio.

We will look at each of these ratios in turn.

Book value per share

This is:

$$\frac{\text{Ordinary shareholders' funds}}{\text{Number of shares}}$$

This book value is the value each share would have if the company's assets and liabilities were sold at their balance sheet (book) value. The market value is the price a potential shareholder is willing to pay to acquire a share in the company. Comparing these two values identifies whether the market values the company at more or less than its book value.

Net dividend

This is the amount of dividend declared in any one year per share:

$$\frac{\text{Paid and proposed dividends}}{\text{Number of shares}}$$

People invest in shares either:

▶ to earn dividends or
▶ to gain capital growth in the value of the share, or both.

The level of dividend and its comparison with previous years is generally regarded as an important indicator of future expectations. However, one danger with this comparison is that dividends are not necessarily just paid out of the current year's earnings but can be paid out of retained earnings. It is therefore important to look at dividend cover in any one year.

Dividend cover

$$\frac{\text{Net profit available to ordinary shareholders}}{\text{Total ordinary dividend}}$$

ACTIVITY **10.12**

The following information is available in respect of Shamar Ltd.

	1994	1995
	£	£
Ordinary shares issued £1	2,500,000	2,500,000
8% preference shares £1	500,000	500,000
Dividend ordinary shares	300,000	250,000
Net profit after tax	287,500	271,900

Calculate dividend per share in pence for both preference and ordinary shares, and dividend cover.

Answer

	1994	1995
Dividend per share in pence preference	8p	8p
Dividend per share ordinary	12p	10p
Dividend cover	287500/340000	271900/290000
	= .85	=.94

The dividend has reduced per share from 1994 to 1995 but the dividend cover has improved. However, this dividend cover is less than one which indicates that the company is not earning enough in either year to pay the dividend and is therefore using past earnings retained to fund the dividend payment. This may be a danger sign for potential investors.

Earnings per share

This is another indicator used widely by the investment community. It represents the amount of profit, in pence, the company has earned during the year for each ordinary share.

For the example of Shamar above the earnings per share in 1994 is:

247,500/2,500,000 = 9.9p

and 1995 is:

231,900/2,500,000 = 9.3p

Earnings per share is:

$$\frac{\text{Net profit available to ordinary shareholders}}{\text{Number of ordinary shares in issue}}$$

Gross dividend Yield

This is calculated from the formula:

$$\frac{\text{Gross dividend}}{\text{Market price of ordinary share}}$$

Shareholders may be willing to accept a low gross dividend yield if there is a greater than average capital growth in share value expected or if the company is a safe investment. Gross dividend is calculated by grossing up the dividend declared in the accounts for basic rate taxation as dividends are always declared and paid net of basic income tax.

For example, in the case of Shamar Ltd if the basic rate of tax is 20% then the gross dividend is

	1994	1995
	£	£
	300,000/80%	2,50,000/80%
	3,75,000	312,500
or per share	15p	12.5p

If the market value per share for Shamar was £1.75 in 1994 and £1.82 in 1995 then the gross dividend yield is:

1994	1995
15/175	12.5/182
= 8.6%	= 6.9%

Price earnings ratio P/E ratio

The formula for this is:

$$\frac{\text{Market price per share}}{\text{Earnings per share}}$$

For Shamar this is:

1994   *1995*
175/9.9   182/9.3
= 17.7   = 19.6

Like the dividend yield the PE ratio will change as the market price per share changes. It represents the market's view of the growth potential of the company, its dividend policy and the degree of risk involved in the investment. In general a high PE indicates the market has a high/good opinion of these factors, a low PE a low/poor opinion of these factors. Another way of looking at the PE is that it represents the number of years' earnings it is necessary to have at the current rate to recover the price paid for the share. For Shamar this was 19.6 years at the 1995 rate of earnings.

DID YOU KNOW ...?

It is not always a sign of weakness if current liabilities exceed current assets. For example, major supermarket chains usually have a negative ratio as they have few debtors and yet take as much credit as possible from suppliers. Their strong cash flow ensures that creditors will be paid when due.

Financial status

It is vital for a business to be able to pay its debts as and when they fall due otherwise its chances of remaining in operation become remote. Thus there is a need to analyse the assets available to meet liabilities. This can be done in the short, medium and long term.

For the short term we use the quick assets ratio or acid test:

$$\frac{\text{Current assets less stock}}{\text{Current liabilities}}$$

Stock is excluded from current assets as it is regarded as less liquid than other assets within that category.

For the medium term the current ratio is:

$$\frac{\text{Current assets}}{\text{Current liabilities}}$$

and for the long term the gearing ratio is:

$$\frac{\text{Long-term debt}}{\text{Shareholders' funds}}$$

Another ratio, interest cover, can also be used:

$$\frac{\text{Net profit before interest and tax}}{\text{Total interest charges}}$$

ACTIVITY **10.13**   Calculate the four liquidity ratios for Rodann Ltd and explain what the f
lated mean.

Answer

	1994	1995
Acid test	$\dfrac{40 - 12 = 28}{18 \quad 18}$	$\dfrac{60 - 16 = 44}{44 \quad 44}$
expressed as	1.6:1	1:1

The ratio has decreased from 1994 to 1995 quite considerably but there are still plenty of liquid assets. The ratio will need careful monitoring to control this downward trend.

	1994	1995
Current ratio	40/18 = 2.2:1	60/44 = 1.4:1

Again this ratio has been substantially reduced but still appears adequate. Monitoring of this downward trend is again required.

	1994	1995
Gearing ratio	not relevant	20/106 = 18.9%

This is low and we would consider this company low geared. If a company is high geared then it may have difficulty meeting the required interest payments.

	1994	1995
Interest cover	not relevant	(22 + 2)/2 = 12

In 1995 the profit covered the required interest payment 12 times indicating no immediate problem for Rodann Ltd.

Notice how consideration of all four ratios helped to build up a picture of the financial status of Rodann Ltd.

Limitations of ratio analysis
. . . .

There are seven principal limitations of ratio analysis:

▶ Differences in accounting policies.
▶ The historic nature of accounts.
▶ Absence of suitable comparable data.
▶ Differences in the environments of periods compared.
    ~~dden~~ short-term fluctuations.
      ~~n~~ the value of money.
      ~~n~~-monetary factors.

~~ese~~ were examined in Activity 10.3; accounting policies, absence of ~~c~~mparable data and changes in environment. Non-monetary factors the fact that nowhere in the analysis is the quality of the product or ~~c~~nsidered, whether labour relations are good or bad. In fact no regard , the goodwill of the business.

gures calcu-

The historical nature of accounts must always be borne in mind as our interpretation of the business is based on this historical information. However, it may not be the best guide as to the future performance, financial status and investment potential.

Short-term fluctuations are also hidden in ratio analysis as our appraisal is based on a balance sheet that provides values of assets and liabilities as at a point in time. For example, consider the following information relating to a company whose year end is 31 December:

	September £	October £	November £	December £
Debtors	2,000	2,100	2,500	5,000
Other current assets	4,000	4,000	3,950	3,900
Current liabilities	5,500	5,600	5,550	5,500
The current ratio for each month is	1.09:1	1.09:1	1.1:1	1.6:1

However, calculating the current ratio by reference to the balance sheet would show a figure of 1.6:1 in December which represents a better view of liquidity than has been the case over the past four months. It is important to remember that the balance sheet only provides a 'snap-shot' of a company at a particular point in time and that considerable changes can occur to that picture in a short period of time. Shamar may well have increased its debtors, and therefore its liquidity position, due to an increased level of sales for the Christmas period.

Changes in the value of money

We all know how inflation affects the value of the pound in our pocket and this is no different for a business. In fact the effects of inflation on our ratio analysis could make the whole analysis invalid. To demonstrate this consider a company with sales last year of £350,000 and sales this year of £400,000. Would you interpret this as an increase in volume of trade of 14%?

If you were informed that the price of the goods sold had been subject to an increase of 10% (inflation) then the increase in volume would only be approximately 4%.

Additional information
••••••••••••••••••••••••••

From the work you have already completed in this chapter you should be able to identify additional information that may help you in assessing the performance, financial status and investment potential of a business.

ACTIVITY **10.14**
•••••••••••••••••

Make a list of additional information that you would like when undertaking a ratio analysis of a company.

Answer

You should have identified several of the following:

▶ Inflation effects on the company.
▶ Does the balance sheet represent the position of the business throughout the year or just at the year end?
▶ Cash flow throughout the year.
▶ Forecast business plans in the form of budgets and cash flows.
▶ Information in respect of the quality of goods and services and other factors affecting the assessment of goodwill in the business.
▶ Industrial averages of ratios.
▶ Differences in accounting policies between businesses.

However, you must be aware that several items in this list may not be available to you as a potential investor as they will not be public information in respect of the business. For example, it would be very difficult, probably impossible, for a potential investor to obtain detailed information in respect of future plans of the business apart from that disclosed in the Chairman's Report in the financial statements.

Summary
. . . .

This chapter has introduced you to the technique of ratio analysis and demonstrated the calculation of such ratios. Ratio analysis was identified as a tool that users of accounts can make use of in order to meet their needs and objectives. However, we noted that there were several limitations in the use of ratio analysis and that these must be borne in mind when making an assessment as to the performance, financial status and investment potential of a business. Not only must you be able to calculate the ratios referred to in this chapter but you must also be able to interpret them in the light of their limitations.

The interpretation is the most difficult part of ratio analysis and requires a great deal of practice and use of common sense! This interpretation is also not definitive – there is no right or wrong answer – as much of the analysis requires subjective judgements to be made by the analyst. The chapter concludes with a few exercises for you to complete in this area.

Further study
. . . .

All introductory texts on bookkeeping or accounting will include the above material and several exercises for you to work through. You will also find analysis of companies in the quality press and accounting journals.

1   Obtain a set of accounts for a supermarket and a manufacturer. You can do
    this by accessing your university library or using the service provided by
    the *Financial Times*.

    Compare and contrast the nature of the current assets and liabilities of
    your two companies.

2   You are given the following information in relation to Olivet Ltd:

PROFIT AND LOSS ACCOUNTS FOR 1994 AND 1995

	1994	1995
	£	£
Sales	100,000	100,000
Cost of sales	50,000	60,000
	50,000	40,000
Expenses	30,000	30,000
	20,000	10,000
Dividends	10,000	10,000
	10,000	–
Retained profits b/f	2,500	12,500
	£12,500	£12,500

BALANCE SHEETS AS AT 1994 AND 1995

	1994	1995
	£	£
Land	21,500	31,500
Buildings	20,000	39,500
Equipment	3,000	3,000
	44,500	74,000
Investments at cost	25,000	40,000
Stock	27,500	32,500
Debtors	20,000	25,000
Bank	1,500	–
	£118,500	£171,500
Ordinary £1 shares	20,000	25,000
Share premium	6,000	7,000
Revaluation reserve	–	10,000
Profit and loss	12,500	12,500
Debentures 10%	50,000	75,000
Creditors	20,000	30,000
Proposed dividend	10,000	10,000
Bank	–	2,000
	£118,500	£171,500

You are required to comment on the financial position of Olivet Ltd as at 1995. Calculate any ratios you feel necessary.

Answers

1 ▶ Debtors – Supermarket: Does not normally have debtors as most business is conducted by cash.
– Manufacturer: Supplies goods on credit therefore its debtors will be quite high.

▶ Stock – Supermarket: Stock turnover periods will be short as items have a limited life.
– Manufacturer: A large amount of money may be tied up in stock and stock turnover periods may be quite long.

▶ Cash – Supermarket: Probably quite low as cash will flow through the business daily but will then be invested so as to earn interest.
– Manufacturer: May have reserves of cash to meet unforeseen events.

▶ Current liabilities – Supermarket: Creditors may be quite high and form a major part of the liabilities of the business.
– Manufacturer: Creditor turnover period will normally be of the order of 40 days. However as he will take a long time to turn these goods into finished products he will need cash available to go on purchasing goods.

In conclusion the current assets of the supermarket may well be much lower than its current liabilities and therefore its current ratio may well be less than 1:1. This is not unsafe for the supermarket, but would be for the manufacturer, as the supermarket has cash flowing through the tills every day. It would therefore not be appropriate to compare a supermarket with a manufacturer. Like must be compared with like in any assessment of the performance, financial status and investment potential of a business.

2 Olivet Ltd.

Ratios	1994	1995
Return on capital employed	$\frac{20 + 5}{88.5} = 28.2\%$	$\frac{10 + 7.5}{129.5} = 13.5\%$
GP percentage	50%	40%
NP percentage	20%	10%
Sales to capital employed	1.13	.77
Return on owners' equity	52%	18.3%
Gearing ratio	56.5%	57.9%
Current ratio	49/30 = 1.6:1	57.5/42 = 1.37:1
Acid test	.72:1	.6:1
Debtors' turnover period	73 days	91 days
Creditors' turnover period	146 days	182.5 days
Stock turnover period	201 days	198 days
Dividend cover	2	1
Interest cover	5	2.3

From the information given in the question we can identify that:

▶   Sales have remained static but cost of sales has increased.
▶   Expenses other than interest have been slightly reduced.
▶   Dividend has remained at 1994 level even though profits were reduced. In fact in 1995 all the profit earned has been paid out in dividend.
▶   Land appears to have been revalued as the revaluation reserve has increased by £10,000.
▶   Further buildings, equipment and investments have been purchased during 1995.
▶   Stock, debtors and creditors have all increased in 1995.
▶   There is a bank overdraft in 1995.

The above would seem to suggest that Olivet has attempted to expand by the purchase of further fixed assets but this does not appear to have produced extra sales.

Ratios of all types have worsened, indeed the ROCE has halved as has the net profit percentage. The return on owners' equity has fallen sharply and the current dividend policy appears somewhat imprudent.

It is possible, of course, that Olivet increased its investment in fixed assets towards the end of the year and therefore these fixed assets will not have generated revenue for a full year. However, even if this is the case the decline in the profit percentages is still a potentially dangerous situation.

Further review questions are available in a separate resource pack which is available to lecturers.

CHAPTER 11

Cash flow statements

Objectives:

By the end of this chapter you should be able to:

▶ Explain the importance of cash flow within the business.

▶ Identify cash flows within a business.

▶ Prepare a cash flow statement.

▶ Explain the relationship between the cash flow statement, profit and loss account and balance sheet within a business.

▶ Identify the difference between the indirect and direct method of preparing a cash flow statement.

▶ Explain the word 'funds' as used in accounting.

Introduction

In previous chapters we have concentrated on preparing financial information for a business based on the concept of profit. You should have already realised that profit does not equal cash and therefore it is quite possible for a business to be making reasonable profits but have very little cash. However, cash is vital to a business. Without it the business cannot purchase stock, pay creditors, wages or any other expenses. Cash is quite often referred to as the 'lifeblood' of a business, without it it will not survive!

A business therefore must pay attention to both its profit and cash position.

Cash flows within a business

At this point in your studies you should be able to complete the following activity quite quickly. If you do have problems return to Chapter 5 and consider the cash transactions that Mr Bean made.

ACTIVITY **11.1**

Identify as many cash flows as you can for a business. Enter them in the table below. Two are already entered for you.

CASH FLOWS

Into the business
▶ Capital contributed in the form of cash

Out of the business
▶ Wages paid in cash

Answer

CASH FLOWS

Into the business
▶ Capital contributed in cash

Out of the business
▶ Wages paid in cash

- ▶ Cash sales
- ▶ Receipts from debtors
- ▶ Cash loans and debentures

- ▶ Sale of fixed assets

- ▶ Rents or other income received
- ▶ Interest and dividends received

- ▶ Cash purchases
- ▶ Payments to creditors
- ▶ Purchase of fixed assets
- ▶ Cash paid for rent, heat, insurance, etc
- ▶ Dividends paid
- ▶ Interest paid
- ▶ Taxation paid

You have, in fact, just constructed a cash account and this is essentially what a cash flow statement is about.

Cash flow statement

Accountants prepare cash flow statements to a given format prescribed by the Accounting Standards Board in FRS 1. This format incorporates all the items you have listed in your table above but identifies cash flows under specific headings.

The format is as follows:

CASH FLOW STATEMENT FOR THE YEAR ENDED XX

Net cash inflow/outflow from operating activities		X
Returns on investments and servicing of finance		
Interest received	X	
Dividends received	X	
Interest paid	X	
Dividends paid	X	
Net cash inflows/outflows from returns on investments and servicing of finance		X
Taxation		
Taxation paid	X	
Net cash outflows from taxation		X
Investing activities		
Payments for intangible fixed assets	X	
Payments for tangible fixed assets	X	
Sale of fixed assets	X	
Net cash outflows/inflows from investing activities		X
Net cash flows before financing		X
Financing		
Issue of shares	X	
Issue of debentures	X	
Redemption of shares	X	
Repayment of debentures/loans		
Issue expenses for shares/debentures	X	X
Increase/Decrease in cash balances		£ X

One item on this cash flow statement, the net cash inflow/outflow from operating activities, does not equate directly to an item on the cash account. We will explain how this figure is derived later in this chapter. To familarise yourself with the cash flow format work through the following activity.

ACTIVITY **11.2**
....

The following information is available in respect of White Rose Ltd for the year end 31.12.95:

▶ Net cash inflow from operating activities was £120,000.
▶ The company received dividends during the year of £45,000, paid an interim dividend of £30,000 and proposed a dividend of £20,000 at the year end. Last year's proposed dividend was £25,000.
▶ The taxation charge for the year was estimated at £55,000 which was £3,000 less than that estimated for the year ended 31.12.94.
▶ Interest was payable during the year on £200,000 of 5% debentures. All interest due had been paid at the year end.
▶ White Rose Ltd had purchased £120,000 of fixed assets during the year to 31.12.95 and fixed assets sold had produced a profit on sale of £10,000. The net book value of fixed assets sold was £50,000.
▶ White Rose Ltd had also issued 50,000 £1 ordinary shares at a premium of 50p. All shares were fully paid at the year end. A loan of £40,000 had also been raised by the company at the same time as redeeming loans of £20,000 at par.

Prepare the cash flow statement for the year ended 31.12.95

Answer

CASH FLOW STATEMENT FOR THE YEAR ENDED 31.12.95

	£000	£000
Net cash inflow from operating activities		120
Returns on investments and servicing of finance		
Dividends received	45	
Dividends paid	(55)	
Interest paid	(10)	
Net cash outflow from returns on investment		
and servicing of finance		(20)
Taxation		
Taxation paid	(58)	
Net cash outflow from taxation		(58)
Investing activities		
Payments for tangible fixed assets	(120)	
Sale of fixed assets	60	
Net cash outflow from investing activities		(60)
Net cash flows before financing		(18)
Financing		
Issue of shares	75	
Issue of debentures	40	
Repayment of debentures	(20)	95
Increase in cash balances		£77

In completing this activity care was required in dealing with the following items to ensure that the cash flow was identified:

▶ Dividends proposed at the year end 31.12.95 were not paid but the proposed dividend from the previous year was.
▶ Tax is not due until nine months after the end of the year so the tax paid is last year's liability.
▶ The actual receipt from the sale of assets was the cash flow not the profit on sale which is the figure included in the profit and loss account.
▶ The cash flow from the issue of shares included the share premium.

Net cash flow from operating activities

This item refers to cash flows in respect of buying and selling goods and expenses incurred. It can, of course, be derived from the cash book by identifying all cash receipts from trading and all cash payments such as payments to trade creditors, payments for wages, rent rates, electricity and so on. This would be the direct method of arriving at the net cash flow from operating activities. However, it can also be derived from the profit and loss account for the year.

ACTIVITY **11.3**

Identify as many items as you can that appear in the profit and loss account before interest, taxation and dividends that do not involve a flow of cash.

Answer

▶ Depreciation – a book entry not a flow of cash.
▶ Profit or loss on sale of assets – the cash receipt of sale price is the cash flow.
▶ Accruals and prepayments – income and expense within the profit and loss account is recognised in accordance with accounting concepts. It is not the cash receipt and payment.
▶ Sales (cash sales and sales on credit) – the cash flow is cash sales and receipts from debtors.
▶ Cost of sales (cash and credit purchases adjusted for opening and closing stock) – the cash flow is the cash spent during the year on purchases and payments to creditors.

Another method, in contrast to the direct method, of arriving at the net cash flow from operating activities would be to adjust the operating profit before taxation, interest and dividends for all the items listed in the answer to Activity 11.3. This is known as the *indirect* method.

The reconciliation of operating profit and net cash flows from operating activities is required as a note to the cash flow statement. The note is formatted as follows:

Reconciliation of operating profit and net cash flows from operating activities:

Operating profit (as per profit and loss account)	X	
Adjustment for items not involving the movement of funds		
Depreciation	X	
(Profit)/loss on sale of assets	(X)	
Amortisation	X	X
(Increase)/decrease in stock		X
(Increase)/decrease in debtors		X
(Decrease)/increase in creditors		X
Net cash inflows from operating activities		£X

Note in the above that:

▶ Depreciation and amortisation charges are added back to the operating profit as these were deducted in arriving at the profit figure. Amortisation is the term used to describe the depreciation of leases.
▶ Profit on sale is deducted.
▶ Decrease in stock and debtors from last year to this is added to the operating profit as this means less cash has been tied up in stocks and debtors. Conversely an increase would mean more cash had been tied up.
▶ An increase in creditors is also added back to the profit figure as this means cash has been kept in the business not paid out to reduce the liability to creditors.

The direct method of arriving at net cash flows from operating activities is formatted as follows:

Cash received from customers	X
Cash paid to suppliers	X
Cash paid to and on behalf of employees	X
Other cash payments	X
Net cash inflow from operating activities	£X

ACTIVITY **11.4**

The following information is available in respect of Red Rose Ltd for the year ended 31.12.95

PROFIT AND LOSS ACCOUNT EXTRACT FOR THE YEAR ENDED 31.12.95

Net profit	120
Net interest charges	30
Net profit before taxation	90
Taxation	15
Net profit after taxation	75
Dividends paid and proposed	40
Retained profit	£35

Net profit of £120 is after charging depreciation of £25 and including loss on sale of assets of £15.

BALANCE SHEET EXTRACTS

	31.12. 94	31.12.95
	£	£
Stock	8	6
Debtors	5	4
Cash	2	3
	15	13
Creditors	7	8

Prepare the reconciliation of operating profit to net cash flow from operating activities.

Answer

Net profit before interest and taxation		120
Adjustments for items not involving the movements		
of funds		
Depreciation	25	
Loss on sale	15	40
		160
Decrease in stock	2	
Decrease in debtors	1	
Increase in creditors	1	4
		£164

Purpose of cash flow statement

The cash flow statement provides information in addition to that provided by a profit and loss account and balance sheet. It identifies the cash flows in a business which are not apparent from the other two statements. It also identifies whether cash has increased or decreased from one year to the next. It does, however, have several drawbacks, some of which it shares with the other statements.

ACTIVITY **11.5**

Identify two drawbacks of a cash flow statement.

Answer

Several clues have already been given to you to answer this question. You should have identified two from the following:

▶ Cash is the 'lifeblood' of an organisation but the cash flow statement is historic. If we are concerned over the liquidity of a business, the ability to pay its debts, then a cash flow forecast would be more useful.
▶ Cash flow from operating activities is derived by either the direct or indirect method. The indirect method uses information from the accruals-based accounting system. If cash flow is what we are interested in then there should

only be one alternative – the direct method. This would also avoid confusion for users who may have difficulty in understanding the reconciliation between operating profit and cash flow.

▶ What is cash? Is it cash in the shop till, cash in the bank, short-term investments? Just what do we mean by cash?

Funds flow

This section will provide you with an answer to the last question raised in the answer to Activity 11.5

We have already looked at the idea of funds in Chapter 2. Identified there was the concept of funds coming into and out of the business – sources and applications. Sources of funds were such items as profit from trading, capital invested and loans taken out. Applications were the purchase of fixed assets and investments. Funds were not necessarily cash funds.

In Chapter 10 you met the phrase 'return on shareholders' funds'. These funds were the total of share capital and reserves, which are certainly not represented solely by cash. Shareholder funds are represented by the business' net assets, that is fixed assets and current assets less current liabilities.

In general, in accounting the word 'funds' is used in connection with the accruals-based accounting system. It is possible to prepare a statement of sources and applications of funds for every business. In fact, prior to the introduction of the cash flow statement requirement in FRS 1 businesses had to prepare such a statement. The statement, instead of arriving at a figure showing the increase/decrease in cash balances, showed the change in working capital. Working capital is the difference between current assets and current liabilities including accruals and prepayments. It is quite feasible for a business to have a net inflow of funds, as defined in terms of working capital, but an actual net outflow of cash. This is demonstrated by the following example.

BALANCE SHEET EXTRACTS

	31.12.94	31.12.95
	£	£
Stock	12	14
Debtors	8	9
Cash	6	5
	26	28
Creditors	12	9
	14	19
Increase in working capital (19–14)		5
Decrease in cash (6–5)		1

The move away from preparing source and application of funds statements to that of preparing cash flow statements is regarded by many as being an important step forward in the provision of information to users.

ACTIVITY **11.6**

Identify two reasons why cash flow statements may be regarded as more useful than funds flow (working capital) statements.

Answer

You should have identified two of the following:

▶ Cash is more objective and verifiable. It is not blurred by estimates of accruals and prepayments.
▶ Cash is more easily understood by users.
▶ Cash flow is a better guide to a business's ability to pay its liabilities than a funds flow.
▶ Working capital is not an indication of the solvency of a business.

Cash, for our cash flow, still needs to be defined. In general, cash is determined as cash on hand and all deposits payable on demand. Deposits payable on demand are defined as those that are easily convertible into cash, that is will mature within three months. This is, in fact quite an arbitrary cut-off and has caused some debate within the accounting profession.

Relationship between the cash flow statement, profit and loss account and balance sheet

In the preparation of cash flow statements so far in this chapter, you have been given the information required. However, some of this information can be deduced from the profit and loss account and the opening and closing balance sheets. For example, you should be able to identify the increase in share capital from the opening and closing balance sheets. The following example illustrates the connections between the three statements and demonstrates the preparation of a cash flow statement by using information from the other two plus additional information.

EXAMPLE **11.1**

The following information is available in respect of Yellow Rose Ltd.

PROFIT AND LOSS ACCOUNT FOR THE YEAR ENDED 31.12.95

Gross profit			140
Depreciation		30	
Interest receivable	(5)		
Interest payable	8	3	
Profit on sale of asset		(8)	
Amortisation of intangibles		20	45
Net profit before taxation			95
Taxation			40
Net profit after taxation			55
Dividends paid and proposed			40
Retained profit			£15

BALANCE SHEETS AS AT

	31.12.94	31.12.95
Fixed assets		
Intangibles	120	140
Tangibles	320	389
	440	529
Current assets		
Stock	30	34
Debtors	24	22
Cash and bank	64	72
	118	128
Creditors due within one year		
Creditors	32	36
Dividends	15	20
Taxation	45	40
	92	96
Net current assets	26	32
	466	561
Creditors due after one year	100	120
	£366	£441
Ordinary share capital	250	280
Share premium	20	30
Revaluation reserve		20
Retained profits	96	111
	£366	£441

The sale proceeds from the sale of fixed assets was £36. All interest due has been received and the interest payable has been paid. The first task to carry out to prepare the cash flow statement is to identify all changes from last year's balance sheet to this year's.

Intangible fixed assets have increased by £20. Amortisation of intangibles for the year was £20, therefore cash of £40 must have been spent.

Tangible fixed assets have changed according to the balance sheets from £320 to £389. However, assets have been bought, sold and depreciated throughout the year. If assets sold produced a profit of £8 and proceeds of £36 then the net book value of assets sold was £28. We can now identify how the assets have changed:

1.1.94 balance	320
Sale of assets	28
	292
Depreciation year 31.12.95	30
	262
31.12.95 balance	389
Therefore purchase	£127

However, a revaluation reserve of £20 has been created during the year. If we assume this is in respect of fixed assets then the figure for the purchase of assets reduces to £107. Current asset changes are easy to identify as stock increase £4, debtors decrease £2 and cash increase £8. Similarly, creditors increase £4.

We need to be more careful when identifying the changes in respect of taxation and dividends. The balance sheet as at 31.12.95 shows the liability remaining in respect of these items, the profit and loss account shows the matched charge for the year.

Thus dividends paid during the year will be:

Balance 1.1.95	15
Charge for year	40
	55
Balance 31.1295	20
Paid	£35
and taxation:	
Balance 1.195	45
Charge for year	40
	85
Balance 31.12.95	40
Paid	£45

The change in creditors due after one year indicates a further loan of £20 raised and the changes in respect of ordinary share capital and share premium, issue of shares for cash of £40.

We can now prepare the reconciliation of operating profit to net cash flow from operating.

Profit before interest and taxation (95 +3)		98
Depreciation	30	
Amortisation	20	
Profit on sale	(8)	42
		140
Increase in stock	(4)	
Decrease in debtors	2	
Increase in creditors	4	2
Net cash inflow from operating activities		£142

CASH FLOW STATEMENT FOR THE YEAR ENDED 31.12.95

Net cash inflow from operating activities		142
Returns on investments and servicing of finance		
Interest received	5	
Interest paid	(8)	
Dividend paid	(35)	
Net cash outflows from returns on investments and servicing of finance		(38)
Taxation		
Taxation paid	(45)	
Net cash outflow from taxation		(45)
Investing activities		
Payments to acquire intangible fixed assets	(40)	
Payments to acquire tangible fixed assets	(107)	
Sale of fixed assets	36	
Net cash outflows from investing activities		(111)
Net cash flows before financing		(52)
Financing		
Issue of shares	40	
Loans raised	20	60
Increase in cash balances		£8

Note the figure derived from the cash flow statement for the increase in cash equates to the increase we identified from the balance sheet 1.1.95 to 31.12.95.

Interpretation of cash flow statements

It is possible to gain an insight into the activities of a business by reviewing the cash flow statement. For example, the cash flow in respect of Yellow Rose Ltd identifies the following facts:

▶ Interest, dividend and taxation payments are more than covered by the cash generated from operating activities.
▶ Acquisition of fixed assets has been financed partly from internal resources and partly from new capital raised in the form of shares and loans.
▶ Working capital displays no significant changes during the year, the small increase in stock being matched by an increase in creditors.
▶ The company could either be expanding or just replacing worn out assets.

Summary

This chapter has introduced you to the cash flow statement. We have reiterated the fact that profit does not equal cash and that for a business to survive it must have cash – it is its 'lifeblood'. A cash flow statement is historic in nature but identifies cash inflows and outflows within a business.

These cash flows are presented in a prescribed format which also includes a reconciliation of operating profit to net cash inflow. However, cash flows from operating profit can be derived by using either the direct or indirect method. The direct method is more appropriate as this identifies cash from customers and cash paid to customers and others, whereas the indirect method arrives at the cash flow by adjusting profit for movements in working capital and items not involving the movement of funds. The majority of businesses though prepare their cash flow using the indirect method as it demonstrates the link between the three required financial statements and does not require the business to adapt their information systems to extract additional information.

This chapter also continued the discussion in respect of the definition of funds, which we began at Chapter 2. The self-test exercises at the end of this chapter provide you with practice in preparing cash flow statements.

Further study
....

All the text books referred to earlier will provide you with further study in this area and you may also find it helpful to read the 'Financial Reporting Standard' in respect of cash flow statements; FRS 1 published in 1991.

SELF-
CHECK
QUESTIONS

1   Identify information provided by a cash flow statement to users that is not provided by a profit and loss account and balance sheet.

2   From the following information in respect of Sparrow Ltd prepare the cash flow statement for the year ended 31.12.95.

BALANCE SHEETS AS AT

	31.12.94	31.12.95
	£000	£000
Fixed assets		
Intangible	237	222
Tangible	637	738
Investments	100	120
	974	1,080
Current assets		
Stock	230	256
Debtors	136	194
Bank	–	26
	366	476
Current liabilities		
Creditors	97	103
Taxation	64	61
Dividends	60	66
Bank overdraft	24	–
	245	230
Net current assets	121	246
Total assets less current		
liabilities	£1,095	£1,326

Ordinary shares of £2	500	520
Share premium	–	130
Retained profits	545	576
Debentures	50	100
	£1,095	£1,326

PROFIT AND LOSS ACCOUNT FOR THE YEARS ENDED

	31.12.94	31.12.95
	£000	£000
Net profit for the year before tax	151	158
Taxation	64	61
Net profit after tax	87	97
Dividends	60	66
Retained profit for the year	27	31
Retained profit b/f	518	545
	£545	£576

Depreciation charged during the year was £187,000 and assets sold during the year produced a profit of £45,000. The net book value of the assets sold was £88,000. No intangible fixed assets have been acquired or sold during the year. Interest charged in the profit and loss account for the year was £12,000 and all of this was paid.

3 Review the cash flow statement prepared in answer to question 2 and summarise any conclusions which may be drawn from it in respect of the financial operations and position of Sparrow Ltd for the year ended 31.12.95.

Answers

1 Cash flow statements identify net cash inflows from operations, net cash inflows from investments in fixed assets, net flows from financing activities and payments in respect of interest, dividends and taxation. None of these are identifiable from the profit and loss account or balance sheet.

It also identifies the extent to which reported profit is matched by cash flows. Thus the distinction between profit and cash flow is clearly made. The user of the statement has more relevant information on which to assess the solvency of the business.

2 Reconciliation of operating profit and net cash flows from operating activities:

		£000
Net profit for the year before tax		158
Add interest charged		12
Net profit before interest and tax		170
Amortisation	15	
Depreciation	187	
Profit on sale	(45)	157
		327
Increase in stock	(26)	
Increase in debtors	(58)	
Increase in creditors	6	(78)
Net cash inflows from operating activities		£249

CASH FLOW STATEMENT FOR SPARROW LTD FOR THE YEAR ENDED 31.12.95

Net cash flow from operating activities		249
Returns on investments and servicing of:		
Finance		
Interest paid	(12)	
Dividends paid	(60)	
Net cash outflows from returns on investments and servicing of finance		(72)
Taxation		
Tax paid	(64)	
Net cash outflows from taxation		(64)
Investing activities		
Payments to acquire tangible fixed assets	(376)	
Payments to acquire investments	(20)	
Sale of fixed assets	133	
Net cash outflows from investing activities		(263)
Net cash flows before financing		(150)
Financing		
Issue of shares	150	
Issue of debentures	50	200
Increase in cash balances		£50

This increase in cash balances equates to the change shown on the balance sheets – balance at bank of £26,000 from an overdrawn balance of £24,000.

3   The cash flow statement identifies the following in respect of the financial operations and position of Sparrow Ltd for the year ended 31.12.95:

▶   Tax, dividend and interest payments were more than covered by the net cash inflow from operating activities.

▶ The outflow of cash in respect of the acquisition of fixed assets and investments has been covered by cash generated from operating, cash generated from sale of assets and the rest from new capital raised by way of share and loan.

▶ Cash raised from new capital has cleared the overdrawn bank balance and left £26,000 in the bank.

▶ Working capital has increased substantially.

▶ It appears that Sparrow Ltd has been expanding its activities by its investment in increased working capital and new assets. Management must ensure that cash flows from operating also increase in line with this expansion.

Further review questions are available in a separate resource pack which is available to lecturers.

CHAPTER 12

Valuation and performance measurement

Objectives:
. . . .

By the end of this chapter you should be able to:

▶ Review valuation theory, including economic value.

▶ Explain why Constant Purchasing Power and Current Cost Accounting failed.

▶ Outline the revaluation accounting approach.

▶ Prepare a simple statement of total recognised gains and losses.

Introduction
. . . .

You have now reached a point in your studies where you should be reasonably confident in your ability to account for fairly complex economic events, and to present the outcomes using a profit and loss account, balance sheet and cash flow statement. You may remember from Chapter 4 that there is a fourth primary statement required by the 'Statement of Principles', and that is the statement of total recognised gains and losses. We will deal with that towards the end of this chapter. Before doing so, however, we should take a more rigorous look at some of the implicit assumptions we have made in preparing all these statements.

Specifically, we need to reconsider the validity of the historical cost concept. There are two aspects to this. First, historical cost may be the simplest and most objective basis for valuing our assets, but it may not be the most relevant and reliable, especially if prices are changing significantly. What, after all, is the use of quantifying a building at what it cost 20 years ago, if, during that time, prices have doubled or trebled? Is it still a relevant and reliable figure to help users make decisions about the entity?

Second, we will take a brief look at attempts that have been made to explicitly allow for the effects of changing prices, and at why they have so far failed. It could be argued that restating our assets at a more current valuation than historical cost is one way of making at least some such allowance, so we will also study the accounting for this process.

Alternatives to historical cost
. . . .

In Chapter 2 we considered replacement cost, net realisable value (NRV), and touched on economic value. To recap, replacement cost is what an asset would cost if we were to replace it today. Strictly, this should be the cost of a similarly part-worn asset. In times of rising prices this will usually be higher than the historical cost. Note, however, that, even when prices generally are rising, the prices of some assets may be rising at a different rate, or even falling. Think, for example, about what has happened to the prices of computers in recent years. Net realisable value is what we could sell the asset for, after allowing for any direct selling costs.

In this chapter we concentrate on the conceptually most difficult of the three alternatives, that is economic value. Having done that, we can consider all the alternatives, together with historical cost, and arrive at a single coherent approach to asset valuation.

Economic value rests on the definition of an asset given in Chapter 3 of the 'Statement of Principles', that is, 'assets are rights or other access to future economic benefits controlled by an entity as a result of past transactions or events'. The essence of an asset is thus the stream of benefits that will flow in to us in the future, because we control that asset. It therefore seems reasonable to value the asset by adding up all those future economic benefits. This is sometimes called the 'value in use' of the asset.

If, for example, an asset is expected to last three years, the products we make using it can be sold for £25,000 per year, and the direct costs of making those products are £10,000 per year, then the net economic benefit is £15,000 for three years. We could then simply add up the benefits, ie £45,000, and use that as the valuation of the asset. We would then show the asset in our balance sheet at £45,000, rather than at its historical cost.

ACTIVITY 12.1

Comparing economic value with historical cost, what are its advantages and disadvantages?

Complete this table by making at least one entry in each box.

Advantages	Disadvantages

Answer

In the advantages box, you should have noted such points as its consistency with the formal definition of an asset, and the fact that it is an up-to-date valuation. The disadvantages include its uncertainty, in that the method assumes that we can predict future incomes and costs with reasonable certainty. This is unlikely. More subtly, the method in its crude form above simply adds together net inflows from different years. This is highly questionable, because of the time value of money.

The time value of money

The time value of money is a concept that states that money has a value, not just in terms of its absolute amount, but also in terms of when that amount is received. If you are offered £100 today, or £100 in a year's time, which would you take? The answer is almost certainly that you would want the money now, perhaps because there is something you urgently want to spend it on, and perhaps because you have realised that, given inflation, that same amount will be worth less in real terms in a year from now. Even without these two reasons, however, you may have realised that if you get the money now, you could invest it for a year, so that the total sum would be £110, if we assume a 10% rate of interest.

Looking at this situation from a slightly different angle, there must be some sum of money which you could receive now, instead of getting £100 a year from now, and be indifferent about which one you got. If we again assume interest at 10%, this amount would be £90.91. It is the amount which you could invest now, at 10%, and expect to receive £100 a year from now (£90.91 + £9.09 = £100.00). The £90.91 is called the Present Value of £100 received in one year, at a 10% discount rate.

Returning to our example of the machine that will yield a net £15,000 for three years, we should now note that simply adding the three lots of £15,000 is not actually adding like to like, because it is expressed in £s at a different point in time, and the time value of money concept tells us that these three amounts are therefore not expressed in the same terms. In a theoretically pure world, we should add the present value of each of the three inflows, since they would then, by definition, all be expressed in £s at the same point in time – the present.

The key to this technique is applying the correct discount factor to each inflow. Fortunately, there is a fairly simple formula for working out what this factor should be,

$$\frac{1}{(1 + r)^n}$$

where r is the rate of interest applicable to the entity – often, slightly inaccurately, called the cost of capital, and n is the number of years before we receive the inflow. The cost of capital is the rate of interest that the organisation or individual would have to pay if they wanted to borrow money. In the case of an individual, it is often called their 'personal cost of capital'.

Note that we will be making a simplifying assumption, namely that the net inflow associated with each year is actually received at the end of that year. If we assume a cost of capital of 10%, then we are finally in a position to work out the economic value of our asset, as follows:

End of year	Inflow	Discount factor	Present value
1	15,000	0.90909	13,636
2	15,000	0.82645	12,397
3	15,000	0.75131	11,270
			£37,303

The base value of this asset that should go in our balance sheet is therefore £37,303. Note that what we paid for the asset, its historical cost, has not figured anywhere in the calculation.

ACTIVITY **12.2**

Ms Lee's entire wealth consists of one investment which cost her £30,000, and which will yield £20,000 for each of the next two years, with no further returns. If her personal cost of capital is 10%, calculate the present value of the inflows today, and hence value her asset.

Answer

Your calculation should look like this:

Year	Inflow	Discount factor	Present value
1	20,000	0.90909	18,182
2	20,000	0.82645	16,529
			£34,711

Putting the valuations together

We now have three alternatives to historical cost as bases for asset valuation. These are:

▶ Replacement cost.
▶ Net realisable value.
▶ Economic value.

In terms of practical accounting, this is not a satisfactory position, because we are faced with trying to determine which is the most relevant, reliable, comparable and understandable basis for any given entity. Not only may opinions vary, but the answer may change as circumstances in the real world change. There are two ways out of this problem. First, we could decide on one as being the most appropriate most of the time, although this would inevitably be a rather arbitrary decision. Second, we could use the more rigorous approach known as the deprival value model. It is usually summarised by the following diagram.

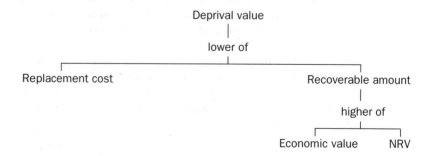

This approach rests on asking two questions.

1   Assuming we have an asset, what should we do with it – keep it and use it, or sell it?

The answer to this question will depend on what would result in the most money for the entity. If we keep it and use it, the benefit is best measured by the economic value method, since this measures the value in use. If we sell, the most appropriate valuation will be the net realisable value (NRV). The higher of these two represents the greatest benefit we could derive from the asset, and is called the recoverable amount.

2   Assuming we were deprived of the asset, would we replace it?

The answer to this second question depends on whether the cost of replacement is more or less than the recoverable amount. If it is less, then it is economically logical to replace the asset, since we can recover more from either using it or selling it than it costs to acquire in the first place. In this case, the most appropriate valuation will be replacement cost. Otherwise, the best valuation will be the recoverable amount, because the consequent non-replacement leaves us with recoverable amount as the best we can do with the asset we are attempting to value.

ACTIVITY **12.3**

A property company owns two plots of land, in Leeds and Bradford, with the following values. It is aware that property prices bear little resemblance to historical costs and therefore wishes to value its property on a deprival value basis.

	Leeds	Bradford
Original cost	£730,000	£185,000
Replacement cost	£815,000	£170,000
Net realisable value	£775,000	£165,000
Estimated economic value (value in use)	£800,000	£180,000

Select the best answer from the list below of respective deprival values for the plots in Leeds and Bradford:

1   £730,000 and £180,000.
2   £800,000 and £170,000.
3   £815,000 and £170,000.
4   £775,000 and £185,000.
5   None of the above.

Answer

Deprival value is the lower of replacement cost and recoverable amount, where the recoverable amount is the higher of net realisable value and economic value. For Leeds, recoverable amount is therefore the higher of £775,000 and £800,000, ie £800,000, and this is lower than the replacement cost of £815,000. The deprival value for Leeds is therefore £800,000. For Bradford, the recoverable amount is the higher of £165,000 and £180,000, ie £180,000. Deprival value is then the lower of this and the replacement cost of £170,000, ie £170,000. The correct answer is therefore (2) '£800,000 and £170,000'.

Finally, note that, in nearly all cases, the economic value will be greater than the NRV – if it were not then no enterprise would be using any asset, since they could derive more from it by selling it second hand, and this is obviously not the case. In other words, the recoverable amount will usually be economic value. Furthermore, when this economic value is then compared with the replacement cost, the outcome will usually be that the replacement cost is lower. If this were not so, then no entity would be buying any asset, and this is again patently not so. In the great majority of cases, therefore, deprival value can be equated with replacement cost.

We therefore have a single, logically coherent alternative to historic cost. This alternative has so far been used in accounting for two things. First, it has been used to help clarify general thinking on asset valuation. Second, and more practically, it has been applied to help address the distortions caused to historical cost accounting by changing prices. The next section of this chapter is thus concerned with a brief look at inflation accounting.

Inflation accounting

Inflation accounting is accounting that makes specific allowances for the effects of inflation. As we will see, it actually includes allowances for changes in prices which are specific to a particular entity. To be pedantic, such accounting is not strictly 'inflation accounting' because inflation is defined as a persistent and *general* rise in prices. Nevertheless, any accounting that makes some explicit allowance for changes in prices, whether general or not, is commonly referred to as inflation accounting.

The need for inflation accounting arises out of the distortions caused within historical cost accounting. Specifically, there are two accounting effects. First, if we buy an asset and record it at historic cost, then its reported value will be increasingly out of date, and often materially lower than a current valuation such as deprival value. Similarly, a liability such as a loan will be recorded in our accounts at its original historical value. A loan of £20,000, for example, is the amount we will show in our balance sheet and it is also the amount we will repay, despite the fact that each of the £s we repay will in real terms be worth less than each of the £s that we borrowed.

Second, inflation will also have an effect on our real profits. Revenues will be in current terms, ie we will sell at today's prices, but the cost of sales will be based on historical cost. We are therefore not comparing like with like, and the effect will be to relatively understate the cost of sales, and so to overstate reported profit. Further, the depreciation charge will be based on a historical asset cost, and thus understated in current terms. Again, the net effect will be to overstate the reported profit. To understand these points more fully, try the next two activities one after the other.

ACTIVITY **12.4**

Realia Ltd recorded sales of £480,000, and purchases of £360,000. Its opening stock cost £30,000 and its closing stock was valued at £35,000. Depreciation was to be provided at 10% straight line on assets which cost £160,000, and other expenses totalled £72,000. Use these figures to prepare a historical cost profit and loss account for the year.

Answer

This should have been a fairly easy exercise, and your answer should be the same as ours, that is:

REALIA LTD
HISTORICAL COST PROFIT AND LOSS ACCOUNT
FOR THE YEAR

Sales		480,000
Cost of sales:		
Opening stock	30,000	
Purchases	360,000	
	390,000	
Closing stock	35,000	
		355,000
Gross profit		125,000
Depreciation (10% x 160,000)	16,000	
Other expenses	72,000	
		88,000
Historical cost net profit		£37,000

Now we take some account of inflation. It seems reasonable to assume that sales, purchases and other expenses took place fairly steadily through the year. Some sales, purchases and expenses will then have taken place early in the year, when prices were relatively low, and some towards the end of the year, when prices were high. Assuming that prices rose fairly steadily throughout the year, and given our first assumption, we can then also assume that the typical transaction took place half way through the year, at an average price level. In other words, the sales, purchases and other expenses shown in our profit and loss account are stated at average prices.

However, the opening stock would be stated at its cost when bought, sometime before the beginning of the year, and the closing stock at a cost that reflects the price level towards the end of the year, when the closing stock was probably bought. Furthermore, the underlying price level for the depreciation would be that when the fixed assets were bought, which could well have been many years ago. The traditional historical cost profit and loss account ignores these differences in price levels, and so does not actually compare like with like.

If we want a more meaningful profit and loss account, then one answer would be to restate the opening and closing stock and the depreciation so that they reflect average, mid-year prices, in the same way that the sales, purchases and other expenses implicitly do.

ACTIVITY **12.5**
....

Realia Ltd knows that if it had bought its opening stock at mid-year prices, it would have cost £33,000, and the closing stock at mid-year prices would have cost £32,000. Finally, it also knows that the cost of its fixed assets at mid-year prices would have been £250,000. Use these figures to redraft the profit and loss account for Realia Ltd. When you have done that, compare it with the original historical cost statement. Which gives the more true and fair view?

Answer

REALIA LTD
PRICE ADJUSTED PROFIT AND LOSS ACCOUNT
FOR THE YEAR

Sales		480,000
Cost of sales:		
Opening stock	33,000	
Purchases	360,000	
	393,000	
Closing stock	32,000	
		361,000
Gross profit		119,000
Depreciation (10% x 250,000)	25,000	
Other expenses	72,000	
		97,000
Price adjusted net profit		£22,000

It is our view that the price adjusted statement presents a more true and fair view, simply because it makes at least some allowance for the fact that the accountant's unit of measurement, the £, changes in size from year to year, because of inflation. The historical cost profit and loss account is presented for all UK companies, and most other entities, but it is distorted whenever inflation is material.

Accountants in the UK have had two major attempts to address this distortion. The first was an approach known as Current Purchasing Power (CPP). If the root problem is that the real value of a £ falls with inflation, then an obvious way to counteract the effects of this would seem to be to develop a system of accounting that uses a unit of currency that is, by definition, current. Monetary items, that is items whose values are expressed and fixed in nominal money terms, such as the £20,000 loan we considered above, always have the same nominal and real value, so need no adjustment. By contrast, non-monetary items, such as fixed assets and stock, should be index-linked, using a general index of inflation. In the UK the obvious index to use is the Retail Price Index. This index linking then compensates for the fall in the value of each £ by attaching a correspondingly greater number of them to each non-monetary items.

The following example is taken from the Appendix to Chapter 5 of the 'Statement of Principles'. It provides a further illustration of the points we have been covering in the last two activities. In particular, the appendix provides a good overview of the alternative approaches that have been taken to accounting under changing prices.

A company begins the year with share capital of £100 and £100 worth of newly purchased stock. Inflation during the year is 5%. The company sells the stock at the end of the year for £200. Replacement cost of the stock is £150.

OPENING BALANCE SHEET

Newly purchased stock	£100
Share capital	£100

Traditional historical cost accounting

PROFIT AND LOSS ACCOUNT

Sales	200
Less: cost of sales	100
Nominal money profit	£100

Current purchasing power

PROFIT AND LOSS ACCOUNT

Sales	200
Less: cost of sales	105
Current purchasing power profit	£95

What the CPP method thus does is uplift the cost of sales by the rate of inflation, so that it is expressed in something like current terms, ie the same terms as the sales. Notice that the effect, when compared with the traditional historical cost accounting approach is to reduce the reported profit by £5. The policy prescription here is that this company should pay a maximum dividend of only £95, not £100. Paying out all the historical cost profit of £100 would, in fact, amount to a distribution of capital.

Notice that paying out a dividend of £100 would leave us with £100, which is what we started the business with, and it would seem that we have therefore maintained capital. In a historical cost world this is true. However, CPP takes the view that true capital maintenance should maintain the original £100 adjusted by 5% inflation, ie £105. The CPP profit calculated above is therefore the most we should distribute if we are to maintain CPP capital.

CPP formed the basis of SSAP 7, but was short lived. The main reasons for its lack of acceptance by accounts preparers and users were:

▶ The use of a general index, such as the Retail Price Index (RPI), is strictly only relevant to a mythical average entity. No business or individual actually experiences average inflation – it always depends on what you buy in a particular period. SSAP 7, however, explicitly required the use of the RPI.

▶ It is not directly relevant to the needs of the specific business, since CPP does not aim to maintain the capital of each particular business, but only of the mythical average business. Organisations in the information technology market tend to experience falling prices, even when inflation is positive. CPP accounting would require even these organisations to account for rising prices.

▶ The process is not easy to understand, takes time to implement, and is therefore expensive.

The issue of the non-specific nature of CPP was addressed by the second attempt at inflation accounting, namely Current Cost Accounting (CCA). This was implemented by SSAP 16 in 1980, and was longer lasting. The essential difference between CPP and CCA is that the latter has a very different view of the capital it is trying to maintain. CCA assumes that the issue is less to maintain the purchasing power of the entity (and hence its owners), than to maintain the ability of the entity to physically do the same things this year as it could last year. If our physical infrastructure allowed us to produce 10,000 tables last year, then the point is to ensure that we can produce the same number again this year, and the money capital needed to do that is incidental.

This 'operating capability' approach implies a basis of valuation which rests on 'value to the business', ie what an asset can do, rather than what it cost. SSAP 16 took the view that this means deprival value. We saw earlier in this chapter that deprival value tends, in practice, to equate with replacement cost. CCA therefore uses replacement cost as a basis for valuing both assets and expenses. Using the same example from Chapter 5 of the 'Statement of Principles' as before, we can again calculate the reported profit, this time using CCA.

Physical capital maintenance

PROFIT AND LOSS ACCOUNT

Sales	200
Less: cost of sales	150
Current cost operating profit	£50

The policy prescription in this case is even more stark. The entity should only distribute a maximum dividend of £50 if it is to maintain the real value of its net assets. SSAP 16 set out a number of adjustments to profit to ensure that funds are retained to allow for:

▶ replacing stock despite the fact that its price has risen – as above
▶ replacing fixed assets, despite the fact that their prices have risen
▶ funding working capital, despite the fact that the absolute amount will have risen in terms of nominal £s.

It also uplifted the value of fixed assets and stock in the balance sheet to ensure that they are fairly represented at something close to their current values, rather than their historical values. All these adjustments will, in principle, make the inflation adjusted accounts more reliable, and perhaps more relevant. However, the increased complexity does also make them less understandable. This was not the only problem with CCA accounting as implemented by SSAP 16. In summary the problems were:

▶ Complexity and hence lower understandability, as above.
▶ The provision of both the traditional, historical cost profit and an inflation adjusted profit, as above. The provision of two profits in the same set of accounts did not improve either the credibility or the understandability of those accounts.
▶ The fact that tax continued to be levied on the historical cost profit.
▶ The conceptual difficulty of much of the process.
▶ The consequent time and expense involved in the production of inflation adjusted accounts.

DID YOU KNOW ...?

Cynical observers would say that the main reason for the demise of SSAP 16 was that current cost profits are significantly less than historic cost profits!

As a result of these problems, many companies stopped producing inflation adjusted accounts around 1983 and 1984. The fact that inflation began to fall probably helped their decision. They were, of course, still producing historical cost accounts, so users had what they were used to. Finally, the Accounting Standards Committee accepted the demise of the standard, and it was formally withdrawn in 1988.

This section on inflation accounting has only scratched the surface of an extensive and difficult topic. Nevertheless, you may have had trouble following the arguments. If so, you are not alone, but a broad understanding of the issues that were tackled will help you in any further studies of accounting. As a final brief check on your understanding, try the following activity.

ACTIVITY **12.6**
• • • • • • • • • • • • • •

Choose the most appropriate response from those listed below. The method of asset valuation which best measures the operating capability of a business is:

1 Net realisable value?
2 Replacement cost?
3 Deprival value?
4 Recoverable amount?
5 None of the above?

Answer

SSAP 16 'Current Cost Accounting' is based on the idea of maintaining the operating capability, and suggests that assets should be valued at their value to the business. This is then defined as net current replacement cost, or, if lower, recoverable amount. In other words, value to the business is based on the deprival value model, and answer (3) is therefore correct. Deprival value will usually turn out to be replacement cost, so choice (2) is reasonable, but not strictly correct.

The Accounting Standards Board (ASB) thinking on the future of inflation accounting currently appears to be that a return to something like SSAP 7 or 16 is unlikely, because of the complexity and widespread scepticism among accountants over the value of the consequent financial statements. Nevertheless, when inflation again becomes significant, there will be a need to allow in some form for the distortions that we have seen occur under historical cost accounting. One possible, albeit partial, answer would be to regularly revalue all fixed assets to some current value, probably replacement cost.

The rationale for this is that fixed assets tend to cost a lot in the first place, and then inflation impacts on them for their relatively long lives. Allowing for the effects of inflation on fixed assets would therefore address a large part of the distortion. It would ensure that the fixed assets are presented at an up-to-date figure in the balance sheet, and that the depreciation charge reflects this more current amount. The next part of this chapter therefore deals with the accounting for such revaluations.

Accounting for revaluations
....

When we revalue an asset our aim is primarily to restate the asset in the balance sheet at a current value. In times of rising prices, this will mean an adjustment upwards. An incidental issue is that the same depreciation policy will then be applied to the higher amount and will itself be a larger charge in the profit and loss account, so resulting in a smaller reported profit. The best way to see all this is to follow an example.

Asif owns a holiday camp, including buildings, which cost £400,000 on 1 January 1990. The depreciation policy has always been to write off the buildings over 40 years on a straight line basis. In the ledger accounts for the year ended 31 December 1996, the following amounts will therefore appear, before any year end adjustments.

BUILDINGS AT COST

1.1.90 Cost	400,000		

PROVISION FOR DEPRECIATION

		1.1.96 Bal b/f (*)	60,000

(*) Six years depreciation at £10,000 per year (400,000 / 40)

As part of the year end accounting, Asif values the buildings at £540,000, and considers that the remaining useful life is another 30 years from now. The first matter is to revalue the buildings in the books. The key to doing this is to open a revaluation account, which will hold the uplift in value from the present net book value (NBV) to the new valuation. Note that this uplift is therefore not £140,000 (540,000 – 400,000), but £200,000 (540,000 – 340,000 (NBV)). The necessary entries will be:

BUILDINGS AT VALUATION

1.1.90 Cost	400,000		
31.12.96 Revaluation account	140,000		
	£540,000		

PROVISION FOR DEPRECIATION

31.12.96 Revaluation account	£60,000	1.1.96	Bal b/f	£60,000
		31.12.96	Profit and loss	18,000

REVALUATION ACCOUNT

	31.12.96	Buildings	140,000
	31.12.96	Depreciation	60,000
			£200,000

You should be able to follow what is going on here. The building account is uplifted to the value we want, with the corresponding credit going to the revaluation account. Notice also, however, that the provision for depreciation account is cleared out, with another credit going to the revaluation account, giving the total uplift on that account of £200,000. Finally, since we have benefited from the building during 1996, we must match some charge against that benefit. In other words, we must make a depreciation charge for 1996.

You may object that we have only just got the value up to where we wanted it and this seems to be immediately reducing it. True, but remember that the purpose of depreciation is not to get the right value in the balance sheet, but to match a cost in the profit and loss account to reflect the using up of the asset in earning the benefits that appear in the profit and loss account. This depreciation charge will be based on the revised estimate of a 30-year life, and will therefore be £18,000, ie 540,000 / 30. This is shown in the provision for depreciation account above.

It may be that we subsequently sell the building. The way to deal with this is to open one final account, namely the sale of assets account. Assuming Asif sells the building on 1 September 1997 for £500,000, the accounting will be:

BUILDINGS AT VALUATION

1.1.90	Cost	400,000			
31.12.96	Revaluation account	140,000			
		540,000	1.9.97	Sale of assets	£540,000

PROVISION FOR DEPRECIATION

31.12.96 Revaluation account	£60,000	1.1.96	Bal b/f	£60,000
1.9.97 Sale of assets	18,000	31.12.97 Profit and loss		£18,000

REVALUATION ACCOUNT

1.9.97 Profit and loss reserve	£200,000	31.12.96 Buildings	140,000
		31.12.96 Depreciation	60,000
	£200,000		£200,000

SALE OF ASSETS

1.9.97 Building	540,000	1.9.97 Bank	500,000
		1.9.97 Depreciation	18,000
		1.9.97 Loss to Profit	
		and loss	22,000
	£540,000		£540,000

The additional entries are mostly straightforward. The balances on the building account and on the provision for depreciation account are transferred to the sale of assets account. The proceeds are debited in the bank account and credited in the sale of assets account. The resulting balance on the sale of assets account then represents the profit or loss on the sale of the building, and is shown in the profit and loss account for the year. In this case it is a loss of £22,000.

The treatment of the balance of £200,000 on the revaluation account is contentious. There are two possibilities,

1   Clear it by transfer to the sale of assets account. Note that this would make the balance on the sale of assets account a credit of £178,000, so that we would report a profit of this amount in the profit and loss account for the year. This is the difference between the cost of £400,000, less the total depreciation charged over the year of £78,000 (60,000 + 18,000), ie £322,000, and the proceeds of £500,000. You might think there is some logic to this.

2   Clear it by transfer direct to the profit and loss *reserve*. In this way it will not pass through the profit and loss *account* for the year, and will not be reported as part of the profit for the year. This is what we have done above. The logic of this approach is that the building is now considered to be worth £540,000 (less depreciation) to Asif, and it is this amount that should be compared with the proceeds. The £540,000, less depreciation, is known as the 'carrying value'.

The treatment of the balance on the revaluation reserve obviously makes a material difference to the profit for the year, and most businesses would probably want to use method 1 above. However, the ASBs prefer the logic of method 2, and FRS 3 now requires that approach. Nevertheless, in order to disclose what the profit or loss would have been if we had compared the proceeds with the depreciated historical cost, FRS 3 also requires that the historical cost result must be shown as a note to the accounts. In Asif's case, this would mean showing a loss of £22,000 in the profit and loss account, and a profit of £178,000 as the 'Note of Historical Cost Profit'. Notice that the difference between the two results is, of course, the balance of the revaluation account.

ACTIVITY **12.7**

Faraday Ltd has always prepared its final accounts to 31 March. The company bought a building on 1 April 1993 for £72,000. Its depreciation policy on buildings has always been to depreciate at 10% pa on a reducing balance basis, but no depreciation is ever charged in the year of a disposal.

When preparing the final accounts for the year ended 31 March 1996, before any depreciation had been charged for that year, it was decided to revalue the building to £100,000. On 1 September 1996, the company sold the building for £95,000.

Write up the ledger accounts for the year ended 31 March 1997, including all opening and closing balances, for:

▶ Buildings account.
▶ Provision for depreciation account.
▶ Revaluation account.
▶ Sale of asset account.

Indicate how the balances would be dealt with in the final accounts at 31 March 1996.

Answer

You will learn more easily and more effectively if you try this activity before you look at the answer. It's your choice!

BUILDINGS

1.4.93 Cost	72,000		
31.3.96 Revaluation account	28,000	1.9.96 Sale of asset	100,000
	£100,000		£100,000

PROVISION FOR DEPRECIATION

		31.3.94 Profit and loss	7,200
31.3.96 Revaluation account	13,680	31.3.95 Profit and loss	6,480
	£13,680		£13,680
1.9.96 Sale of asset	£10,000	31.3.96 Profit and loss	£10,000

REVALUATION

		31.3.96 Cost	28,000
1.9.96 Profit and loss reserve	41,680	31.3.96 Depreciation	13,680
	£41,680		£41,680

SALE OF ASSET

1.9.96 Buildings	100,000	1.9.96 Depreciation	10,000
1.9.96 Profit – Profit and loss	5,000	1.9.96 Bank	95,000
	£105,000		£105,000

You should be able to follow our answer, since the logic is the same as in the Asif example. Remember that reducing balance depreciation takes a fixed percentage of the net book value every year.

In the balance sheet at 31 March 1996, the building and depreciation will be shown under fixed assets as usual, except that it will be described as being 'at valuation', rather than as 'at cost'. The revaluation account is a capital reserve (ie not available for dividend payments), and will be shown with shareholders' funds.

There is just one matter remaining to be dealt with in this chapter, and that is the further reporting of revaluation gains, and similar gains and losses. We have already seen that any balance on the revaluation account is a capital reserve, and is taken direct to the profit and loss reserve when realised on a sale. Pending such a sale, we have recognised an uplift in the value of the building, but hold it as a capital reserve because it is unrealised (ie the asset has not been sold). Nevertheless, we have recognised that a gain has occurred during the year, and it is arguable that such a gain should be explicitly reported in its own statement, rather than left implicit within the note of reserves. Such a statement is called the statement of total recognised gains and losses.

Statement of total recognised gains and losses

You may recall from Chapter 4 that this statement is identified as one of the four primary statements in Chapter 6 of the 'Statement of Principles', along with the balance sheet, profit and loss account, and cash flow statement. It is also required by FRS 3 and is defined there as a primary statement. It differs from the profit and loss account by including not just the realised profit for the year but also all unrealised gains and losses.

If, for example, Asif had reported a profit of £145,000 for the year ended 31 December 1996, then his statement of total recognised gains and losses for the year ended 31 December 1996 would be:

Profit for the year	145,000
Surplus on revaluation of buildings	200,000
Total gains recognised since the last annual report	£345,000

Such a short and simple statement will often be all that is needed. Indeed, if there are no unrealised gains or losses, the company will simply report this fact, instead of producing the statement. In more complex enterprises, you may come across gains and losses on foreign exchange, and even prior year adjustments. These are beyond the scope of this book.

Summary

This has been a wide-ranging chapter, covering some difficult ideas. We have followed a train of argument that started with an introduction to the theory of valuation and concentrated on the new ideas of economic value and deprival value. We then looked at a major application of these ideas, namely inflation accounting. This topic would rate a book to itself, but we explored the need for some allowance for changing prices in our accounting, and the main efforts that have so far been made to tackle the problems.

We concluded with a look at the uses and mechanics of revaluations needed if our assets and profits are to reflect at least some changing values, and finally reviewed the statement of total recognised gains and losses. In

Chapter 13 we shift the emphasis of study, and consider the need for and techniques of control in accounting.

Further study
. . . .

The material in this chapter is contentious and difficult, and, with the exception of the accounting for revaluations, does not usually make much of an appearance in basic 'how to' texts on financial accounting. The most authoritative statement on inflation accounting must still be the *Handbook of Accounting for Changing Prices* (Accounting Standards Committee (the forerunner of the Accounting Standards Board) 1985). It is effectively its attempt to draw lessons from the two failed accounting standards, and, given the topic, is very readable.

If you are interested in the valuation issues raised in this chapter, or are simply required to know more, then *Financial Reporting* (Alexander and Britton, 1996, Chapman and Hall) includes an approachable and more thorough exploration. It is pitched at a higher level, and may be more suitable for second and third year undergraduate studies.

SELF-
CHECK
QUESTION

It is conceivable that UK accounting and reporting for fixed assets could be changed to a system based on one of the valuation methods dealt with in this chapter, perhaps deprival value. List three reasons for such a change, and three reasons for retaining historical cost as the base method of valuation.

Answer

This is a difficult and contentious area. Nevertheless, the answer attempts to outline the main points for and against such a development. You should have listed some or all of the same points.

For change
1   The meaning of the balance sheet figure is uncertain, given that it is not only subject to subjective amounts of depreciation, but also out of date.
2   Periodic revaluations depend on the decisions of individual companies, and there is thus little consistency between the balance sheets of different companies. This makes any comparative analysis very difficult, if not meaningless. A requirement for all to adopt another valuation could largely remove the inconsistency.
3   It is theoretically incorrect to add together amounts for assets bought at different times, which, as a result of inflation, are thus not expressed in the same currency.

For retaining historical cost
1   Historical cost is objective, and hence relatively easily audited.
2   The simplicity of historical cost makes it a cheaper method to implement, since no time need be spent in determining an alternative valuation.
3   It is probably more easily understood by non-accountants.
4   Its widespread acceptance allows for better comparison between companies.

Further review questions are available in a separate resource pack which is available to lecturers.

Control of accounting systems

Objectives:
. . . .

By the end of this chapter you should be able to:

▶ Outline the main features of control in a financial accounting system.
▶ Explain the function of internal and external audit.
▶ Prepare a bank reconciliation statement.
▶ Prepare control accounts.

Introduction
. . . .

So far in this book, we have tended to assume that bookkeeping procedures and the preparation of final accounts will be carried out by competent people of integrity, who never make mistakes. This is obviously unlikely. This chapter therefore deals with the issue of the controls in accounting systems, which enable us to address the effects of any failings.

Many of the techniques that we examine in this chapter have their roots in traditional manual accounting systems. Such systems are becoming increasingly rare, in any but the smallest organisations, because of the growing cost-effectiveness of computer-based systems. Nevertheless, the principles of control remain, although they may be implemented very differently in a computer system. This chapter looks at the basic principles and at how they have traditionally been applied, and Chapter 14 explores the impact on such controls of the introduction of computers to accounting.

The need for controls
. . . .

We identified above three requirements of those involved in the accounting function if financial statements are to show a true and fair view. These are requirements in terms of:

▶ avoidance of mistakes
▶ competence
▶ integrity.

It is worth considering a response to each of these requirements in turn. First, it is as common for accountants to make mistakes as for anyone else. Arithmetic errors are probably less common since the advent of computers, but errors of principle are still possible. Errors of principle include, for example, entering a transaction twice, or omitting it entirely, or making an entry in the wrong account. It would be quite possible, for instance, to record a purchase invoice from J Smith as a purchase invoice from a customer called L Smith.

Some errors, such as a one-legged entry, ie entering only the debit or only the credit, will be shown up by a trial balance that does not balance. The trial balance is thus a basic, but very effective, control on the accuracy of bookkeeping. If you are unsure exactly what a trial balance looks like and how it is constructed, you can, and should, revise it now from Chapter 5. There are two other widely used controls, the bank reconciliation and control accounts, which we study later in this chapter.

Second, financial statements can fail to show a true and fair view because of a lack of technical ability on the part of those involved in their preparation. Mistakes can be made even if you know what you are supposed to be doing, but they are more likely if you are unsure about appropriate techniques of accounting and the rules concerning the presentation of financial information. Third, those involved in the preparation of financial statements may be tempted to bend those rules in order to present a more favourable picture of the entity. If your annual bonus is linked to the reported profit of your organisation, you may occasionally be tempted to adopt an accounting treatment that results in a higher profit, rather than one that you objectively believe to show a more true and fair view. Both of these possibilities are, in principle, addressed by the existence of audit.

Audit
·······

There are two types of audit, external and internal. External audit is carried out by persons from outside the organisation, who should be both expert and independent. They investigate the accounting systems and transactions and then ensure that the financial statements have been prepared in accordance with the underlying books, and with the law and accounting standards. The purpose of an external audit is for the auditor to be in a position to express an opinion on whether the financial statements being reported on show a true and fair view or not. A satisfactory 'clean' audit report provides considerable reassurance to the users of the accounts that those accounts are reliable. This is so obviously fundamental to the purpose of financial statements that an external audit is required by the Companies Act 1985. This Act requires all limited companies, except the smallest, to have, and to pay for, an external audit. The Act then requires the auditors to report to the shareholders of the company on whether, in their opinion, the financial statements do actually show a true and fair view.

Notice what the purpose of an external audit is not. It is not an attempt to find fraud, and it is not a management control. Fraud may be discovered during an audit, and the auditor will usually be well placed to provide advice to management on potential improvements in the internal control systems, but these benefits are incidental. The auditor's report is addressed, not to the management, but to the members (shareholders). Nevertheless, the reassurance as to the truth and fairness of the statements will usually also be of value to all the other users of those statements, that is all the users we considered back in Chapter 1.

Internal audit is a management tool, which aims to verify that accounting procedures are being carried out as they should be. It often has the incidental benefit of recommending improvements to those systems. Internal auditors tend to be found only in larger organisations, where the cost is justified by the benefits of monitoring relatively complex accounting systems. Standards and procedures in internal audit are thus a matter for the management of individual organisations to determine, whereas external audit is governed by extensive regulation. A detailed exposition of audit regulation would fill this book, and would probably not thrill you. What follows is a brief summary of the major issues that you should appreciate in relation to external audit, arranged under three headings, Who are external auditors?, Procedures of external audit, and Reporting of external audit.

Who are external auditors?

The essential point is that external auditors should be both expert and independent. The Companies Act 1985 empowers the Secretary of State to nominate 'Authorised Bodies', whose members can audit UK companies, provided they are registered as auditors with those bodies. The relevant bodies at the moment are:

▶ Institute of Chartered Accountants in England and Wales (ICAEW).
▶ Institute of Chartered Accountants of Scotland (ICAS).
▶ Institute of Chartered Accountants in Ireland (ICAI).
▶ Chartered Association of Certified Accountants (ACCA).
▶ Association of International Accounts (AIA).

Independence should be ensured by the requirement in the Companies Act that an 'officer or servant' (ie an employee) of the company, or their partner or employee, is ineligible for appointment as auditor of a company. Furthermore, they should not normally be reliant on the one company for more than 15% of their total income.

It has been proposed by the European Union that preparing the accounting records of audit clients should be prohibited, although it is currently permitted by statements on ethics by the professional bodies. The objective of the proposal is to prevent accountants from suppressing information, or failing to notice their own errors, by insisting that audits should be carried out by someone independent of the preparer of the accounts. It is supported by most other European Union countries.

Auditors are notionally appointed by, and report to, the shareholders of the company. A simple majority vote at the company's annual general meeting is sufficient to appoint, or remove, them. In practice, the choice of auditors is often delegated to the directors. Indeed, the Companies Act allows directors to appoint auditors if a vacancy occurs between general meetings. Such vacancies usually occur because the auditor has resigned. They may do this at any time, provided they confirm to the shareholders that there are no matters connected with the resignation that the shareholders should be aware of. This language can be interpreted to mean that auditors should tell the shareholders if the directors are pressurising the auditors to resign, perhaps because they are finding evidence of a lack of total integrity.

Procedures of external audit

The Auditing Practices Board is to auditing what the Accounting Standards Board is to accounting. It has published both mandatory 'Auditing Standards', notably on operational standards and on the audit report, and advisory 'Auditing Guidelines'. The detail of these is beyond the scope of this book, but note that the practice of auditing is increasingly becoming as tightly regulated as the practice of accounting. Of particular impact is the Auditing Standard on the audit report.

Reporting of external audit

The audit report is the auditor's opinion, addressed to the shareholders, on whether the financial statements show a true and fair view. The audit report should state:

▶ which financial statements have been audited
▶ the fact of compliance with auditing standards in doing the audit
▶ usually, an emphasis that it is the directors' responsibility to prepare the financial statements and the auditors' purely to audit them
▶ the audit opinion
▶ the identity of the auditor, and the date of the report.

A qualified audit report is one in which the auditor has reservations that have a material effect on the financial statements. The circumstances giving rise to a qualification will be either:

▶ where there is a limitation on the scope of the audit, and hence an unresolvable uncertainty, which prevents the auditor from forming an opinion, or
▶ where the auditor is able to form an opinion, but, even after negotiation with the directors, disagrees with the financial statements.

In either of these cases, the audit report must also include a statement of the issue or disagreement, and the auditor's estimate of the financial effect. The particular form of the qualification depends on how material the auditor considers the problem to be. If it is so pervasive and fundamental that the misstatement results in the statements not showing a true and fair view then the auditor must state this in his or her report. Less fundamentally, it may be that the problem results in a serious misstatement of the accounts, but that they do still have some value. In this latter case, the audit report should state the problem, and then continue by saying that 'except for the effects of the matter' the accounts do give a true and fair view.

ACTIVITY **13.1**

For each of the following situations, decide which audit report you, as auditor, would give. Following on from the explanation above, your choices are:

▶ a clean report
▶ an 'except for' report
▶ a 'the accounts do not show a true and fair view' report.

1   The inclusion of a material debt from a company that is known to be in liquidation.
2   A fraud involving £1,800 is discovered in a large public company.
3   Controls over the cash accounting system were found to be non-existent, and records incompletely kept, so that there was no way of verifying the amount of cash sales included in the accounts.
4   In a supermarket chain, stock has been valued at selling price, which is very much higher than cost.

Answer

First, we should say that making a judgement about the correct form of audit report is a highly skilled activity, requiring extensive knowledge and experience. In particular, any judgement needs to be made in the light of the overall impact on the accounts, and particularly of the materiality of each issue. In the absence of such fuller information, our answers can be no more than good indications of what an auditor would probably decide. Furthermore, we have only attempted to cover the main features of an audit report, and you should be aware that more complex audit opinions are possible. These, however, would be the subject of a specialist book or course in auditing.

Nevertheless, we would write an 'except for' opinion for situations 1 and 3. The inclusion of what is almost certainly a bad debt will result in materially incorrect debtors and profit figures, and the accounts are therefore unlikely to show a true and fair view. However, the rest of the accounts will be unaffected, and it should not be necessary to give an adverse opinion. In situation 3, the cash sales figure may well be right, but we have been unable to determine this, so our report should explain this problem of a limitation on the scope of our audit, and again report that 'except for' this issue, the accounts show a true and fair view.

Situation 2 is easier, in that a misstatement of £1,800 will almost certainly not have a material effect on the truth and fairness of the accounts of a large public company. In this case, the audit report should make no mention of the issue, and a clean report can be given.

Finally, situation 4 is an example of a fundamental misstatement. Stock will be a very large item in the accounts of a supermarket, and a treatment that conflicts with SSAP 9 'Stocks and Long-Term Contracts' will almost certainly have such a pervasive impact on the accounts as to mean that they do not show a true and fair view. The report should therefore be adverse, ie 'the accounts do not show a true and fair view'.

A qualified audit report is usually regarded as a serious matter, because it significantly reduces the reliability of the financial statements. This may then mean, for example, that a potential lender will not lend.

Finally, you should be aware that there is a continuing debate over whether an audit is of real benefit to very small companies. The shareholders, to whom the audit report is nominally addressed, tend to also be the directors, managers and much of the workforce. What then is the benefit of using the traditional financial statements to tell them about their business? They already know. If the financial statements are of little value, so must the related audit report be. The counter argument is that outsiders, such as lenders and the Inland

Revenue, are also interested in the business and would benefit from the financial statements, and hence from an audit report that enabled them to rely on the truth and fairness of those statements.

Before we move on from this introduction to auditing, use the following activity to test your basic knowledge.

ACTIVITY **13.2**

Select the best answer or answers in each of the following cases.

1   Which of the following can not be appointed as a company auditor:
    (a) A director?
    (b) An employee?
    (c) An ex-employee?
    (d) A member of the Chartered Institute of Management Accountants?
2   Which of the following circumstances would probably result in a qualified audit report:
    (a) The loss of the cash book?
    (b) Gross inaccuracies in the register of shareholders?
    (c) The omission of a cash flow statement?
    (d) Discovery of the theft of £200 petty cash?

Answers

The correct answers are (a), (b) and (d) for question 1, and (a) and (c) for question 2. If this doesn't make sense, go back and re-read the material above on the audit.

Audit, particularly external audit, can thus have a valuable function in ensuring that financial statements are prepared competently and objectively. As we noted earlier, control to guard against mistakes feeding through the accounting system undetected can be helped through the use of bank reconciliations and control accounts.

Bank reconciliations

We saw in Activity 13.2 the fundamental importance of the cash book, that is our own record of amounts in and out of our bank account. It is possible that deliberate or accidental mistakes will be made in writing it up, but fortunately there is an independent record of exactly the same transactions. That independent record is, of course, the bank statement.

The balance in the cash book should be the same as the balance on the bank statement. This independent record can therefore provide an excellent check on the accuracy and completeness of our cash book. In practice, however, the two balances may not be the same. There may, for example, be amounts we have received and paid in to our bank, and which we have therefore entered in the cash book, but which have not yet cleared through the banking system. The two balances will therefore differ by the amount of the 'uncredited lodgement'.

However, if we can identify all such items in transit, we can allow for them and so still reconcile the two balances. Such a summary of items in transit, which reconciles the bank statement balance with the cash book balance is called a bank reconciliation statement. Its purpose is to verify the cash book balance, and, by inference, all entries in that cash book.

ACTIVITY 13.3

List four items which might cause the cash book balance not to immediately agree with the balance per the bank statement.

Answer

The items we have identified are as follows:

1   A very common transit item is an unpresented cheque. This is a cheque that you have entered in the cash book but which has not yet been presented to the bank.
2   The opposite item is the uncredited lodgement that we have already seen. This is an amount you have paid in to the bank, and entered in your cash book, but which has not yet been received by the bank and entered on the bank statement.
3   The bank may have charged interest or bank charges, or have given you interest on your account, but you will usually only find out about these when you receive the bank statement. Until you then enter them in the cash book they will also be sources of difference.
4   You may have made a mistake in writing up your cash book, or the bank statement may be wrong.

There are two broad reasons why these differences occur, and the distinction is crucial. First, there are legitimate reasons, such as items 1, 2 and 3 above. Second, there are mistakes, either by you or by the bank. The purpose of a bank reconciliation statement is to allow for such all legitimate differences. Any residual difference must then have been caused by an error.

Items 1 and 2 in the list above are items that we have entered in our cash book but which the bank has not yet entered on the bank statement. All we can do is list them as part of the reason why the two balances disagree, ie they will form part of the bank reconciliation statement. Conversely, item 3 is an item that the bank have entered up but we haven't. We can therefore eliminate this source of difference before we prepare the bank reconciliation statement. In other words, we should complete the writing up of the cash book to take account of items that are so far only on the bank statement. Such items will then no longer be a source of difference.

ACTIVITY 13.4

Gloria started business with £200 in her account at the bank. During June she issued the following cheques:

1st   £86 to Garside Books
4th   £480 to Fletcher Cars

13th   £300 to Harker Ltd
27th   £430 to Fletcher Cars
30th   £182 to Plant Supplies

She also recorded the following amounts paid into the bank;

4th   £490 from Darley Building
15th   £38 from a cash sale
20th   £780 from Darley Building
30th   £75 from a cash sale

Write up the cash book for the above transactions, remembering to include the opening £200, and to show the closing balance. You should be able to do this by thinking back to what you learnt about the writing up of ledger accounts earlier in this book. Write up the cash book as simply another ledger account.

Answer

CASH BOOK

1st Bal b/f	200	1st Garside Books	86
4th Darley Building	490	4th Fletcher Cars	480
15th Cash sale	38	13th Harker Ltd	300
20th Darley Building	780	27th Fletcher Cars	430
30th Cash sale	75	30th Plant Supplies	182
		30th Bal c/f	105
	£1,583		£1,583

ACTIVITY **13.5**

At the end of the month, Gloria receives the following bank statement. Note that it is in overdraft (O/D) at some points during the month, ie there is a negative balance. Check each item against the cash book and so identify which items are not common.

BANK STATEMENT

Date	Detail	Payments	Receipts	Balance £
1	Balance b/f			200
4	Cheque	86		114
6	Cheque	480		366 O/D
8	Counter credit		490	124
16	Cheque	300		176 O/D
17	Counter credit		38	138 O/D
22	Counter credit		780	642
30	Cheque	430		212
30	Charges for June	20		192

Answer

The items you should have identified are:

> ▶ The cheque paid out on 30 June to Plant Supplies for £182 is not on the bank statement.
> ▶ The cash sale of £75 on 30 June similarly does not appear on the bank statement.
> ▶ The bank statement shows charges of £20, which have not been entered in the cash book, because Gloria did not know about them until she received the bank statement.

ACTIVITY 13.6

Recalculate the cash book balance after the bank charges have been entered, ie complete the writing up of the cash book.

Answer

The revised balance will be the existing balance of £105, less the bank charges of £20, ie the cash book balance, written up as far as Gloria is able, will be £85. It is this amount which we must reconcile to the balance per the bank statement of £192.

Hopefully, we know the reasons for the whole of the difference. It should be attributable to the cheque paid on the 30 June and the cash sale paid in on the same date. All that remains is to set these items out formally to prove that this is the case. In order to do so, you need to be aware of how the bank balance is affected by the items in transit. A cheque drawn on our bank account will be deducted from our account balance by our bank. In other words, the balance will go down. Conversely, an uncredited lodgement will increase the bank balance when it reaches the bank. Providing we start with the balance per the bank statement, unpresented cheques should therefore be deducted, and uncredited lodgements should be added.

ACTIVITY 13.7

Bearing the above in mind, about the direction of adjustments, draft a bank reconciliation statement for Gloria at 30 June. It should start with the balance per the bank statement, then adjust for the unpresented cheque, and the uncredited lodgement, and so arrive at the balance per the cash book.

Answer

As always, you will learn faster and more easily if you discipline yourself to trying the activity before you look at the answer.

GLORIA
BANK RECONCILIATION STATEMENT AT 30 JUNE

Balance per bank statement	192
Less: unpresented cheque; 30 June, Plant Supplies	182
	10
Add: uncredited lodgement; 30 June, cash sale	75
Balance per cash book, as adjusted	£85

ACTIVITY **13.8**

Consolidate your knowledge now by outlining the purposes of a bank reconciliation statement. You may find it most helpful to do this by creating a list of the purposes.

Answer

Our suggested list would include these points:

▶ The bank reconciliation statement constitutes a comparison between the cash book and the independent bank statement, allowing for items in transit.

▶ It thus provides a check on the completeness and accuracy of the cash book.

▶ Agreement of the two adjusted balances provides a high level of assurance of the accuracy and completeness of the cash book.

▶ Non-agreement of the two adjusted balances indicates an error, probably in the cash book, since errors on bank statements are less frequent.

▶ A trial balance difference may have indicated an error somewhere in the accounting system; the same amount showing up as a bank reconciliation difference indicates that any search for an error can be restricted to the bank accounting system.

We thus have a way of verifying the bank account in our books. However, it is still possible that we will make mistakes in the writing up of our other accounts. Fortunately, control accounts provide a way of checking the accuracy of our sales and purchase ledgers.

Control accounts

Think back to your earlier studies about how sales and purchase ledgers are written up. You should recall that individual accounts in the sales ledger are written up by posting sales invoices and cash receipts from customers. In practice, the sales invoices would not be entered up one by one directly in the sales account and individual customer accounts, but would usually first be listed and summarised. This listing is called a 'sales journal' or 'sales day book'. It does not form part of the double entry system, and so was not covered in the earlier chapters on double entry bookkeeping. Nevertheless, it becomes significant once we turn our attention to control accounts.

This sales journal is no more than a listing of sales invoices as they are sent out, but it does offer the opportunity to total all the invoices, usually monthly, and to post just the total to the sales account, instead of having to post the sales one by one from the individual invoices. Entries into individual customers' accounts would, however, still have to be posted individually, in order to record sales to each customer. Receipts from each customer would, of course, be entered from the cash book, but note that such receipts could also be totalled in the cash book for the month.

Now imagine that, as well as doing all that, for the same month we also posted the total amount of sales invoices from the sales journal and the total amount of receipts from debtors in the cash book. In other words, we would make just one total entry from the sales journal, and one total entry from the cash book, to a new account, created for the purpose. This new account is called either a total account or a control account. In this case it would be the sales control account, but you could create a purchases control account in exactly the same way. The total postings would be from the purchases journal (a listing of purchase invoices) and from the total of payments to creditors in the cash book.

Notice that we now have two sales ledgers (and two purchase ledgers), one made up of individual accounts, and one made up of the control account. Both of these sales ledgers should record the same transactions, one customer by customer, and one in total, but both for the same month. The implication is that the total of the balances on the individual ledger accounts should add up to the same as the balance on the single control account. This is the point of the control account. What we have created is a check on the accuracy of the individual sales ledger accounts. If the total of the balances on the individual accounts is the same as the balance on the control account, then we can be reasonably confident that the individual accounts have been written up correctly.

This can be invaluable if the trial balance does not agree, and we are therefore faced with looking for one or more mistakes somewhere in the accounting system. If, however, we prepare a sales control account and the balance agrees with the total of individual sales ledger balances, then we can be reasonably confident that the mistakes are not in the sales ledger. This dramatically reduces the search we have to undertake. If we prepare a purchase control and that also agrees with the total of the individual purchase ledger accounts, then we can also eliminate the purchases sub-system as a source of error. We now know the trial balance difference must be somewhere in the nominal ledger, and we can focus our search there. What we have achieved is a way of checking the accuracy of the sales and purchases ledgers in isolation.

It is, of course, always possible that we make the same mistake in preparing the control account as we did in writing up the individual accounts. In this case the control account would agree with the total of the individual accounts, and we would have failed to detect the error. Control accounts are not as effective as bank reconciliations because they check against an internally produced source, rather than against an independent source, such as a bank statement.

You may have wondered what happens to the integrity of the double entry system if there are two sales ledgers in existence. The answer is that *either* the total of the individual accounts *or* the control account forms part of the double-entry. There is no absolute rule about which forms part of the double entry system, although it is obviously easier to list a control account in a trial balance, rather than hundreds of individual accounts. Understanding that only one of the control account, or the individual accounts goes into the double entry system is fundamental to understanding control accounts.

If the individual accounts are put into the trial balance then the control account is known as a memorandum account. On the other hand, if the control account balance is included in the trial balance, then the individual ledger accounts form the memorandum. A memorandum is just that, a working note of detail, which is outside the double entry system.

ACTIVITY **13.9**

Identify which of these errors can affect the agreement of the sales control account:

	Error	Affects agreement?
A	Posting the total of the sales journal to the purchase ledger control account	
B	Omission of entry from control account only	
C	Making the same mistake in the individual account as in the control account	
D	Posting the correct amount to the wrong account in the individual accounts	
E	Omission of entry from individual and control account	

Answer

You should have answered yes in the boxes against errors A and B, and no against the others. Error A will result in the same difference in the sales control and in the purchases control – a good indication of what has happened. It is worth noting that three errors will not be shown up by the control account technique. Nevertheless, it is a fairly easy and cheap technique, and typically found in all but the most basic accounting systems.

ACTIVITY **13.10**

The following information has been taken from the records of Garside Books. Prepare the sales ledger account for the year to 31 December 1996. It can be written up in exactly the same way as an individual sales ledger account.

	£
Debtor balances at 1 January 1996, per control account and per list of balances	14,890
Sales for the year to 31 December 1996, per sales journal	203,680
Cash received from debtors, per cash book	205,905
Bad debts written off	400

Answer

SALES LEDGER CONTROL

	£		£
1.1.96 Bal b/f	14,890	31.12.96 Cash book	205,905
31.12.96 Sales journal	203,680	31.12.96 Bad debt	400
		31.12.96 Bal c/f	12,265
	£218,570		£218,570

ACTIVITY **13.11**
••••••••••••••••••

A list of the balances on the individual debtors' accounts in Garside Books' sales ledger at 31 December 1995 totalled £11,771. Investigation reveals:

1 An invoice for £263 to Sandringham was entered twice in the sales journal and subsequently posted twice to the customer's account.

2 An invoice for £485 to S Patel was correctly entered in the sales journal but was subsequently posted to I Patel's account in the purchase ledger.

3 A receipt of £78 from Foster was correctly entered in the control account, but entered as £87 in the individual debtor's account.

Correct the control account and/or the list of individual debtor balances as necessary and so reconcile the total with the balance on the sales control account. You may find it helpful to deal with each item in both the control account and the individual account, before considering the next.

Answer

Our approach is to consider whether Item 1 will result in a control difference. It appears to have been entered twice in the individual account, and in the control account. It will be included twice in the control account because that is, of course, written up from the sales journal, where it has been entered twice. While this is a mistake which needs correction, it will not help us to agree the control account to the total of individual balances.

We then consider Item 2. The sales journal treatment, and hence the control account is correct. However, the individual account for S Patel will be understated by the omission of the invoice for £485. This must therefore be added to the total of the individual balances. Note that it will also need to be corrected in I Patel's account in the purchase ledger, but that is not our immediate concern.

Item 3 is also correct in the control account, but the individual account for Foster will have been credited with £9 too much. This therefore needs to be added back, so increasing the balance on Foster's individual account.

The net effect of all this can be summarised as follows:

Existing total of individual balances	11,771
Add: Omission of sales invoice to S Patel	485
Correction of over credit to Foster	9
Balance per sales control account	£12,265

If we now make correcting entries in the accounts of S Patel and Foster, the total of the individual accounts will then agree with the balance on the control account. Notice what the construction and use of the control account has done for us. It has enabled us to detect a problem with two accounts in our sales ledger, which it is quite possible we would not otherwise have found until the mistakes had damaged our relationship with those customers.

Summary
· · · · · · · · · · ·

This chapter has introduced a key issue in accounting – that of control. We have seen how a lack of control can open up an entity to both mistakes and deliberate fraud, and how the achievement of a true and fair view may be compromised. Albeit briefly, we have looked at two broad approaches to ensuring a minimum level of control within the accounting systems of our organisation. These are the use of audit, both internal and external, and the use of bookkeeping controls, notably the bank reconciliation and the control account.

None of these controls will ensure the integrity of our accounting records and financial statements, either individually or together. However, what they will do is significantly increase the likelihood of achieving something close to such integrity. In the case of external audit, we have seen that the benefits of the control are considered so important that an audit is required by the Companies Act 1985.

Chapter 14 examines the role of the computer in accounting systems, and includes a look at the control features involved in such systems.

Further study
· · · · · · · · · · · · · · · · ·

Most introductory books on financial accounting will include alternative expositions of the mechanics of bank reconciliations and control accounts. Control issues are usually more fully covered in books on auditing.

**SELF-
CHECK
QUESTION**

For each of the following issues, select the single most appropriate answer. Our answers are at the end of the questions. If you get any wrong, then re-read the relevant part of this chapter.

1 Which of the following is an error of principle:
    (a) Entering a sales invoice for £89 as £98 in the customer's account?
    (b) Not using a control account?
    (c) Entering a sales invoice twice?
    (d) Adding up the cash book incorrectly?

2 A main purpose of an external audit is:
    (a) To enable the auditors to detect fraud.
    (b) To enable the directors to use correct accounting policies.
    (c) To enable auditors to report on the truth and fairness of the accounts.
    (d) To enable the shareholders to monitor the managers.

3 A clean audit report implies that:
    (a) The auditors believe that the accounts show a true and fair view.
    (b) The directors believe that the accounts show a true and fair view.
    (c) The shareholders believe that the accounts are reliable.
    (d) The auditors have not detected any fraud or error.

4 Which of the following are required by law to have an external audit?
    (a) Small limited companies?
    (b) Sole traders?

(c) All limited companies?

(d) Larger limited companies?

5 The purpose of a bank reconciliation statement is to:

(a) Detect cash book errors.

(b) Make sure the cash book includes all bank interest and charges.

(c) Highlight items in transit within the banking system.

(d) None of the above.

6 If a bank reconciliation statement starts with the balance per the bank statement, and that balance is in overdraft, then, in the reconciliation statement, any unpresented cheques should be:

(a) Added to the balance per the bank statement.

(b) Subtracted from the balance per the bank statement.

(c) Omitted from the statement.

(d) Added back and then subtracted once the bank balance is positive.

7 The balance on a sales control account should agree with:

(a) The total of both individual sales ledger and individual purchase ledger balances.

(b) The total of individual sales ledger balances.

(c) The trial balance total.

(d) The balance on the purchase ledger control account.

8 The purpose of a purchase ledger control account is to ensure that:

(a) All errors in the writing up of the purchases system are detected.

(b) Most errors in the writing up of the purchases system are detected.

(c) The purchases figure in the financial statements is correct.

(d) The creditors figure in the financial statements is correct.

Answers

1(c), 2(c), 3(a), 4(d), 5(a), 6(a), 7(b), 8(b).

Further review questions are available in a separate resource pack which is available to lecturers.

Information technology and accounting

Objectives:

By the end of this chapter you should be able to:

▶ Outline the main features of hardware systems, including networks, and associated software as applied to financial accounting.

▶ Review the uses of IT in financial accounting.

▶ Describe other uses of IT relevant to the accounting function.

Introduction

We noted in Chapter 13 that accounting has become ever more reliant on the use of computers. In all but the smallest entities, it has now become most unusual to find an accounting system that is not computer based to some degree. The purpose of this chapter is to introduce some of the concepts and terminology of computer-based accounting, and to consider the use and control of such systems.

You will probably be aware of the current pace of change in computing, in terms of the power of hardware, the sophistication of software, and the spectacular growth in the ability to inter-connect with other computing systems. This implies that any description of current practices would be seriously out of date before you came to read this. We will therefore deal less with the current practicalities and more with the principles of accounting in a computer environment.

Nevertheless, this chapter starts with a brief overview of hardware and software, including the use of networking. Much of what we have to say here may be familiar to you, in which case you can skim it. We then move on to consider our main concern, which is the use and control of accounting software. Finally, we will take a brief look at other forms of information technology (IT) which are relevant to the accountant.

Hardware and software

Computers are excellent at repetitively processing large amounts of data. Since this is what routine bookkeeping entails, it is not surprising that accounting was one of the first commercial functions to be computerised. In the early days, this meant the use of mainframe computers, that is single, physically big computers which inherently centralised computing. Access to this power was through dedicated 'dumb' terminals, ie terminals which had no computing power of their own, but simply allowed input to, and receipt of processed data from, the central computer. The advent of the personal computer from 1975, and more especially the introduction of the IBM personal computer (PC) in 1982, started to change this picture.

The increasing power of the PC has gradually shifted computing towards processing by the end user, so that individuals can carry out much of their work locally. This has advantages in terms of flexibility, but can cause difficulties in terms of sharing data. In the days when there was only a single computer, it was implicit that everyone used their terminals to access the same data. Once PCs acquired the power to process data locally, the question arose of how to ensure that many different versions of the same data were not created. The answer usually adopted is the network.

Networks

A network is a number of computers connected together, usually for one or more of three main purposes. First, as noted above, their inter-connection allows for a single set of data to be maintained, since all will use and update the one set of data. This single data set will be held on one of the computers in the network. This means, for example, that the organisation's list of its employees should always be up to date and correct. Contrast this with what could happen if a number of employees all started with the same set of data, but then each amended it as they saw fit. The organisation would be generating multiple employee lists, with no assurance over which was the most reliable.

Second, a network allows for some resources to be shared. The usual example given is a fast laser printer, which may be expensive but infrequently used. It would therefore make economic sense to share this printer by connecting it to the network and allowing any PC to use it when needed. This argument is probably becoming less valid as printer prices fall, but may still be true for other peripherals, such as multiple CD ROM drives. These are discussed later in this chapter.

Third, connecting PCs together allows them not only to share data, but also exchange messages. At its simplest, a network facilitates electronic mail, usually abbreviated to e-mail. E-mail software enables users to write and send messages, and attached files, to each other over the network. In a local environment this may be of marginal benefit over traditional internal post and telephone, although it will usually be faster than internal post. The real benefits of e-mail are seen when messages are sent over larger distances, including internationally. At a more sophisticated level, the ability to exchange data with other computers allows the functioning of the Internet. This is covered in more detail later in this chapter.

LANS and WANS

Networks are commonly divided into two types, Local Area Networks (LANs), and Wide Area Networks (WANs). LANs are usually constructed using wiring specifically installed for the purpose within a single organisation. They are typically the means of the data sharing discussed earlier. WANs tend to use lines installed by a third party, and are often also telephone lines. They are often leased, and used to provide connection with other closely related organisations. A WAN could be used, for example, to connect a holding company in London with its subsidiaries in Edinburgh and Paris. This would allow the subsidiaries to submit monthly accounts, budgets and other reports quickly, and in a format that would be immediately usable by software at the holding company. Additional hardware need only be a modem, that is a box of electronics which converts the digital signals used by a computer into the analogue (continuous) signals still used by many telephone lines. A modem at the receiving end converts back again.

Software
....

Software is of two types, operating system and application software. Operating system software is the basic command software that enables the hardware to function. There are a number of commercial operating systems, with the best known probably being DOS. This was originally developed for use on the IBM PC, but will also work on any compatible computer, ie one with the same hardware architecture. More recently, the overlaying of Microsoft's 'Windows' system on top of DOS has resulted in an easier to use interface between the computer and the user. In late 1995, Microsoft released 'Windows 95'. This is a radically reworked operating system, but still performs the same basic function, that of issuing commands to the hardware. Larger computers have tended to use alternative operating systems, notably UNIX.

Operating systems software provides very basic functionality. In order to do serious work, a computer also needs applications software. Under this heading come the many word processors, spreadsheets, databases, accounting software, e-mail packages, graphics programs, and so on. The next section of this chapter considers one such application, namely accounting software. To put the use of such software in its proper context, we should first consider the nature of accounting systems.

Accounting systems
....

There is little point in looking at the computer-based option unless we are very clear about exactly what we want from our accounting system. This means making our accounting needs and wants explicit in terms of:

▶ Sources of and types of data to be dealt with.
▶ The information to be extracted from the system by way of management information, financial statements (eg a balance sheet), statutory returns (eg a VAT return), and anything else we think might be useful to any of the people we might regard as having a right to such information.
▶ An acceptable level of costs for running this accounting system.

Only after a thorough consideration of at least these matters will we be in a position to assess the pro's and con's of introducing computers into our accounting.

The options available for an accounting system include recording transactions in an *ad hoc* way – on the backs of envelopes etc. Such a system would be called incomplete records. In other words, it is that approach to accounting which does not rely on the maintenance of a full set of double entry records. Many small organisations do, in fact, rely on such an approach. More usual is the sort of full double entry system that we have seen in previous chapters.

ACTIVITY **14.1**

Why do you think most accounting systems rely on double entry if an incomplete record system can, perhaps, produce the information we require?

Answer

While the answer to this question will be dependent on the specific organisation, and particularly on its information needs, some of the key reasons can be listed as:

▶   It is easier and faster to extract information from a complete double entry system, than from a system where the data is unorganised.
▶   Double entry imposes an automatic control on the accuracy and completeness of the accounting. Most, though not all, mistakes will result in an unbalanced set of books. Furthermore, we saw in Chapter 13 that such a control can be supplemented by a bank reconciliation and control accounts. Similar mistakes would probably not be noticed in an incomplete record system.
▶   Final accounts are, accordingly, easier to prepare and more reliable where they are based on double entry.

A comprehensive accounting system, based on double entry principles thus has considerable advantages. Computers offer the possibility of combining these advantages with speed of processing and arithmetic accuracy. However, implementation of any system, whether manual or computer based, should start with a consideration of what we want from that system.

Information needs

Two of the key influences on how we plan and implement an accounting system are the type of raw data and the requirements of the end users. There will be many types of raw data, ranging from delivery notes to bank statements and from time sheets to petty cash vouchers.

ACTIVITY **14.2**

1   List five source documents for accounting information that you think would be relevant to a trading company. You may find it helpful to think about an organisation you are familiar with, and the types of documentation it has to deal with.
2   Identify three separate reports or statements that you would want to extract from the accounting system, other than final accounts, such as the balance sheet.

Answers

This is a deliberately open-ended activity, since any answer will be dependent on the particular organisation. Nevertheless, you could have suggested, among other things, that source documents would include:

▶ sales invoices, giving details of amounts charged to customers
▶ sales credit notes, showing amounts due to customers because of goods returned, overcharges, etc
▶ purchase invoices and credit notes, giving the same details as the equivalent sales documents, but in respect of our purchases from suppliers
▶ bank statements, showing bank charges, interest received, etc
▶ cheque stubs, recording details of amounts paid
▶ paying in slips, detailing amounts received into our bank account.

The information statements that we might want could include, for example:

▶ a list of outstanding debtors
▶ a list of outstanding creditors
▶ a forecast of cash flows in and out of our bank account over the next few months
▶ a statement of stock in hand
▶ a summary of actual expenditure, compared with budgeted expenditure.

Once we are clear about the need for a comprehensive system, have clarified the data to be dealt with, and have decided on the information statements we want from our accounting system, we can move on to consider implementation.

The options at this point are to have a system custom written for us or to buy a general system 'off the peg'. The latter will obviously be much cheaper and is, therefore, the usual approach. Occasionally, a specialist software supplier will be able to marginally customise a standard package, and this may achieve the best of both worlds.

Many accounting systems have been designed as modular systems. This means that they are divided into separate, self-contained programs for different parts of the total accounting system. There is thus one module available for dealing with the sales ledger, and other, separate, modules for purchases, nominal, stock, etc. This has had advantages in that users only had to buy those parts of the system that they needed. A business that only sells for cash would therefore not need to acquire the sales ledger module. This approach also had the incidental benefit of reducing the demands on the hardware.

As hardware power has risen and prices have fallen, however, the rationale for modular systems has become less obvious. It is now more common to find that accounting software is integrated, so that all functions are, in principle at least, part of a seamless whole. This is obviously a simpler approach and ought to make the software easier to use.

Implementation

It only remains to successfully implement such a package. This will require not only suitable hardware and software, but also an organised approach to the implementation. In particular, we must consider how the data can be accurately transferred from the old system to the new, and make contingency plans in case the new system fails in any unforeseen way. Data loss is a serious problem and could result in the collapse of the organisation.

A typical process for the transfer of an accounting system from a manual to a computer-based system would include:

1   Ensuring that the manual system is up to date.
2   Installing hardware and software as determined by the issues considered above. This might include spare hardware and back-up software, preferably on a separate site, to be used in case of damage to, or failure of, the main hardware.
3   Entering all existing data onto the software. Given the importance of this step, it should preferably be verified, even though this is an expensive process. This could be done, for example, by re-entering all data and comparing the two sets.
4   Running both the existing manual system and the new computer system for a period. Again, this is expensive, but it is essential to be sure that the new system works adequately before ending the old system. This process is known as parallel running.
5   Once the computer-based system is running reliably, the old system can be discontinued. Note that the new system must include suitable control procedures, analogous to control accounts etc, before it can be considered to be satisfactory. Control in a computer-based accounting environment is covered next.

Control issues
....

We saw in Chapter 13 how controls within an accounting system can help to guard against fraud, mistakes and incompetence. This is no less true in a computer-based system. Think about what we need to achieve. We need an accounting system that at least minimises error and fraud, and certainly a system that detects it. One of the great benefits of a computer-based system is that arithmetic error should normally be eliminated, and the software should not allow entries that do not balance. While these are significant improvements, it will still be possible to make errors of principle, such as posting a repair invoice to an electricity account, or crediting the wrong customer with a receipt. Some of these errors may be deliberate. One of the key controls in this respect is the audit trail.

An audit trail is simply a listing of transactions, including a note of who entered the transaction. This enables both the organisation and its auditors to trace the accounting treatment of a transaction, to ensure that it has been dealt with correctly. Alternatively, it allows the identification of an error, and who made it. For routine transactions, this may mean no more than the software attaching a number to each transaction and keeping a record of who logged in to make that transaction. This, of course, implies that there must be some way of ensuring that only the correct person is able to log in with their personal identification.

The usual answer to this control problem is to use a password. This has the additional benefit of preventing anyone other than the nominated person from writing up the accounts. It is possible to set various levels of password protection so that, for example, the sales ledger clerk can only access the sales ledger and cash book receipts, the assistant accountant can access any ledger, but only the chief accountant can access the software which allows the preparation of final accounts. Passwords can't be relied on by themselves, since people tend to forget their passwords, tell them to those helping them 'temporarily', use easy to guess words, or leave their PC unattended after logging in.

A second benefit of an audit trail is then to at least trace what entries have been made. This is particularly important with the more recent versions of accounting packages. Early versions of accounting software effectively adopted the double entry metaphor, so that they explicitly required both source and application to be identified. This was later refined, so that the software took care of one leg of the double entry. Recording the cash book receipt of £100 from a customer called Jack, for example, would automatically also credit Jack's account in the sales ledger. Nevertheless, a mistake, such as entering the receipt as being from Jill, would still require an explicit double entry to correct the error, in this case debiting Jill's account and crediting Jack's. In other words, it has not been possible to simply go back to Jack's account and cross out the entry and then make it in Jill's instead. This has ensured that the audit trail was always very clear, if rather laboured.

The latest generation of accounting software for smaller businesses has adopted a more intuitive approach, where such a crossing out and new entry is exactly what is done. Jack's account would therefore retain no record of the original mis-posting. The audit trail would include the correcting error, but it is still questionable whether the lack of any record in Jack's account maintains a full and obvious audit trail for control purposes.

The use of nominated persons, passwords and an audit trail should protect reasonably well against accidental or deliberate fraud. Note, however, that an audit trail is only of use if someone reads it, and picks up any anomalies. In a larger organisation, this will usually be included within the internal audit function. In a smaller organisation, it may only be done by exception, when a problem becomes apparent for other reasons. There still remains the problem of what to do if the computer system breaks down.

Back up

The main control over this possibility is the use of back ups. This means that there must always be at least two sets of the same data, and many organisations will use three sets of data. At the start of the day, there will thus be, say, two sets of data, A and B. Set A will be used as a starting point for that day's transactions, so that by the end of the day it will include not only the transactions that are on Set B, but will also have had that day's transactions overlaid onto it. If there is any disaster during the day and Set A is lost, Set B can be used, and all that will have been lost will be the transactions for the day up to the point of the disaster. It would not be a major issue to re-enter these on Set B. If all goes well, then Set

B can be backed up from Set A at the end of the day so that we again start the next day with two sets of data. It will improve the control if set B is kept off-site until needed. There is obviously a danger of a fire or other problem when Set B is being backed up from Set A, and both sets could then be lost. This is why some organisations work with three sets of data, so allowing the third set to always be off-site. Sets B and C can then be backed up in rotation, and the worst that could happen is that we would lose one day's entry of transactions.

We have already noted in this chapter the use of parallel hardware, so that there is something to run the software on in the case of a major disaster. It will obviously be expensive to keep otherwise redundant hardware, so one alternative would be to come to a mutual arrangement with another organisation running the same software, so that each could use the other's facilities, perhaps overnight, and so maintain processing pending replacement of its own facilities. This may, of course, not be possible, so a number of commercial firms have arisen which offer such facilities to a number of companies, in exchange for a fee.

We have covered a wide range of topics so far in this chapter. Before we move on the final section, try the next activity, which is designed to help you consolidate these topics.

ACTIVITY **14.3**

Arturo Ltd is considering changing from its existing hand-written accounting system to a computer-based system. Outline the procedures that you will implement in order to ensure that there is no loss of data, and no subsequent failure of the new system. You may find it most effective to organise your answer as a list of points – we have.

Answer

Our suggested answer summarises much of what has been covered earlier in this chapter. For more detail on any of these points you should therefore refer back.

▶ Identify the data sources and required outputs, and so clarify the required system. This should help to ensure that the system will be sufficiently comprehensive to accurately deal with all data.
▶ Similarly, suitable software and the necessary hardware will improve the chances of avoiding data loss, especially in the transfer period.
▶ Parallel running will provide some reassurance about the reliability of the computer-based system, before the manual system is discontinued.
▶ Once the new system is running, it is essential that frequent and regular back-up copies are taken of the data. If done conscientiously, this should ensure that any data loss is restricted to only whatever data has been input since the last back-up.
▶ Contingency plans for back-up hardware and software will guard against the effects of a disaster, such as a major fire.

The wider picture

The final part of this chapter is concerned with uses of information technology other than accounting software that may still be of relevance to the accountant.

The first area to look at is other applications software, especially word processors and spreadsheets. Word-processing software basically allows the user to create letters, reports, etc, but more recent versions have included the ability to incorporate graphics, and facilities such as indexing, spell checkers and tables of contents which allow for the production of more extensive books and articles. The use of Windows enables data to be transferred relatively easily between word processors and other applications, including spreadsheets.

Spreadsheets are an electronic version of the accountant's traditional working paper with many columns and rows. You have already seen one major example of such a working paper in the use of the extended trial balance in Chapter 7. A spreadsheet not only allows text and numbers to be placed in the cells of the spreadsheets, but then also enables formulae to be included, which refer to that text and, more usually, to those numbers. This then means that totals and other calculated figures can be automatically computed, and then recomputed if any underlying figure changes. This ability to very quickly recalculate enables the user to try out 'what if' scenarios, ie changing figures, perhaps as a result of changing underlying assumptions, so that alternative courses of action can be tested. Most of the more modern spreadsheets allow calculations to include references to more than one spreadsheet.

A third major application is the database. However, constructing a useful database is a much more complex matter than constructing a spreadsheet to automatically add up a budget, or using a word processor to write the notes to the accounts. Accordingly, it is far less common to find databases being seriously used by end users. Note that most word processors permit the maintenance of simple databases, such as a list of names and addresses, and this will therefore often be a valid alternative to a full database package.

Finally, we have already touched on the use of e-mail. Other common uses of information technology by accountants tends to fall into a similar area, in that they are concerned with the acquisition and communication of information. Other than e-mail, there are broadly two ways this can be done. The first is CD ROM. CD ROM stands for 'Compact Disk Read Only Memory', and each CD ROM disk can currently hold as much as 600 megabytes of data – enough to store a major encyclopaedia, including all the diagrams and pictures! Larger capacity disks are being developed.

The real power of CD ROM sources, however, lies not just in their huge capacity, but in the ability of software to search that data for the items that you are interested in. You can then print out your search results, or, better still, save the data onto your floppy disk. In particular, there are now a number of commercial CD ROMs which contain data about UK companies, usually including the full annual report and accounts. Saving such data in spreadsheet format would, for example, enable the user to calculate ratios for a number of companies, and so make the sort of inter-firm comparisons we covered earlier in this book. More simply, it is an effective method of acquiring names of directors, addresses of registered offices, discovering who the auditors are, and so on.

Supplementing CD ROMs are the on-line sources. Some of these are commercial and concerned specifically with UK company data. They extend the information available from CD ROMs by providing ready calculated ratios, and by providing additional information, such as share prices, and often by presenting that information graphically. Being commercial, there is usually a substantial charge for using such services. Increasingly, however, on-line services include data sources which come under the heading of the Internet.

The Internet is a network of networks. Note that it is therefore not a formal system, controlled by any one body. It is possible for an organisation to connect its own network to this system of other networks. Setting up such a 'gateway' is, however, expensive, and smaller organisations tend to use a gateway set up by a commercial provider, and pay a rental for doing so. Whatever the route followed, connection to the other networks that make up the Internet allows access to all other 'sites'. A site is a computer whose owner has allowed access, perhaps out of enlightened self-interest, since others will hopefully then do the same for you. Many of these sites are discussion groups of very variable quality and usefulness. Some are sources of information, and thus of potentially more use to accountants.

At the moment, attempts to make the Internet more commercial, and to charge for information are stalled by difficulties in securely collected fees for doing so, and also by the prevailing anarchic spirit of the Internet. There are fears that the advent of large corporations onto the Internet, charging fees, will destroy the existing benefits of the mutual support that has so far been its culture. We are not going to attempt to predict the outcome.

Summary
············

This chapter has been concerned with the costs and benefits of computer-based accounting. We have looked at the necessary hardware and typical software, as well as at the associated control issues. It is a fast changing area of accounting, so we have tried to restrict ourselves to coverage of principles, rather than discussion of particular systems. Above all, it is important that you appreciate that there is more to using an accounting package than simply knowing which keys to hit.

This has been the last chapter that introduces new material. Chapter 15 attempts to pull together much of what this book has been about, through the use of one large case study. Accounting is about synthesising data and communicating it in a way meaningful to the users. The case study is one way of synthesising your knowledge and understanding acquired so far, and then using it to produce useful information. We strongly recommend that you try it.

Further study
·················

The problem with any book on information technology, whether connected with accounting or not, is that it very rapidly becomes out of date. We have attempted to avoid the problem by restricting this chapter to broad categories and principles, and not looking at specific systems. For more detail on the categories and principles, we suggest you browse introductory books on computing. For up-to-date details of current applications of information technology in accounting, the best source we know is the wide range of computing magazines and journals now available. Try your library for these, looking for articles specifically on accounting packages and developments.

SELF-
CHECK
QUESTION

Are you familiar with accounting software? You may have used such software at work, but many of you are likely to be studying accounting before starting full-time work. Nevertheless, most higher educational establishments have some sort of accounting software for use by students. While it is often older versions of popular commercial packages such as Sage or Pegasus, it is still useful to try setting up accounts, entering a few transactions and extracting the results. Only in this way will you properly grasp many of the issues raised in this chapter, especially in relation to control.

When you use the package, try entering deliberate mistakes, and see which the software will pick up, and which it won't. Think about how your wider accounting system could prevent or detect the latter errors. Would a bank reconciliation help, for example? Wider still, what would you do now if the disk on which you have just saved your transactions were to be lost or corrupted?

Even if you can't get access to such a package, try to get hold of one of the newer generation of accounting packages, such as Quicken or Money, which are aimed at use in the small business, or for domestic accounting. Restricted or evaluation editions of such packages are occasionally given away with computing magazines. At the very least, browse such magazines looking for reviews of accounting packages.

Your overall aim is to get a feel for what accounting software can do, and how it typically does it. It is only through getting as close to the use of accounting software as your circumstances permit that you will be able to relate the practicalities of accounting to the inevitably rather general points that have been covered in this chapter.

Further review questions are available in a separate resource pack which is available to lecturers.

CHAPTER **15**
················

The finale

Objectives:
··············

By the end of this chapter you should be able to:

▶ Prepare a profit and loss account from cash flow and appropriate balance sheet information for a company.

▶ Redraft financial statements prepared using non-UK accounting practices.

▶ Prepare a report to users analysing and comparing a non-UK and UK company.

Introduction
·················

The style of this chapter is somewhat different to those previous in that there is no new information to learn. If you work through this chapter diligently it will identify for you those items that you have not thoroughly understood.

This chapter also has something of an international flavour and is in essence a case study.

Case study
··············

Bairstow Holdings plc is investigating the possibility of investing in one of two companies. The first, Hamilton Engineering Ltd, is a UK company, and the accounts for the year ended 31 December 1997 are available. The second is an overseas competitor to Hamilton Engineering, called Kriton Manufacturers SA. Kriton is incorporated in the central European country of Ecudia. Bairstow Holdings has also obtained the annual report and accounts for Kriton, but has found that the accounts are significantly different from those of Hamilton.

In particular, the accounting regulations in Ecudia do not require the publication of an income statement. However, they do require a cash flow statement, although in a non-UK format, and a balance sheet. As assistant accountant for Bairstow Holdings, you have been asked to use the available information about Kriton to redraft the overseas accounts in a format consistent with generally accepted accounting practice in the UK. Having thus prepared accounts for Kriton which are comparable to those of Hamilton, you are also required to analyse their respective positions and prospects, and so to recommend which company, if either, Bairstow should invest in.

Accounts for Kriton Manufacturers SA

All amounts are expressed in the local currency, the 'Ecu' (E).

CASH FLOW STATEMENT

Receipts

From customers	654,836
Interest received	12,900
Fixed assets sold	105,040
Debentures issued	150,000
	*£*922,776

Payments

To suppliers for goods purchased	362,573
To suppliers for other expenses	151,353
Purchases of fixed assets	278,200
Costs of debenture issue	2,150
Tax paid	63,045
Dividends paid	40,257
Interest paid	5,238
	*£*902,816
Increase in bank balance	*£*19,960

BALANCE SHEETS		*1997*		*1996*
Fixed assets				
Land and buildings		588,933		465,287
Machinery		659,314		590,721
Vehicles		34,941		54,020
		1,283,188		1,110,028
Current assets				
Stock	90,200		86,582	
Trade debtors	44,877		43,084	
Bank	39,532		19,572	
	174,609		149,238	
Current liabilities				
Trade creditors	(31,613)		(33,365)	
Other creditors	(5,045)		(4,502)	
Tax	(42,919)		(63,045)	
Dividends	(42,300)		(40,257)	
Contingencies	(56,000)		–	
		(3,268)		8,069
		1,279,920		1,118,097
Debentures		450,000		300,000
		*£*829,920		*£*818,097

Share capital	500,000	500,000
General reserve	329,920	318,097
	£829,920	£818,097

Notes to the accounts

Fixed assets

You discover that the fixed assets of Kriton are depreciated in accordance with the fiscal policy in operation in Ecudia. Thus depreciation for the year to 31 December 1997 of £85,343 has been reflected in the Kriton accounts. If the depreciation charge had been based on the same policy as in Hamilton, then the depreciation charge would have been £103,445 for the year, ie an additional £18,102.

The fixed asset figures in the balance sheet of Kriton reflect the depreciation charged over the years, that is they are at net book value, in accordance with Ecudian generally accepted accounting practices. If the total provision for depreciation brought forward at the beginning of 1997 had been calculated on the same basis as for Hamilton, it would have been an extra £46,578. In other words, the net book value as at 1st January 1997 would have been reduced by that amount.

Other expenses

Research and development costs of Kriton are written off to the income statement as and when they are incurred. They form part of the other expenses on the cash flow statement.

All contingencies, no matter how remote, are also included in this income statement. You estimate that £56,000 in expenses has been accrued for. It is very unlikely to ever become due. You also note that this type of contingency would not normally be accrued for in the UK.

Stock

Standard accounting practice in Ecudia is to value stock at selling price. The valuations at historical cost for Kriton would be £65,900 at 31 December 1996 and £67,250 at 31 December 1997.

Issue costs

Debenture issue costs are written off in the year in Ecudia.

HAMILTON ENGINEERING LTD FINANCIAL STATEMENTS
BALANCE SHEETS AS AT 31 DECEMBER

		1997		1996
		£		£
Fixed assets		850,976		793,465
Current assets				
Stock	23,472		26,574	
Debtors	36,457		38,563	
Bank	6,453		–	
	66,382		65,137	

Current liabilities

Creditors	(29,756)		(27,463)
Tax	(37,465)		(29,465)
Bank	–		(350)
		(839)	7,859
		851,815	801,324
Debentures		150,000	200,000
		£701,815	£601,324
Share capital		600,000	600,000
General reserves		101,815	1,324
		£701,815	£601,324

PROFIT AND LOSS ACCOUNT
FOR THE YEAR ENDED 31 DECEMBER

		1997		*1996*
		£		*£*
Sales		524,536		395,764
Cost of sales		284,657		269,472
Gross profit		239,879		126,292
Depreciation	65,655		59,685	
Expenses	32,657		28,675	
Interest paid	7,500		10,000	
		105,812		98,360
Net profit before tax		134,067		27,932
Taxation		33,576		29,465
Retained profit for the year		100,491		(1,533)
Dividends		–		–
Retained profit b/f		1,324		2,857
Retained profit c/f		£101,815		£1,324

Notes
▶ No fixed assets were sold during the year but £124,844 were bought.
▶ Research and development expenditure is charged to the profit and loss.
▶ Stock is valued at historical cost.
▶ The debentures were redeemed at nominal value.

Required

1 Draft a profit and loss account for Kriton Manufacturers SA for the year ended 31 December 1997. Refer to Chapter 7 if you need to refresh your knowledge of how to do this.

2 Redraft the income statement for Kriton prepared in answer to part 1, in accordance with UK generally accepted accounting practice (ie the accounting practice of Hamilton Engineering Ltd).

3 Redraft the balance sheets at both 31 December 1997 and 31 December 1996 for Kriton, in accordance with UK generally accepted accounting practice (ie the accounting practice of Hamilton Engineering Ltd).

4 Redraft the cash-flow statement for the year ended 31 December 1997 in accordance with best UK practice, adopting the indirect method of reporting. Refer to Chapter 11 if you need to refresh your knowledge of how to do this.

5 Calculate the following ratios for both Kriton, using your newly drafted accounts, and for Hamilton, for both 1996 and 1997, as far as the information allows:

(a) Gross profit.
(b) Net profit.
(c) Return on capital employed.
(d) Return on owners equity.
(e) Gearing.
(f) Current.
(g) Quick.
(h) Debtors' collection.
(i) Creditors' payment.
(j) Stock turnover.
(k) Sales to capital employed.

Refer to Chapter 10 if you need to refresh your knowledge of how to do this.

6 Use the ratios as a basis for your recommendation to the directors of Bairstow Holdings plc on which company, if either, they should invest in. Refer to Chapter 10 if you need to refresh your knowledge of how to do this.

Answers

1 **KRITON MANUFACTURERS SA**
PROFIT AND LOSS ACCOUNT
FOR THE YEAR ENDED 31 DECEMBER 1997

Sales (654,836 – 43,084 + 44,877)		656,629
Opening stock	86,582	
Purchases (362,573 – 33,365 + 31,613)	360,821	
	447,403	
Less closing stock	90,200	357,203
Gross profit		299,426
Expenses (151,353 – 4,502 + 5,045)	151,896	
Depreciation	85,343	
Contingency	56,000	
Profit on sale of assets (note 1) (105,040 – 19,697)	(85,343)	
Debenture issue costs	2,150	
Interest received	(12,900)	
Interest paid	5,238	
		202,384
Net profit before tax		97,042

Tax		42,919
Net profit after tax		54,123
Dividends		42,300
		11,823
Retained profit b/f		318,097
Retained profit c/f		£329,920

Note 1

Opening assets valuation		1,110,028
Add purchase new assets		278,200
		1,388,228
Less depreciation for the year		85,343
		1,302,885
Closing asset valuation		1,283,188
Thus net book value assets sold		£19,697

2 **KRITON MANUFACTURERS SA**
   PROFIT AND LOSS ACCOUNT
   FOR THE YEAR ENDED 31 DECEMBER 1997
   IN ACCORDANCE WITH UK GAAP

Sales		656,629
Opening stock	65,900	
Purchases	360,821	
	426,721	
Less closing stock	67,250	
		359,471
Gross profit		297,158
Expenses	151,896	
Depreciation	103,445	
Contingency	–	
Debenture issue costs	2,150	
Interest received	(12,900)	
Interest paid	5,238	
Profit on sale of assets	(85,343)	
		164,486
Net profit before tax		132,672
Taxation		42,919
Net profit after tax		89,753
Dividends		42,300
Retained profit for the year		47,453
Retained profit b/f (note 1)		250,837
Retained profit c/f		£298,290

Note 1: Adjustment to retained profit b/f

Retained profit b/f as per balance sheet	318,097
Less previous years' depreciation	(46,578)
Less revaluation of closing stock 31 December 1996	(20,682)
Retained profit b/f	£250,837

3 **KRITON MANUFACTURERS SA**
BALANCE SHEET AS AT 31 DECEMBER 1997
UNDER UK GAAP

Fixed assets (1283188 – 46578 – 18102)			1,218,508
Current assets			
Stock		67,250	
Debtors		44,877	
Bank		39,532	
		151,659	
Current liabilities			
Trade creditors	31,613		
Other creditors	5,045		
Taxation	42,919		
Dividends	42,300		
	121,877		
			29,782
			1,248,290
Debentures			450,000
			£798,290
Share capital			500,000
General reserve			298,290
			£798,290

KRITON MANUFACTURERS SA
BALANCE SHEET AS AT 31 DECEMBER 1996
AS PER UK GAAP

Fixed assets			1,063,450
Current assets			
Stock		65,900	
Debtors		43,084	
Bank		19,572	
		128,556	
Current liabilities			
Trade creditors	33,365		
Other creditors	4,502		
Tax	63,045		
Dividends	40,257		
	141,169		
			(12,613)
			1,050,837

Debentures		300,000
		£750,837
Share capital		500,000
General reserve		250,837
		£750,837

4 **KRITON MANUFACTURERS SA**
   CASH FLOW STATEMENT
   FOR THE YEAR ENDED 31 DECEMBER 1997
   AS PER UK INDIRECT METHOD

Cash inflow from operating activities (note 1)		140,910
Returns on investments and servicing of finance		
Interest paid	(5,238)	
Dividends paid	(40,257)	
Interest received	12,900	
Net cash outflow from investments and servicing of finance		(32,595)
Taxation		
Tax paid		(63,045)
Net cash flow from investing activities		
Purchase of assets	(278,200)	
Proceeds of sale of assets	105,040	
Net cash outflow from investing activities		(173,160)
Net cash outflow before financing		(127,890)
Net cash inflow from financing		
Debenture issue		147,850
Net cash inflow for the year		19,960
Change in cash and bank		£19,960

Note 1

Operating profit for the year before tax, interest and dividends		
(132,672 + 5,238 – 12,900)		125,010
Add back:		
Depreciation	103,445	
Issue costs	2,150	
Less profit on sale	(85,343)	
		20,252
		145,262
Increase in stock	(1,350)	
Increase in debtors	(1,793)	
Decrease in trade creditors	(1,752)	
Increase in other creditors	543	
		(4,352)
		£140,910

5 We have shown our ratios in two separate tables for ease of reference. The first table shows the ratios themselves, while the subsequent table shows the underlying calculations. Note that not all ratios can be calculated for Kriton, in the absence of a profit and loss account for 1996. Such restrictions are often a feature of accounts analysis, and conclusions and recommendations have to be determined from what information is available.

	KRITON		HAMILTON	
	1997	*1996*	*1997*	*1996*
Gross profit	45.3%		45.7%	31.9%
Net profit	0.7% (note 1)		25.6%	7.1%
Return on capital employed	0.8% (note 1)		12.7%	1.1%
Return on shareholders' funds	0.6% (note 1)		14.3%	(0.5)%
Gearing	36.0%	28.5%	17.6%	25.0%
Current	1.24	0.91	0.99	1.14
Quick	0.69 ·	0.44	0.64	0.67
Debtors' collection	25 days		25 days	35 days
Creditors' payment	32 days (note 2)		38 days	37 days
Stock turnover	68 days		30 days	36 days
Sales to capital employed	0.53		0.62	0.49

Note 1
The 'raw' net profit figure is £89,753. Using this gives a net profit to sales percentage of 13.7%. However, our view is that this would be an unreliable figure, since it includes a very substantial profit on the sale of fixed assets, which is unlikely to be repeated, and is therefore a poor guide to future performance. The figure we have used for profit therefore excludes this profit on sale of fixed assets, and is consequently on £4,410. The same figure has then also been used for the next two ratios. Note that our identification of a sustainable profit here is a contentious issue – the essential thing is to be consistent in any such adjustment policy.

Note 2
Since only the cost of sales figure is available for Hamilton, we have also used the cost of sales figure for Kriton's ratio calculation. Strictly, the denominator should, of course, be the purchases figure, but our approach has the key merit of consistency.

The answers above have been calculated from the following fractions. You should be able to identify the amounts involved below from the accounts.

	KRITON		HAMILTON	
	1997	*1996*	*1997*	*1996*
Gross profit	$\dfrac{297158}{656629}$		$\dfrac{239879}{524536}$	$\dfrac{126292}{395764}$
Net profit	$\dfrac{4410}{656629}$		$\dfrac{134067}{524536}$	$\dfrac{27932}{395764}$
Return on capital employed	$\dfrac{9648}{1248290}$		$\dfrac{107991}{851815}$	$\dfrac{8467}{801324}$
Return on shareholders' funds	$\dfrac{4410}{798290}$		$\dfrac{100491}{701815}$	$\dfrac{(1533)}{301324}$
Gearing	$\dfrac{450000}{1248290}$	$\dfrac{300000}{1050837}$	$\dfrac{150000}{851815}$	$\dfrac{200000}{801324}$
Current	$\dfrac{151659}{121877}$	$\dfrac{128556}{141169}$	$\dfrac{66382}{67221}$	$\dfrac{65137}{57278}$
Quick	$\dfrac{84409}{121877}$	$\dfrac{62656}{141169}$	$\dfrac{42910}{67221}$	$\dfrac{38563}{57278}$
Debtors' collection	$\dfrac{44877}{656629} \times 365$		$\dfrac{36457}{524536} \times 365$	$\dfrac{38563}{395764} \times 365$
Creditors' payment	$\dfrac{31613}{359471} \times 365$		$\dfrac{29756}{284657} \times 365$	$\dfrac{27463}{269472} \times 365$
Stock turnover	$\dfrac{67250}{359471} \times 365$		$\dfrac{23472}{284657} \times 365$	$\dfrac{26574}{269472} \times 365$
Sales to capital employed	$\dfrac{656629}{1248290}$		$\dfrac{524536}{851815}$	$\dfrac{395764}{801324}$

6 Analysis and recommendations

The following points should be included in any report you prepare for Bairstow plc.

▶ The absence of a profit and loss account for Kriton for 1996 means that some ratios can not be calculated.

▶ The net profit figure to be used for Kriton for 1997 is subject to debate over the repeatability of the profit on the sale of the fixed assets.

▶ The gross profit percentages for 1997 are very similar between the two companies, but the net profit percentages indicate that Kriton's expenses are substantially more than Hamilton's, in relation to their respective turnovers. This indicates that serious attention needs to be given to Kriton's expenses.

▶ The poor net profit in Kriton is also reflected in return on capital and on shareholders' funds ratios; that is they are much lower for Kriton than for Hamilton. It is also worth noting that Hamilton's ratios have improved since 1996. Kriton thus appears a less attractive possibility as an investment than Hamilton, if the objective is a high return on that investment.

▶ The gearing ratio has increased in Kriton, while it has fallen in Hamilton. The high gearing implies high interest charges, which is likely to leave little profit as a return for investors. Again, the implication is that Kriton is unattractive as an investment, relative to Hamilton.

▶ The relative positions of the two companies as regards liquidity show Kriton to be in the stronger position. Both its current and quick ratios have improved significantly over 1997, while Hamilton's position has worsened, as evidenced by the same two ratios. This may imply a concern over the future ability of Hamilton to meet its obligations in the short term, despite its relatively good profitability.

▶ Both debtor collection and creditor payment periods are similar for the two companies, as far as can be determined from the limited information available for Kriton. Credit management policies and practices are probably therefore similar in the two companies.

▶ The stock turnover period, however, is much longer in Kriton than in Hamilton. This is surprising, given that they are in the same industry, albeit operating in different countries. It may be that Kriton's relative inability to move its stock quickly is a cause of its relatively poor profitability.

▶ The similarity of the sales to capital employed ratios suggest that both companies are similar in their ability to generate sales from a given level of investment.

▶ Overall, Kriton's problems seem to stem from its high level of expenses, relative to turnover, compared with what Hamilton has been able to achieve. This area should certainly be investigated before any decision to invest in Kriton is made. Furthermore, it may well be productive to investigate why Kriton has been unable to shift its stock as quickly as its competitor.

▶ The better investment would therefore appear to be Hamilton. However, any decision to invest should take into account the alternative investments open to Bairstow. At its simplest, these could include, for example, placing the money in a deposit account. This would, of course, probably be a significantly safer investment than putting money into Hamilton, and the question of relative risk should be considered alongside that of relative return.

Summary

This final chapter has attempted to pull together many of the issues that you have studied in this book. It has been an extensive case study, and it is likely that you did not find it very easy. However, we recommend that you return to it at least once more, since you should find it an excellent way to revise and consolidate your understanding.

Index